Good Night Stories for Rebel Girls

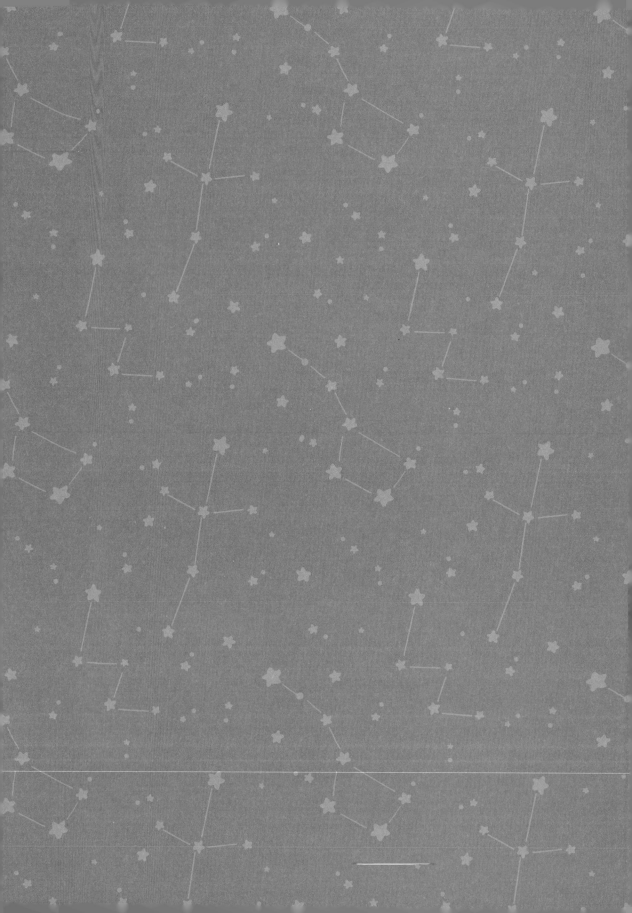

Good Night Stories for Rebel Girls

ELENA FAVILLI

100 IMMIGRANT WOMEN WHO CHANGED THE WORLD

REBEL GIRLS

Good Night Stories for Rebel Girls and all other Rebel Girls titles are available for bulk purchase for sale promotions, premiums, fundraising, and educational needs.
For details, write to sales@rebelgirls.com

This is a work of creative nonfiction. It is a collection of heartwarming and thought-provoking bedtime stories inspired by the life and adventures of 103 heroic women. It is not an encyclopedic account of events and accomplishments of their lives.

www.rebelgirls.com

Printed in China, 2021
10 9 8 7 6

Art Director: Giulia Flamini
Graphic Designer: Annalisa Ventura
Cover Design and Lettering: Cesar Iannarella

ISBN: 978-1-7333292-9-3

Good Night Stories for Rebel Girls : 100 Immigrant Women Who Changed the World
is FSC® certified.

MIX
Paper from
responsible sources
FSC® C124807
FSC
www.fsc.org

OTHER BOOKS FROM REBEL GIRLS

Good Night Stories for Rebel Girls

Good Night Stories for Rebel Girls 2

Good Night Stories for Rebel Girls:
100 Real-Life Tales of Black Girl Magic

Good Night Stories for Rebel Girls:
The Chapter Book Collection

I Am a Rebel Girl: A Journal to Start Revolutions

Rebel Girls Champions

Rebel Girls Climate Warriors

Rebel Girls Lead

Rebel Girls Powerful Pairs

Questions for Rebel Girls

To the rebel girls of the world:

Cross boundaries

Demand freedom

Make your mark

And, when in doubt, remember

The future is yours.

CONTENTS

BONUS! AUDIO STORIES!

SCAN TO HEAR MORE!

Download the Rebel Girls app to hear longer stories about some of the extraordinary women in this book. You will also unlock creative activities and discover stories of other trailblazing women. Whenever you come across a bookmark icon, just scan the code, and you'll be whisked away on an audio adventure.

PREFACE

Dear Rebels,

To those of you who are picking up a Good Night Stories for Rebel Girls book for the first time, I want to say, "Welcome!" And to those of you who are joining us for the second or even third time, "Welcome back!" In this book, I am excited to share with you 100 stories of incredible women who moved from one country to another, experiencing some form of immigration over the course of their lives.

This is also a personal topic for me, as I am an immigrant myself. Good Night Stories for Rebel Girls was created by two women—me (Elena Favilli) and Francesca Cavallo—who moved from Italy to the United States and who wanted to share their vision for a more equal world with all of you. I came to the US when I was 23 years old to attend University of California, Berkeley. This country is now my home, where I have built this company, written these books, and met all of you. As you can see, Francesca is not writing this third book with me, but that same inspiration we shared at the start of our journey continues to drive this series.

People often ask me what it means to be a Rebel Girl, and there can be many definitions—just like we are all different from one another. At her heart, a Rebel Girl is someone who tries to make the world better for herself and the people around her, no matter the risks. In the following pages, you will read stories about women who embody the spirit of the Rebel Girl, leaving their birth countries for a multitude of reasons. Some of these women actively chose to seek new opportunities, while others left out of necessity.

You will explore the Amazon with Emilie Snethlage, part scientist, part explorer, who moved from Germany to study the plants and animals of the Brazilian rainforest. You will dance with Yuan Yuan Tan whose career as a ballerina began with the flip of a coin and brought her from China to her new home in the United States. And you will fight for what's right with Muzoon Almellehan, who fled war in Syria to settle in England, finding strength in books, campaigning for girls' education, and becoming one of the youngest UNICEF Goodwill Ambassadors to date.

Immigration is rarely thought of as a woman's story, but more than half of all immigrants are women. The women featured in this book have already made an impact on the world just by forging their own paths across borders. They also happened to accomplish great things in their new homes. But whatever an immigrant hopes to achieve through their journey, I hope you will finish this book with an understanding that movement from one country to another is a human right.

As you dive into each of these stories, it might help to think about times you've wanted to move from one place to another. Have you ever wanted to move to a different classroom? A different team? What about a different city? That is exactly what these immigrant women did, on a larger scale. Let their courage and perseverance be a reminder to you, Rebel Girls, that you should always fight for your beliefs no matter where they take you.

Yours,
Elena Favilli

ADELAIDE HERRMANN

MAGICIAN

Once upon a time, there was a girl with a flair for the dramatic. While other Victorian girls learned housekeeping skills, Adelaide practiced acrobatics, dance, and a new sport called trick cycling.

One night, Adelaide saw a magic show in London that changed her life. The magician, Alexander Herrmann (known as Herrmann the Great), asked for a volunteer, and Adelaide eagerly raised her hand. The magician set her ring on fire and made it reappear on a ribbon tied around a dove's neck!

A few months later, when Adelaide moved to New York City, she ran into Alexander again. They got married and together became one of the country's most successful magic acts. Herrmann the Great was the star, and Adelaide played supporting roles, including a dancer and a human cannonball!

In 1896, Alexander suddenly died. Adelaide was left alone with their magic show, a warehouse of props and animals, and a mountain of debt. But soon it became clear that only one person had the experience to continue Herrmann the Great's **legacy**—Adelaide herself.

For more than 30 years, Adelaide performed as the Queen of Magic. After a fire tore through her warehouse, Adelaide insisted she'd rise like a phoenix from the ashes. And she did. She continued to tour before finally retiring in her seventies.

AUGUST 11, 1853–FEBRUARY 19, 1932
UNITED KINGDOM → UNITED STATES OF AMERICA

"SELF-CONFIDENCE AND ASSURANCE ARE MOST ESSENTIAL TO THE SUCCESSFUL MAGICIAN."
—ADELAIDE HERRMANN

ILLUSTRATION BY
CAMILLE DE CUSSAC

ALICE GUY-BLACHÉ

FILMMAKER

Once there was a girl named Alice who spent her childhood crisscrossing the globe from France (her mother's home) to Chile (her father's home) to Switzerland (where she lived with her grandmother). When she grew up, Alice became a secretary at a camera company turned film studio. Filmmaking was a new and exciting art form. The very first films were nothing like today's movies. They showed people doing ordinary things—a group of workers simply leaving a factory or a train racing along a track.

Alice thought these films were boring and wondered: *What if film could be used to tell a story?* So she borrowed camera equipment and created her first motion picture, *The Cabbage Fairy*. It was only about one minute long, but it was one of the first films to tell a fictional story.

Eventually, Alice became the studio's head of production and experimented with new ways to make films and add special effects. She married a fellow filmmaker, Herbert Blaché, and they moved to the United States. In 1910, Alice opened her own film studio called the Solax Film Company and eventually built a state-of-the-art production studio. It was the largest film studio in the country.

Herbert became the company's president so Alice could be free to make movies. She became the world's first woman filmmaker, creating about 1,000 films—many of which survive today. Alice made her last film in 1920 and was forgotten for a long time, but today's filmmakers owe a lot to this pioneering director and producer.

JULY 1, 1873–MARCH 24, 1968

FRANCE ➜ UNITED STATES OF AMERICA

ILLUSTRATION BY
HELEN LI

"THERE IS NOTHING
CONNECTED WITH THE STAGING
OF A MOTION PICTURE THAT
A WOMAN CANNOT DO
AS EASILY AS A MAN."
—ALICE GUY-BLACHÉ

ANGELICA ROZEANU

TABLE TENNIS PLAYER

Once upon a time, there was a young Romanian, Jewish girl who was a natural athlete, but she didn't have a favorite sport—at least, not at first. Angelica loved swimming, tennis, and cycling. But one day, as Angelica later described it, a new sport found her.

When she was around eight years old, Angelica got scarlet fever. Scarlet fever was a serious illness, and it took a long time to get better. Angelica's brother, Gaston, wanted to find a way to entertain his sister as she recovered. He brought home a paddle, ball, and net, and introduced Angelica to table tennis.

Angelica was a quick learner. With dancer-like footwork and quick reflexes, she began to play competitively and won her first national championship when she was 15! In 1940, however, her athletic career suddenly stopped. Romania joined forces with Nazi Germany. As a result of the many restrictions put on Jewish people in Romania at the time, Angelica was unable to play the sport she loved.

When the war ended, Angelica once again picked up her paddle. In 1950, she became the first Romanian woman athlete to win a world championship. That year, she also became president of the Romanian Table Tennis Commission. Over her career, Angelica won at least 15 national championships and 17 world championships. In 1960, after experiencing more **discrimination** in her home country, Angelica **immigrated** to Israel. In 1981, Angelica was inducted into the International Jewish Sports Hall of Fame.

OCTOBER 15, 1921–FEBRUARY 21, 2006
ROMANIA → ISRAEL

"I PREFERRED TABLE TENNIS OR PERHAPS, IF YOU LIKE, TABLE TENNIS PREFERRED ME."
—ANGELICA ROZEANU

ILLUSTRATION BY MAGGIE COLE

ANITA SARKEESIAN

JOURNALIST AND MEDIA CRITIC

Anita loved video games. As a little girl growing up in Canada, she begged her parents for a Nintendo Game Boy of her own. When she was in high school, she spent hours playing on the computer. Video games were fun, and they made her happy.

But as she got older, she noticed something that bothered her. There were hardly any female game characters—and extremely few strong, positive female ones.

This wasn't the first time Anita had noticed something amiss in the media. When she was younger, Anita had seen that people from Iraq— the country her parents were from—were often portrayed on television as scary or bad. She didn't see any representations that looked like the people she loved. Anita realized that sometimes the media told stories that weren't accurate or left important things out.

Anita started her own website, a blog called *Feminist Frequency*. She posted a series of videos in which she talked to viewers about the way women were depicted in video games.

Her videos were smart and funny, and made people in the gaming industry think about how to make their products better for men and women alike. But some men who saw the videos didn't want to hear any new ideas. They called her ugly names. Some even threatened to hurt her.

Anita refused to be silent, and the more she spoke up, the more people listened. Today there are more women than ever in video games—both as characters on the screen and as engineers designing them.

BIRTHDATE UNKNOWN

CANADA ➜ UNITED STATES OF AMERICA

ILLUSTRATION BY
JENNY MEILIHOVE

"THERE IS SO MUCH VALUE
TO SPEAKING UP FOR WHAT
YOU BELIEVE IS RIGHT,
EVEN IF THE COSTS FEEL
INSURMOUNTABLE."
—ANITA SARKEESIAN

ANNA WINTOUR

EDITOR IN CHIEF

Once there was a girl who had a style all her own. From a young age, Anna was captivated by the world of fashion. It called to her from the glossy pages of magazines and the vibrant London streets where she lived. Anna's father, a respected newspaper editor, encouraged his daughter's interests. With his help, Anna got her first job at a high-end boutique when she was 15 years old. Shortly afterward, she started taking fashion design classes. But she quickly grew tired of them. *You either know fashion or you don't,* she thought. And it was clear: Anna *knew* fashion.

At 20, Anna got her first job at a fashion magazine. For the next few years, she worked at many different magazines in London and New York. In 1988, Anna was hired for the job that made her famous in the fashion world. She became editor in chief of *Vogue*. Right away, Anna was determined to follow her instincts. For her very first cover, she had a model wear a $10,000 jeweled top with a pair of ordinary jeans. It was so unusual that at first some people thought it was a mistake. But Anna wasn't afraid to try new things.

Thirty years later, Anna is still the editor in chief of *Vogue*. Although she is known for her trademark look—a bob haircut and oversized sunglasses—she is more than simply a style icon. Her bold ideas, take-charge attitude, and focus on **philanthropy** have helped change the world of magazines and fashion for the better.

BORN NOVEMBER 3, 1949

UNITED KINGDOM ➜ UNITED STATES OF AMERICA

ILLUSTRATION BY
MEEL TAMPHANON

"PEOPLE RESPOND WELL
TO SOMEONE WHO'S SURE
OF WHAT THEY WANT."
—ANNA WINTOUR

ANNE HIDALGO

POLITICIAN

Born in San Fernando, Spain, Ana Maria Hidalgo and her family moved to France when she was a child. They lived in a working-class neighborhood full of fellow immigrants. Ana Maria grew up speaking two languages—Spanish to her parents and French to most everyone else. As a teenager, Ana Maria changed her name to Anne and became a French **citizen**. Today she has both French and Spanish citizenship.

In school, Anne studied social services and law, planning to one day work in government. After moving to Paris, she worked in civil service for many years and eventually became deputy mayor in 2001. Anne spent 13 years as deputy mayor, working for the people of Paris. But she wanted to do more.

In the 2014 elections, Anne ran for mayor. Some people didn't think she would win because of her immigrant background, but more people seemed to think this experience made her a good candidate—and they were right. She won the election! For hundreds of years, Paris had been an important center for politics, business, art, and fashion, and it had had many leaders—from military generals to kings to mayors. But no woman had ever been in charge, until Anne.

Since taking office, Anne has championed climate change issues. She wants to help create a greener world, and she knows the importance of starting right where you are: "My vision for Paris is as a green city where we can all breathe fresh air, share open space, and enjoy our lives."

BORN JUNE 19, 1959

SPAIN ➞ FRANCE

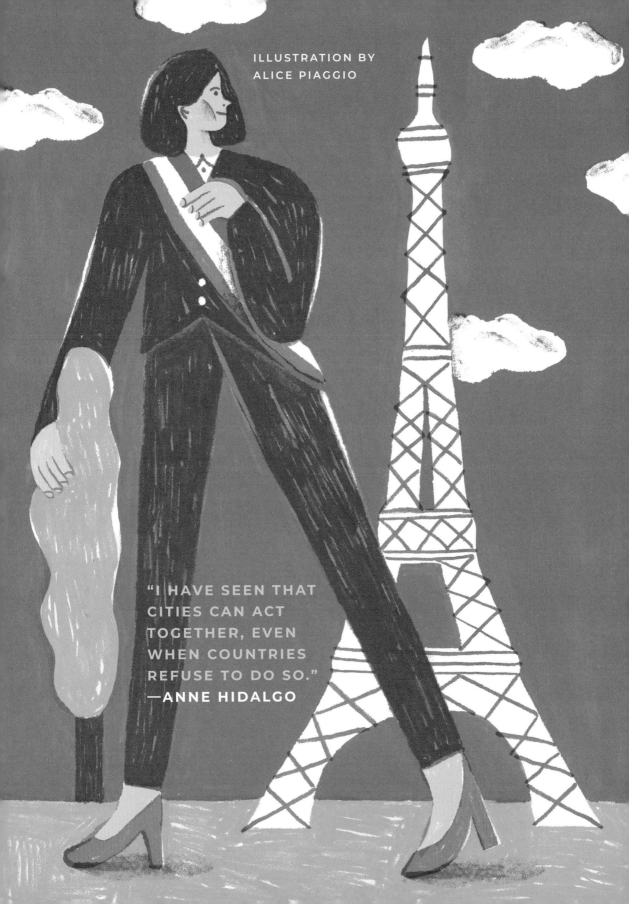

ILLUSTRATION BY
ALICE PIAGGIO

"I HAVE SEEN THAT
CITIES CAN ACT
TOGETHER, EVEN
WHEN COUNTRIES
REFUSE TO DO SO."
—ANNE HIDALGO

ANNE WAFULA STRIKE

PARALYMPIAN

One day in Kenya, a two-year-old girl named Anne became very, very sick. Her worried parents took her to a hospital, where doctors wrapped her in stiff plaster that made it impossible to move. When Anne got better, she could no longer walk. She had contracted polio and was paralyzed from the waist down.

Many people in Anne's village did not understand what polio was. The local healer said she was a victim of evil magic. Her neighbors called her a snake because she had to crawl everywhere to get around.

Her body worked differently now, but Anne refused to stop moving. She learned to use crutches, and her father found a special school that taught children with disabilities. Anne excelled at school. She became the first person in her family to go to university.

Later, when Anne was working as a teacher in Kenya, she fell in love with a fellow teacher named Norman. They decided to get married and move to Essex, England, where Norman was from.

One day, while exercising at her local track, a coach noticed Anne circling the track in her wheelchair and asked if she had ever tried competitive racing. It turned out that Anne was fast—very fast. Two years later, in Athens, Anne became the first wheelchair racer from east Africa to compete in the Paralympic Games.

In 2006, Anne became a British **citizen**. The next year, she won a bronze medal at the Paralympic World Cup before a cheering crowd as an athlete competing for her new home—Great Britain.

BORN MAY 8, 1969
KENYA ➡ UNITED KINGDOM

ILLUSTRATION BY
LUISA RIVERA

"I CONSIDER MYSELF
AN ESSEX GIRL FROM AFRICA."
—ANNE WAFULA STRIKE

ANNIKA SÖRENSTAM

GOLFER

Once upon a time in Sweden, there was a girl who didn't want to sit on the sidelines. Annika was a confident athlete who played tennis and soccer, and raced down the slopes as an Alpine skier. When she was 12, she started playing golf at summer camp. "I was determined to figure it out," Annika said.

Annika eventually joined a team and became a very good golfer. But there was a problem. In the junior tournaments, the winners gave victory speeches. Annika was shy, so she lost on purpose, getting second place instead of first. Annika's coaches noticed. They had the rules changed, so both the winner and runner-up had to give speeches. Annika decided that if she had to give a speech either way, she might as well win!

After high school, Annika played golf for the University of Arizona. She won the NCAA tournament as a college freshman, and a year later, she left school to be a professional golfer.

Over the next two decades, Annika became one of the most successful female golfers of all time. She won 90 tournaments, was inducted into the World Golf Hall of Fame, and was the first woman to play on the PGA Tour in its 58-year history. The year before she retired, Annika started her own brand and a foundation to introduce girls to golf. "My goal now is to inspire others to pick up the game," Annika said.

BORN OCTOBER 9, 1970

SWEDEN → UNITED STATES OF AMERICA

"I DON'T PLAY FOR FAME
OR ACCOLADES.
FOR ME, IT'S ALL ABOUT
PERFORMANCE AND
SATISFACTION."
—ANNIKA SÖRENSTAM

SCAN TO HEAR MORE

ARIANNA HUFFINGTON

AUTHOR AND CEO

Once there was a girl named Arianna who read everything she could find, and nothing could distract her—not even the trucks at the fire station across the street from her family's apartment in Athens.

When she was just 17, Arianna moved to England and eventually won a scholarship to attend Cambridge University. Some of the other students made fun of her Greek accent when she spoke. But Arianna refused to be silent. Instead, she spoke up more, first as president of Cambridge's famous debating club and later in her life as a journalist and TV commentator.

Arianna moved to the United States in 1980 and eventually cofounded a website, the *Huffington Post*, to share the viewpoints and ideas from people all over the world. As she grew her business, Arianna also continued to write books, make speeches, and advocate for causes she cared about. She often worked 18 hours a day and hardly ever slept!

Then came a day that changed Arianna's life. One minute she was busy returning emails and making phone calls. The next she was on the floor. She had collapsed, and the fall broke her cheekbone and cut open her face. She went to see doctors who told her she was suffering from burnout. If she didn't change her hectic schedule, she was going to get very sick.

Arianna adjusted her life, realizing that when she took care of herself she was also more effective and more productive. Later, she started a new company, Thrive Global, that teaches people how to care for themselves while doing the work they love.

BORN JULY 15, 1950

GREECE → UNITED STATES OF AMERICA

"WE THINK, MISTAKENLY, THAT SUCCESS IS THE RESULT OF THE AMOUNT OF TIME WE PUT IN AT WORK, INSTEAD OF THE QUALITY OF TIME WE PUT IN."
—ARIANNA HUFFINGTON

ILLUSTRATION BY FANNY BLANC

ASMA KHAN

CHEF

One day in India, a girl stood on a magnificent fortress that had belonged to her **ancestors**. Her father pointed at the slums below. "It is an accident of birth," he said. "You could have been there, or you could have been here. Use your life to make a difference, because being in a position of privilege, you have a duty. To lift others up."

But Asma didn't feel powerful. She was a second-born daughter. In India, sons were so important that a second daughter was often a disappointment. She vowed to make her family proud.

Asma eventually married and moved to England, where she earned her PhD in law. She was terribly homesick. As Asma passed a neighbor's house, she smelled the familiar foods of her childhood. Asma longed to cook these recipes herself. She took a trip to India and asked her mother to teach her.

When Asma returned to London, she hosted supper clubs in her home. She became friends with other South Asian immigrant women and invited them to cook with her. Their dinners became so popular that Asma opened her own restaurant, which specialized in homestyle Indian food. But food was just one part of Asma's mission. She also wanted to empower women. She started a nonprofit to celebrate the births of second daughters in India and began employing an all-women staff in her restaurant. Many were second-born daughters like Asma. "I've watched these women grow, stand tall, be proud," Asma said. "This is what happens to women when other women stand by them."

BORN CIRCA JULY 1969

INDIA ➜ UNITED KINGDOM

"WE NEED TO UNITE TO PROTECT THE RIGHTS OF THE NEXT GENERATION OF WOMEN AND WOMEN TODAY WHO ARE STRUGGLING."
—ASMA KHAN

ILLUSTRATION BY PAOLA ROLLO

BANA ALABED

Once there was a happy girl who lived in the city of Aleppo, Syria, and her name was Bana. Bana loved to swim with her father, make up songs and games with her friends, and explore the beautiful flowers in her family's garden.

When Bana was two, her world began to change. War broke out in Syria. There was fighting in the streets and she couldn't play outside anymore. Many of her friends and relatives moved away to different countries. Some of them were hurt or even killed. Bana and her family felt sad, alone, and very afraid.

A few years later, her own city was attacked. For weeks, bombs fell on Aleppo. Bana and her family couldn't get food, water, or medicine. They desperately needed help. With the assistance of her mother, Fatemah, Bana posted messages on Twitter. Though it was difficult and dangerous, Bana bravely reported her experiences to the public. On days when their internet wasn't working, neighbors would invite them over to use theirs, in the hopes that the world would understand what ordinary people were facing in Aleppo and help them.

Eventually, Bana and her family had to leave Syria and start a new life in Turkey. At first, Bana was scared to go to a new country, but when she got there, she saw that there was no war. She could go to school again, and she was so happy.

Bana wants to be a teacher when she grows up. "I want to change everything," Bana said. "I don't want war anymore."

BORN CIRCA JUNE 2009
SYRIA ➡ TURKEY

"DO WHAT YOU CAN DO AND BELIEVE IN YOURSELF BECAUSE YOU MAKE THE FUTURE."
—BANA ALABED

ILLUSTRATION BY
TATHEER SYEDA

CARMEN HERRERA

ARTIST

Growing up in Havana, Cuba, with six siblings and two journalist parents, Carmen loved to draw. She went to college to study architecture but stayed only one year. There were lots of protests in Cuba, and the university was often closed. But at architecture school, Carmen said later, "an extraordinary world opened up to me that never closed: the world of straight lines."

Carmen got married and moved with her husband to New York, where he lived. All the while, Carmen made art—bold, bright geometric paintings and sculptures. Though other artists admired her work, she never got to show her paintings in museums and galleries the way male artists did.

Carmen eventually sold her first painting in 2004, when she was 89 years old. At an age when many artists put away their easels and retired, Carmen was just getting started.

Every morning, Carmen took a seat before the big, beautiful window in her New York City apartment. She picked up her sketchbook and drew whatever inspired her: the lines and angles of the shadows, the memory of a landscape.

After decades as a painter, Carmen reached the peak of her artistic fame. Museums around the world showed her work, and she kept painting every day, well after her one hundredth birthday. After all, why should she stop? "I've painted all my life," she said. "It makes me feel good."

BORN MAY 30, 1915

CUBA ➡ UNITED STATES OF AMERICA

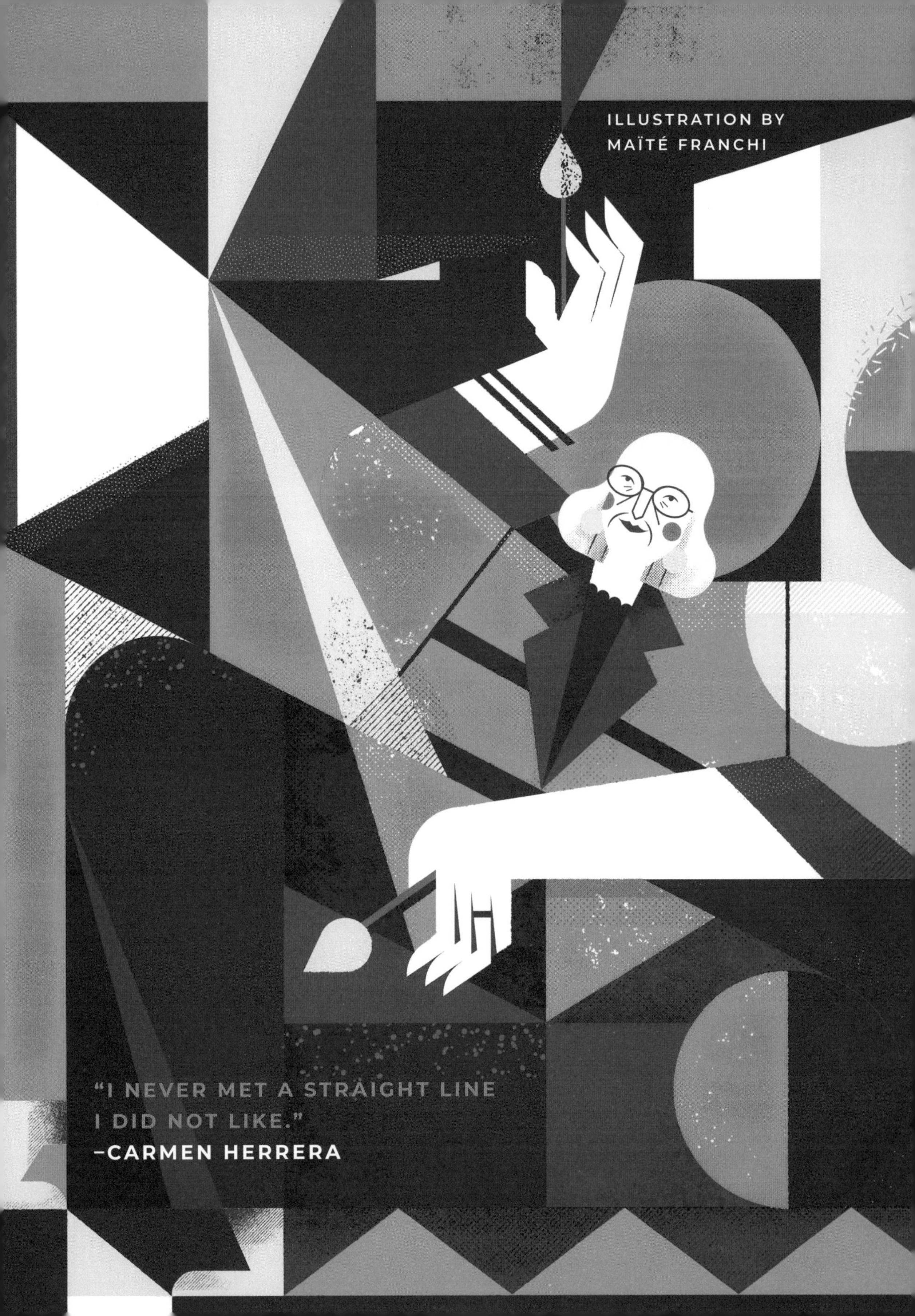
ILLUSTRATION BY
MAÏTÉ FRANCHI
"I NEVER MET A STRAIGHT LINE
I DID NOT LIKE."
–CARMEN HERRERA

CARMEN MIRANDA

SINGER AND ACTRESS

SCAN TO HEAR MORE

Maria do Carmo Miranda da Cunha was born in a small town in Portugal. But by the time she moved to Brazil as a baby, her father had given her a nickname, Carmen, after the famous opera.

Carmen dreamed of a career in show business and recorded some of her first albums singing popular Brazilian songs.

After her first hit record, in 1930, Carmen became a star in Brazil, singing and dancing her way through a series of movie musicals. By 1939, she created her signature look: colorful flowing dresses, platform shoes, and elaborate headdresses.

In June 1939, Carmen and her band performed in a Broadway show. American audiences were captivated by her. Carmen's next stop was Hollywood, where she made more than a dozen films and became the highest-paid actress in the country.

But as Carmen's international success grew, she became less popular back home. Some Brazilians thought she encouraged stereotypes of Latinx people and that she wasn't a true Brazilian because she hadn't been born there. She responded by recording a defiant song in Portuguese called "Disseram Que Eu Voltei Americanizada" ("They Say I've Come Back Americanized"). Through her perseverance and resilience, Carmen showed that a person can be more than one thing and be from more than one place.

FEBRUARY 9, 1909–AUGUST 5, 1955
PORTUGAL → BRAZIL AND UNITED STATES OF AMERICA

ILLUSTRATION BY
SONIA LAZO

"I INVENT MY HATS, I INVENT
MY SHOES, I INVENT MY DRESS.
I HAVE THE IDEAS FOR MY
SONGS, AND I KNOW EXACTLY
WHAT PEOPLE LIKE."
—CARMEN MIRANDA

CAROLINA GUERRERO

JOURNALIST AND PRODUCER

Once there was a girl named Carolina who always wanted to learn something new. In Colombia, where she grew up, she taught people how to scuba dive. When she moved to New York City, she became an art dealer and designer. Later, she organized workshops, art shows, and cultural festivals all over North and South America.

The world was so rich and full, Carolina thought. How could anyone limit themselves to just one place, one language, one **culture**?

In her new home in New York City, Carolina loved to listen to radio programs that told deep, important stories about things she would otherwise never have known about. But these programs were only in English. What about the people, like herself, who spoke Spanish? Why wasn't there a place where they could tell their stories, in their own language?

Carolina decided to start a podcast of her own. *Radio Ambulante* would be a storytelling podcast by and for Spanish speakers. Once a week, the podcast would introduce listeners to firefighters in Peru or punk rockers in Mexico, astronomers in Argentina or soccer stars in Brazil. Carolina became the CEO, the person responsible for making sure *Radio Ambulante* grew and thrived as a business.

The first show was shared in 2011, and today millions of people around the world listen in every week. With *Radio Ambulante*, Carolina brings people together through the power of storytelling.

BIRTHDATE UNKNOWN

COLOMBIA ➔ UNITED STATES OF AMERICA

ILLUSTRATION BY
NOA DENMON

"THERE IS NOTHING LIKE
RADIO AMBULANTE....
WE CELEBRATE A LANGUAGE,
A COMMON LANGUAGE, TO
TELL THOSE STORIES."
—CAROLINA GUERRERO

CHINWE ESIMAI

FINANCIAL EXECUTIVE

Once there was a girl who believed it was more important to shine bright than blend in. When Chinwe was a teenager, her family moved to the United States from Nigeria. In the US, Chinwe realized the way she looked and spoke made her stand out—and not always in a positive way. She also noticed that other immigrants—especially women of color—often tried to disappear into the crowd.

Chinwe eventually earned a degree from Harvard Law School. In her work as a lawyer and later as a professor, she noticed the same troubling thing: immigrant women sometimes downplayed their differences in order to succeed. One of her students was an immigrant from China who never spoke in class even though she was very smart. The student didn't think she should speak up or try to lead until her accent had faded. But Chinwe believed cultural differences—including her own—were strengths. She wanted other women to believe it too.

Chinwe started a leadership website and blog. It was a place where immigrant women could find advice to help them become leaders, especially in the business world. Chinwe wrote from her own experience. Eventually, she became a managing director and chief anti-bribery and corruption officer at an investment banking company where she was the first person to hold that title. And she did it all without hiding who she was. Chinwe said, "I think it's very important to view our background and our **culture** as a positive because that's something unique that you bring to the table."

BIRTHDATE UNKNOWN

NIGERIA ➜ UNITED STATES OF AMERICA

ILLUSTRATION BY
D'ARA NAZARYAN

"EVERYONE'S VOICE
IS IMPORTANT."
—CHINWE ESIMAI

CLARA JULIANA GUERRERO LONDOÑO

BOWLER

There was no place Clara loved more than the bowling alley, and no sound she loved more than the heavy *crash!* of a ball knocking down all 10 pins at once. Clara's grandfather, parents, and brother all loved to bowl. By the time Clara was nine, she was a bowler too. And she was really good at it, winning bigger and bigger tournaments as time went on.

But at Clara's first national tournament for young bowlers, she had a bad game and lost. So she vowed to work even harder.

By the time she was 18, Clara had made the Colombian national bowling team. She was one of the best bowlers in her country and was even voted the sport's Amateur Athlete of the Year. Still, Clara had bigger dreams. The largest bowling tour in the world was in the United States, and the best college bowling team in the US was at Wichita State University.

Moving to a brand-new country would be a challenge, but Clara was willing to try it. It paid off: with Clara on the roster, Wichita State won the national championships!

Clara graduated in 2006 with a degree in international business—and an even better game. In 2009, after winning two gold medals at the women's world championships, Clara was voted Bowler of the Year by the World Bowling Writers. She was also named Athlete of the Year in Colombia—the first time a bowler had been awarded that honor.

BORN APRIL 22, 1982

COLOMBIA ➡ UNITED STATES OF AMERICA

ILLUSTRATION BY AMALTEIA

"MOVING TO A NEW COUNTRY WITH A DIFFERENT CULTURE FAR AWAY FROM HOME TO FOLLOW YOUR DREAM HELPS MAKE YOU STRONGER AS A PERSON."
—CLARA JULIANA GUERRERO LONDOÑO

CLARA LEMLICH SHAVELSON

ACTIVIST

By the time **activist** Clara Lemlich was 23 years old, she had been arrested 17 times. Clara and her family had escaped anti-Jewish violence in the Russian Empire, from a country currently known as Ukraine, when she was a teenager. But life in America was difficult. As soon as they arrived, Clara started working at one of the many clothing factories in New York City. The factories were dark, dirty, and unsafe, and they employed thousands of women who sat at sewing machines from sunrise to sunset. Workers didn't have many rights, and there were few laws to protect them.

Americans had started to form unions—groups of workers who band together—which they believed would give them a voice to fight for their rights. At the time, most unions were led by men and didn't let women get involved. But Clara insisted that unions needed women in order to succeed. Clara organized her fellow workers, wrote articles, and asked people to strike. One day, she gave a passionate speech in **Yiddish** at a union meeting. Her speech led to a huge labor strike that brought about important changes such as better wages and working conditions.

Clara was unfairly arrested over and over for her activism, but she never backed down. She worked hard on causes like women's **suffrage** and helped renters who had unfair landlords. Her passion for justice among working-class people shaped her entire life.

MARCH 28, 1886–JULY 12, 1982
UKRAINE ➜ UNITED STATES OF AMERICA

"I THINK THE WOMEN WHO BUY AND WEAR THE BEAUTIFUL CLOTHES DO NOT KNOW HOW IT IS FOR THE GIRL WHO MAKES THEM.... OR THEY WOULD CARE AND WOULD TRY TO HELP HER."
—CLARA LEMLICH SHAVELSON

ILLUSTRATION BY LISA LANOË

CLAUDIA RANKINE

POET AND PLAYWRIGHT

Once there was a seven-year-old girl named Claudia whose family left their tropical island home for a new life in New York City.

Life in crowded, gritty New York City was very different from life in Jamaica. Claudia's mother wanted her to be proud of being Jamaican, but Claudia also wanted to fit in. She looked like other black Americans, but she didn't share some of their **culture**. Claudia spent a lot of time reading and thinking about her new world. Eventually, she would turn these thoughts into stories and poems.

Later, Claudia earned college degrees in literature and poetry and began to teach at a university. She continued to watch, listen, and write. In 1994, she published her first poetry collection. Since then, Claudia's poetry has won many important awards, and she's written several plays. In 2014, one of her books became the first book of poetry to ever hold a place on the *New York Times* bestseller list for nonfiction.

But Claudia doesn't write poetry for the awards. Instead, she sees her poems as conversations with her reader. These conversations are often about difficult topics, like **racism**. But Claudia believes that hard conversations can lead to understanding. "It's our job to see the person in front of us," she said, "and if that means having an uncomfortable conversation, have that conversation. Please."

BORN CIRCA 1963

JAMAICA ➜ UNITED STATES OF AMERICA

ILLUSTRATION BY
NICOLE MILES

"I WASN'T WAITING TO BE
CHOSEN—YOU DON'T WRITE
WITH THE FREEDOM THAT I DO
IF THAT'S WHAT IS ON YOUR MIND."
—CLAUDIA RANKINE

DANIELA SCHILLER

· · · · · · · · · · · · · · · · · · ·

NEUROSCIENTIST

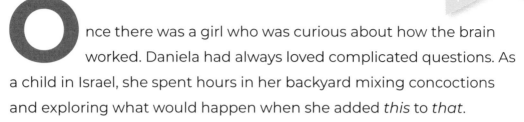

Once there was a girl who was curious about how the brain worked. Daniela had always loved complicated questions. As a child in Israel, she spent hours in her backyard mixing concoctions and exploring what would happen when she added *this* to *that*.

But there were some questions Daniela couldn't answer. For a sixth-grade class project, she tried to interview her father about his experiences during the **Holocaust**, but his memories were too painful to share.

She wanted to understand why fear and painful memories were so powerful. So she became a scientist who studied the part of the brain that controlled emotion and memory. She also wanted to help people like her father who had lived through terrible things. After getting her PhD in cognitive neuroscience, Daniela moved to the United States and got a job with an important research lab. Scientists were learning how to use medication to change the way people felt about their bad memories. They would no longer cause fear, sadness, or pain.

Later, Daniela made her own amazing discovery: it was possible to change bad memories *without* using medication. She realized if a person experienced something pleasant while thinking about a bad memory, that would help change how they felt about it. Since that discovery, Daniela has continued to study the brain and is now the leader of her own research lab. Her groundbreaking work is being used to bring healing and hope to people who—like her father—are living with trauma and anxiety.

· ·

BORN OCTOBER 26, 1972
ISRAEL ➜ UNITED STATES OF AMERICA

ILLUSTRATION BY
IRENE RINALDI

"WE AREN'T A SLAVE
TO OUR PAST. IF YOU
ARE STUCK WITH A BAD
MEMORY...IT'S NOT
EXACTLY THE TRUTH
AND YOU CAN REVISE IT."
—DANIELA SCHILLER

DANIELA SOTO-INNES

CHEF

Once there was a girl who believed that food should bring people joy. It was a lesson she learned in her family's kitchen in Mexico. Daniela spent her childhood helping her grandmother in her bakery and learning recipes from her mother. "I knew it was the thing that made me the happiest," she said.

When Daniela was 12 years old, her family moved from Mexico City to Texas. Two years later, she got her first restaurant job and attended culinary school soon after. But when Daniela started working in restaurants, she was disappointed by what she saw: kitchens were not joyful places. The staff worked long hours, and the chefs were harsh bosses. Daniela decided that if she ever ran a restaurant, she would do things differently.

She didn't have to wait long. Her career as a chef started in Mexico City, and when Daniela was just 24, she was asked to lead a Mexican-inspired restaurant in New York City. The restaurant became a huge success, and it allowed Daniela to combine both her Latin American and American roots in experimental ways.

In 2016, Daniela won the James Beard Award for Rising Star Chef. Eventually, she opened another restaurant and has won even more awards. To Daniela, her greatest success is the community she's created and a staff that feels like family. Her kitchens are always full of laughter, dancing, and singing—just like in the kitchen of her childhood.

BORN AUGUST 26, 1990
MEXICO ➔ UNITED STATES OF AMERICA

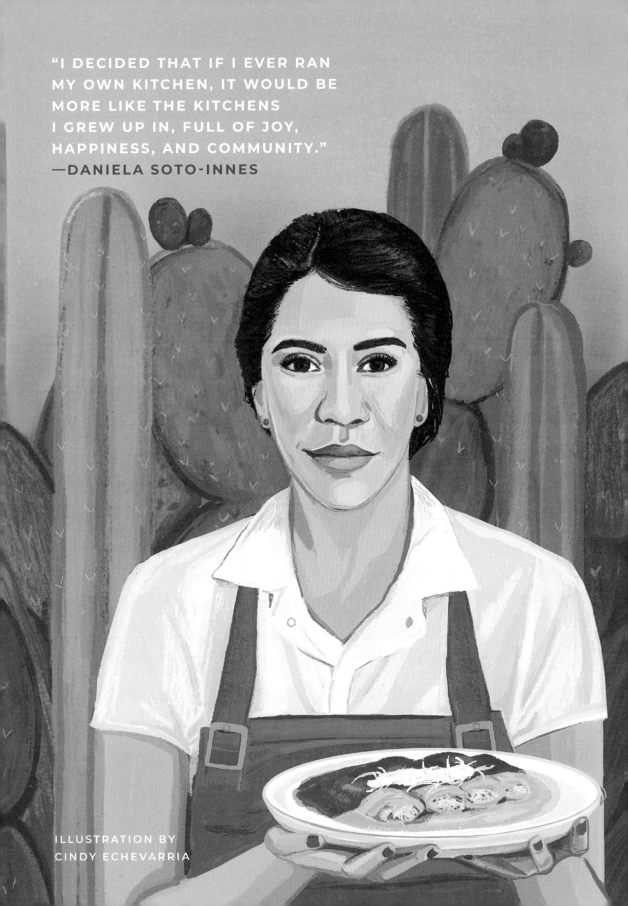

"I DECIDED THAT IF I EVER RAN MY OWN KITCHEN, IT WOULD BE MORE LIKE THE KITCHENS I GREW UP IN, FULL OF JOY, HAPPINESS, AND COMMUNITY."
—DANIELA SOTO-INNES

ILLUSTRATION BY
CINDY ECHEVARRIA

DAPHNE KOLLER

COMPUTER SCIENTIST AND ENTREPRENEUR

Once upon a time, there was a girl named Daphne who loved to learn. She loved math and computers, and started programming when she was 12 years old. When she was a young teenager, Daphne told her parents she was bored in high school. She wanted to go to college instead.

Daphne was only 17 years old when she graduated from university in Israel. Soon after, she decided to move to the United States to get her PhD. Daphne arrived on July 4, 1989. It was Independence Day in the US—a good day, she decided, to start a life in her new country.

By studying artificial intelligence and centuries-old ideas about decision-making, Daphne found new ways to teach computers to make predictions. Her research helped doctors figure out how cancer spreads, how to prevent illness in premature babies, and other lifesaving work.

Because of her own experiences in school, Daphne also knew the importance of a flexible education. She wanted to connect students with the knowledge they craved, even if they didn't have money or means to get to a classroom.

With her business partner, Daphne started Coursera, a company that would allow people all over the world to take university classes online. Since then, Daphne has been elected to the American Academy of Arts and Sciences and named one of the world's most influential people by *Time* magazine.

BORN AUGUST 27, 1968
ISRAEL → UNITED STATES OF AMERICA

ILLUSTRATION BY FANNY BLANC

"THE WORLD IS NOISY AND MESSY. YOU NEED TO DEAL WITH THE NOISE AND UNCERTAINTY."
—DAPHNE KOLLER

DIANE VON FÜRSTENBERG

FASHION DESIGNER

In fairy tales, when a woman becomes a princess, she lives happily ever after in a castle. But when a young Belgian woman named Diane married a German prince, she didn't want to live a sheltered life. She wanted to *do* something. "I decided to have a career," she said. "I had to be someone of my own."

After Diane von Fürstenberg and her husband moved to the United States and had two children, she started to design her own clothing line: Diane von Fürstenberg Studio. One day, Diane combined a wrap-style shirt and skirt into a simple long-sleeved dress that tied at the waist: a wrap dress. The design was a success. Made from soft fabric with no zippers or buttons, the wrap dress was comfortable and easy to wear. It was a style that was formal enough for office work but fashionable enough to wear after work too. In 1975, Diane's studio made 15,000 wrap dresses a week, and by 1976, she had sold more than five million dresses!

Today Diane von Fürstenberg owns one of the most successful fashion empires in the world. Her designs are worn by women everywhere, including royalty and movie stars. Diane also uses her success to mentor and help other women. "I did not know what I wanted to do," Diane said, "but I knew the kind of woman I wanted to be."

BORN DECEMBER 31, 1946

BELGIUM → UNITED STATES OF AMERICA

"I WANT TO EMPOWER
EVERY WOMAN."
—DIANE VON FÜRSTENBERG

ILLUSTRATION BY
ELISA SEITZINGER

DOREEN SIMMONS

SPORTS COMMENTATOR

Once upon a time, there was a girl who dreamed of seeing what life was like in a country different from her own. After college, she traveled far from home—first to Singapore and then to Japan. In Japan, Doreen became captivated by the country's favorite sport: sumo wrestling.

Growing up in England, Doreen had loved to watch a sport called cricket. She watched it every Saturday and took careful notes about what she saw. Years later, when Doreen learned about the complicated world of sumo wrestling, she did the same thing. She became an expert.

"I took up sumo watching just like I did cricket, taking notes with my own homemade scorecard—oh, and learning Japanese frantically," Doreen said.

Doreen traveled all over Japan to watch tournaments and wrote a magazine column about sumo. It was rare for a woman—especially a woman who wasn't Japanese—to be part of the inner world of sumo, but Doreen was not afraid to do the unexpected. In 1992, she was hired as a part-time commentator for sumo matches on national TV in Japan. She helped viewers understand what they were seeing. The TV network depended on Doreen for her expert knowledge. In 2017, the Japanese government awarded Doreen with the Order of the Rising Sun, one of the country's highest honors, to celebrate her contributions to Japan's **culture**.

MAY 29, 1932–APRIL 23, 2018
UNITED KINGDOM ➡ JAPAN

"EVERYTHING IN MY LIFE
CHANGED FROM BLACK AND
WHITE TO GLORIOUS COLOR.
AND I'VE BEEN LIVING IN
GLORIOUS COLOR EVER SINCE."
—DOREEN SIMMONS

ILLUSTRATION BY
PETRA BRAUN

EDMONIA LEWIS

SCULPTOR

Once upon a time, there was a little girl called Wildfire. Born in New York to an Afro-Haitian father and a mother who was Mississauga Ojibwe, Wildfire became an orphan at a young age and was taken in by her mother's sisters.

When Wildfire was a young woman, she dropped her Ojibwe name and started to use her other given name, Mary Edmonia Lewis—or just Edmonia, for short. Edmonia attended one of the first American colleges that allowed students of color, but she experienced terrible **racism** there. She was even falsely accused of poisoning two white classmates and put on trial. The jury decided that Edmonia was innocent, but she was forced to leave college without graduating.

Around 1863, Edmonia moved to Boston to become a sculptor. In those days, people thought sculpting was only for men.

As the first American woman of color to become a professional sculptor, Edmonia attracted attention from white **abolitionists**. But she dreamed of living in a place where people paid more attention to her skill than to her **ethnicity**.

Around 1865, Edmonia moved to Rome and joined a community of artists. In 1876, she created a sculpture of Cleopatra in honor of America's one hundredth anniversary. Sadly, most of Edmonia's art hasn't survived, but this sculpture did. It disappeared for a century until it was discovered in a Chicago mall covered in paint, and it now lives at the Smithsonian American Art Museum.

CIRCA 1844–SEPTEMBER 17, 1907

UNITED STATES OF AMERICA ➜ ITALY

"I HAVE A STRONG SYMPATHY
FOR ALL WOMEN WHO HAVE
STRUGGLED AND SUFFERED."
—EDMONIA LEWIS

ILLUSTRATION BY
MONICA AHANONU

EILEEN GRAY

ARCHITECT AND FURNITURE DESIGNER

Once there was a girl named Eileen who left Ireland to study drawing at a famous London art school. As she wandered the streets one day, she ducked into a shop where craftspeople were repairing old lacquer screens. Seeing her excitement, they eventually invited her to help out. And so, Eileen traded her drawing pencils for tools when she discovered a new passion: furniture design.

A few years later, Eileen moved to Paris to study art and learn from Japanese lacquer master Seizo Sugawara. The two artists opened a workshop together, and people began to buy Eileen's unique and eye-catching furniture. She loved to experiment with unexpected materials like glass, chrome, and steel tubes, and challenge old design methods. Eileen eventually opened her own gallery, where she sold her furniture, light fixtures, and handwoven carpets.

Over time, Eileen's interest changed from furniture design to modern architecture. She read architecture books, took drafting lessons, and joined architects at their building sites. She also drew plans of her own. Eileen's first—and most famous—building was a villa she called E-1027. The house was white and rectangular like a row of sugar cubes and was perched on a cliff overlooking the Mediterranean Sea. It was filled with Eileen's modern furniture. Eileen continued to work and create until she died at age 98. By then she had gained the reputation as a pioneer in the modern design movement.

AUGUST 9, 1878–OCTOBER 31, 1976
IRELAND → UNITED KINGDOM AND FRANCE

"TO CREATE, ONE MUST FIRST QUESTION EVERYTHING."
—EILEEN GRAY

ILLUSTRATION BY
JOSEFINA SCHARGORODSKY

ELENA PONIATOWSKA

JOURNALIST

Once upon a time, there was a girl named Elena who was born to a wealthy family in France descended from Polish royalty.

When Elena was around nine years old, her family moved to Mexico to escape World War II. She wanted to learn more about her new home and the people who shared it with her. One of the best ways to do that was to become a reporter. It was a reporter's job to pay attention, write things down, and ask questions—and Elena loved asking questions! She got her first job at a newspaper when she was 21.

Elena was drawn to stories that other writers overlooked: those of poor people, Indigenous people, prisoners, and women. She wrote dozens and dozens of works, including essays, nonfiction books, articles, novels, poetry, and books for children.

Elena also told stories that other journalists were too afraid to write about. When soldiers attacked peaceful **protesters** in Mexico City in 1968, Elena was brave enough to write about it. Though she was threatened, Elena believed that her book about the attack should be published. It was published all over the world and became a bestseller, helping survivors and their families understand what happened that night. When the government tried to give her a prize for the book, she refused it. The people they should be honoring, she said, were the victims.

In 2014, Elena received the Cervantes Prize, the highest honor for writing in the Spanish language.

BORN MAY 19, 1932

FRANCE ➡ MEXICO

ILLUSTRATION BY
CRISTINA MARTÍN

"I WAS ALWAYS ASKING
TOO MANY QUESTIONS, AND
I'LL BE THAT WAY UNTIL I DIE."
—ELENA PONIATOWSKA

ELISA ROJAS

LAWYER

When a girl named Elisa was born, the doctors were worried. Something was different about this baby, they said. Her body was shaped differently. Some of her bones broke at birth.

Her parents did not care. When they looked in Elisa's eyes, all they saw was a smart and spirited girl looking back at them.

Elisa was born with a genetic condition that made her bones break easily. She would always need to use a wheelchair to get around. But Elisa was bright and curious, and did not see why that should stop her from chasing her dreams. Her parents didn't, either. The family moved from Chile to a new home in France so Elisa could have better opportunities: not just for her medical care but for her brilliant mind too.

Elisa excelled in school and decided to become a lawyer. She passed her exams, but it took 18 months to find a law firm willing to hire a woman who used a wheelchair.

Elisa was a great lawyer, but practicing law wasn't always easy. She often arrived at courthouses to represent her clients to find that she was not able to get into the building. Elisa was furious. She had the right to access those places just as much as any other person in France. Her disability wasn't the problem. The problem was people's refusal to treat her as an equal.

Elisa helped form a group that fought to make laws fair for people with disabilities. She is still fighting today.

BORN APRIL 30, 1979

CHILE ➜ FRANCE

"WE WANT SIMPLE RESPECT FOR OUR RIGHTS."
—ELISA ROJAS

ILLUSTRATION BY
ANNALISA VENTURA

ELISABETH KÜBLER-ROSS

PSYCHIATRIST

One summer night in Switzerland, three tiny girls were born right in a row: Elisabeth, Erika, and Eva. From the beginning, Elisabeth was determined to make her own way in the world. Even before she finished school, Elisabeth knew she wanted to be a doctor. Her bold plans made her father angry, so at 16 years old, Elisabeth left home, working odd jobs and volunteering in wartime hospitals.

In 1951, Elisabeth went to medical school in Switzerland to become a psychiatrist. After marrying a fellow doctor, Elisabeth moved to the United States. At her new job in a hospital, she worked with patients who were sick with illnesses that could not be cured. She was shocked by how these patients were treated. The medical staff seemed to know very little about death and how to talk about it. Elisabeth believed that death was a normal part of life and that people should be able to talk about it in honest ways. She convinced the hospital to allow her to provide counseling and care for the patients.

For the rest of her career—as a psychiatrist, professor, and author—Elisabeth taught medical students, doctors, and nurses to be honest and compassionate toward dying patients. She developed the well-known theory of the five stages of grief, and her work changed many attitudes in the medical community. Her work inspired the creation of a hospice system, special clinics that care for terminally ill patients. In 2007, Elisabeth was inducted into the National Women's Hall of Fame for her pioneering work.

JULY 8, 1926–AUGUST 24, 2004
SWITZERLAND ➔ UNITED STATES OF AMERICA

"THE ULTIMATE LESSON ALL OF US HAVE TO LEARN IS UNCONDITIONAL LOVE, WHICH INCLUDES NOT ONLY OTHERS BUT OURSELVES AS WELL."
—ELISABETH KÜBLER-ROSS

ILLUSTRATION BY JENNIFER POTTER

ELIZABETH NYAMAYARO

HUMANITARIAN

Once upon a time, there was a girl who dreamed about working for the United Nations. Elizabeth was eight years old when a terrible famine happened in Zimbabwe. But, one day, help arrived. A young woman in a blue uniform came to her village and handed out food. She told Elizabeth, "As Africans, we must all uplift each other." The woman worked for the United Nations, an organization that encourages countries to work together to solve problems and help people. This moment sparked Elizabeth's dream to help others.

After a second famine struck, Elizabeth was sent to live in Harare, Zimbabwe's capital, with an aunt. At 10 years old, Elizabeth started attending school, where she experienced inequality and **prejudice** for the first time. Because she couldn't speak English and was behind in reading and writing, her classmates looked down on her. It was a difficult experience. But this made Elizabeth even more determined to help others who were mistreated.

Elizabeth later left Zimbabwe to chase her dream in London. With lots of hard work, her childhood dream came true: she got a job at the United Nations! As a senior director there, Elizabeth helped launch an important worldwide movement for gender equality called HeForShe. The movement encouraged all genders to work together to speak out against stereotypes and **discrimination**. Elizabeth made a home for herself in New York, but she carries her African continent in her heart. She even started a nonprofit to help people there. "Africa has given me so much and made me who I am," Elizabeth said. "I want to be part of the solution."

BIRTHDATE UNKNOWN

ZIMBABWE → UNITED STATES OF AMERICA

"WE ALL CAN AND SHOULD MAKE A DIFFERENCE."
—ELIZABETH NYAMAYARO

ILLUSTRATION BY MARIAN BAILEY

EMILIE SNETHLAGE

ORNITHOLOGIST

When Emilie attended the University of Berlin for the first time around age 30, she was an eager student. She wanted to study natural history.

Despite being a bright student, Emilie unfortunately was also an invisible one. Women weren't allowed to officially enroll in college yet in Germany, so Emily had to sit behind a screen when she attended class. Despite this unfair treatment, Emilie earned her doctorate in 1904 and began her career as a zoological assistant at the Berlin Natural History Museum.

But a bigger adventure was waiting. In 1905, Emilie was hired to be a zoological assistant at Museu Paraense Emílio Goeldi, a museum and research institution in Belém, Brazil. When she boarded the boat for her journey, it was the first time she had traveled so far outside her own country.

From then on, Brazil was Emilie's home. Part scientist, part explorer, she studied the animals of the Amazon, and she trekked to remote parts of the rain forest to collect specimens. Emilie became best known for her work as an ornithologist, a scientist who studies birds. In 1914, she became the first woman director of a scientific institution in South America. She also published a book about Amazonian birds that was 530 pages long! At least five animal species, including two bird species, have been named in her honor.

APRIL 13, 1868–NOVEMBER 25, 1929

GERMANY ➔ BRAZIL

ILLUSTRATION BY
BODIL JANE

"I KNOW THE BIRDS
SO WELL, THAT I KNOW
WHAT KIND OF BIRD IS
IN FRONT OF ME EVEN
BEFORE IT LANDS."
—EMILIE SNETHLAGE

EMMY NOETHER

MATHEMATICIAN

Once there was a girl whose mind came alive whenever she studied math. In Emmy's day, women were not welcome in college classrooms in Germany. She had passed exams that would have allowed her to teach English and French to girls, but Emmy didn't want to follow that path.

In 1904, the University of Erlangen allowed women students for the first time, and Emmy enrolled immediately. By 1907, she had earned her PhD in mathematics. For the next seven years, Emmy taught at that same university alongside her father, who was also a mathematician.

Because of unjust rules about women teachers, the university refused to pay Emmy, but she earned the respect of other mathematicians during that time, including two of her former teachers. One day, those teachers asked for Emmy's help. They were struggling with some problems related to Albert Einstein's new theory of relativity. In the process of working with them, Emmy proved a new mathematical result. It's known today as Noether's theorem, and it's an important part of physics. She also helped start a new branch of mathematics called abstract algebra.

Around 1923, Emmy began teaching at the University of Göttingen. She was devoted to her classes, but when the Nazis came to power in Germany 10 years later, the university fired all professors who were Jewish like Emmy. Emmy left for the United States, and today she's considered one of the most important mathematicians of the twentieth century.

MARCH 23, 1882–APRIL 14, 1935
GERMANY ➜ UNITED STATES OF AMERICA

ILLUSTRATION BY
ELENI DEBO

"MY METHODS ARE REALLY
METHODS OF WORKING
AND THINKING."
—EMMY NOETHER

FATMA IPEK ALCI

Once upon a time, there was a nurse named Fatma who moved from Turkey to Sweden so she could use her skills to take care of sick people there.

The first neighborhood where she and her family lived was a very nice place. Then her daughter got sick, and when the local hospital couldn't help her anymore, Fatma's family moved to Stockholm, the capital of Sweden, which had a bigger hospital.

The new neighborhood was very different. It wasn't safe. Young people were getting into trouble, damaging markets and other local businesses. Some people were afraid to leave their houses.

Fatma didn't think this was right. She cared about her new community, so she met with other parents to try to figure out how to fix the problems. Under Fatma's direction, they organized teams of local neighbors to walk around the area at night to help everyone feel safe.

She also realized that young people were getting into trouble because there was nothing for them to do. She convinced the government to open a job center for teenagers in their area, which helped. She even started taking classes in private security herself.

In 2017, Fatma was named Hero of the Year by a Swedish newspaper for her work in the community.

BORN CIRCA 1954
TURKEY → SWEDEN

ILLUSTRATION BY
LACI JORDAN

"WE HAVE TO SAVE OUR YOUTH....
I'M NOT A COP, BUT I'M A MOTHER,
I'M A GRANDMOTHER, I'M AN AUNT.
I THINK ABOUT MY GRANDKIDS,
MY NEIGHBORS' CHILDREN."
—FATMA IPEK ALCI

FRIEDA BELINFANTE

SCAN TO HEAR MORE

CELLIST AND CONDUCTOR

Once there was a girl named Frieda who lived and breathed music. Her father was a professional pianist, so it was no surprise that Frieda was a natural musician. She played the cello from a young age and eventually set out to become a professional musician like her father. Things didn't exactly go as planned. After graduating from a conservatory in Amsterdam in 1921, Frieda applied to be a high school music teacher. The school hired a man instead, believing he'd be better at disciplining students. Ultimately, that frustrated teacher quit, and Frieda was hired in his place. She was a capable teacher and—quite unexpectedly—a talented conductor. The head of Amsterdam's royal concert hall asked Frieda to be the conductor and artistic director for their chamber orchestra, making her the first woman conductor of a chamber orchestra in Europe.

World War II interrupted Frieda's career. She bravely joined the Dutch **resistance** even though she was of Jewish heritage and a lesbian. After being pursued by the Nazis, Frieda disguised herself as a man and escaped to Switzerland by crossing the Alps on foot.

After the war, Frieda **immigrated** to the United States and became a music professor at the University of California, Los Angeles. She also became the conductor and artistic director of the Orange County Philharmonic. As director, she insisted the concerts have free admission so more people could hear their music. "I pioneered in music," Freida said when she was in her nineties. "I liked that, to bring music where it wasn't."

MAY 10, 1904–APRIL 26, 1995
NETHERLANDS → UNITED STATES OF AMERICA

23

ILLUSTRATION BY
GOSIA HERBA

"I'VE ALWAYS BEEN
A PERSISTENT PERSON.
I DON'T TAKE NO FOR
AN ANSWER. IF IT CANNOT
BE DONE, I WOULD SAY,
'WE'LL SEE.'"
—FRIEDA BELINFANTE

GERALDINE COX

HUMANITARIAN

Once there was a girl named Geraldine who longed to experience life outside her small Australian town. She finally got to travel abroad when she was 19 years old and spent a year working as a secretary in a London office. When she returned to Australia, her desire to know more about the world was even stronger.

At age 26, Geraldine worked for Australia's Department of Foreign Affairs and was assigned to the office in Phnom Penh, Cambodia. This changed the course of her life. At that time, Cambodia was experiencing a bitter civil war. In the years that followed, Geraldine's job sent her all over the world: to the Philippines, Thailand, and Iran. In Cambodia, meanwhile, millions suffered under a brutal **dictator** named Pol Pot. Geraldine followed this news with a heavy heart and longed to return. She cared deeply about the country and its people.

When she was 50 years old, Geraldine moved back to Cambodia and volunteered at an orphanage. The war and Pol Pot were long gone, but the country was still very poor and recovering from years of hardship.

Then more fighting broke out. The orphanage workers were scared, but Geraldine refused to leave behind the 60 children living there. She founded her own orphanage, Sunrise Cambodia, to help children whose families couldn't care for them. She even set up schools and training programs. Over the years, thousands of children in Cambodia have called Sunrise home. They call Geraldine *M'Day Thom*—Big Mother.

BORN CIRCA 1945

AUSTRALIA ➞ CAMBODIA

"EVERYONE WANTS
TO BE NEEDED."
—GERALDINE COX

GERALDINE HEANEY

ICE HOCKEY PLAYER AND COACH

A screaming crowd filled the arena at the gold-medal game between Canada and the United States at ice hockey's first-ever women's world championships. A Canadian named Geraldine got the puck and fired so hard that her body flew through the air—just as the game-winning goal sailed into the net.

Geraldine was born in Northern Ireland. When she was just a baby, her parents decided to move the family to Canada. When they arrived, they learned their new country was passionate about a sport called ice hockey.

As soon as she was old enough to skate, Geraldine followed her older brothers to the ice rink so she could play too. Not many girls played ice hockey. But Geraldine didn't care. She just loved to play. By the time she was 13, she had signed with a semiprofessional women's team. Within a decade, she'd be a member of the women's national team.

During her time on Canada's national team, Geraldine won seven world championships, a silver medal at the 1998 Olympics, and a gold medal at the 2002 Olympics, her final international tournament. She was only the third woman to be inducted into the Hockey Hall of Fame.

Geraldine played her last professional game in 2004, at the Canadian national championship. Just as she had almost 14 years earlier, Geraldine scored the game-winning goal to win the gold. This time, however, she was three months pregnant with her first child.

After Geraldine stopped playing ice hockey professionally, she became a coach, passing on her love of the game to other young women.

BORN OCTOBER 1, 1967

NORTHERN IRELAND → CANADA

"I WAS TOLD, 'GIRLS DON'T PLAY HOCKEY'.... BUT I JUST IGNORED ALL THAT."
—GERALDINE HEANEY

ILLUSTRATION BY
PAOLA ROLLO

GERDA TARO

PHOTOGRAPHER

Once there was a fearless girl who used her camera to tell the truth about the world. Gerta Pohorylle grew up in Germany, but she was forced to flee after the Nazis came to power. At 23, she moved to Paris, where she met and fell in love with a fellow Jewish **refugee**, Endre Friedmann. Endre was an adventurous photojournalist, and as Gerta worked as his assistant, he taught her all he knew. Soon, Endre and Gerta were working as a team and traveled to Spain to photograph the Spanish Civil War.

Gerta and Endre faced a lot of **prejudice** due to political intolerance and anti-Semitism in Europe. Together, they invented an alias, a fake American photographer they called Robert Capa to avoid **discrimination** and to command higher prices for their work. At first, Gerta and Endre both published their photos under this name. After a while, however, only Endre used the name Robert Capa, while Gerta published under the name Gerda Taro.

The couple traveled through Spain and to the front lines of the civil war. They took photos of soldiers and refugees, and documented how the violent war hurt ordinary people. Gerta was a bold photographer, and traveled to increasingly dangerous places. In 1937, tragedy struck: Gerta died while photographing the Battle of Brunete. She is considered the first woman war photographer to die in battle. In Paris, more than 10,000 people lined the streets to pay their respects at her funeral and honor her bravery.

AUGUST 1, 1910–JULY 26, 1937

GERMANY ➡ FRANCE

ILLUSTRATION BY
MARTA GIUNIPERO

GLORIA ESTEFAN

SINGER

Once there was a shy girl who grew to love the spotlight. When Gloria's family left Cuba in 1959, there was a **revolution** happening there. They built a new life in Florida, where Gloria and her siblings went to school, her mother got a job, and her father volunteered to fight in the Vietnam War. When he returned, he was very sick.

Gloria spent her teen years taking care of her father. During this difficult time, her love of music grew. "When my father was ill, music was my escape," Gloria said. Gloria's love of singing eventually led to the stage. She met a fellow Cuban immigrant named Emilio, who asked her to join his band.

Gloria and Emilio soon got married, and eventually, Gloria became a solo artist. She sang in English and Spanish, becoming popular in the US and overseas. In 1990, however, Gloria's music career nearly ended. The band's tour bus got into an accident, and Gloria was badly hurt. Doctors told her she might never walk again. But less than a year later, she was back onstage.

Gloria and Emilio became a powerful force in music and in business. Between them, they have released more than 20 albums, won 26 Grammys, and produced a musical. They own a recording studio, a publishing company, restaurants, hotels, and part of a football team! In 2017, Gloria received the Kennedy Center Honors for her contributions to American **culture**. She was the first Cuban American to ever receive the award.

BORN SEPTEMBER 1, 1957
CUBA ➜ UNITED STATES OF AMERICA

"MUSIC IS MY FIRST LOVE."
—GLORIA ESTEFAN

ILLUSTRATION BY
NAN LAWSON

GOLDA MEIR

POLITICIAN

Once there was a girl who was born to be an **activist**. When Golda was in school, she noticed that some students didn't have textbooks because they couldn't afford them. Golda rallied her friends to hold a fundraiser to buy textbooks for their classmates. She and her family had **immigrated** to the US only a few years ago. They had left their home in the Russian Empire, from a country currently known as Ukraine, because Jewish people were no longer safe there.

In America, Golda trained to become a teacher and taught **Yiddish** at a school in Milwaukee. She also joined a group of political activists who believed Jewish people should have their own country in the Middle East where their **ancestors** had first lived. Eventually, Golda and her husband, Morris Meyerson, moved to the Middle East themselves and joined a community called a kibbutz.

In 1948, Golda was one of two women to sign Israel's declaration of independence. For over two decades, she worked in Israel's government. When she was asked to take a Hebrew last name, she changed it from Meyerson to Meir, which means "illuminate."

When she was about 68, Golda wanted to retire, but people urged her not to. Then one day, Israel's prime minister unexpectedly died, and Golda, then secretary-general, became prime minister. A few months later, her political party won the election, and she served as prime minister for four and a half more years. She was Israel's fourth prime minister and, to this day, the only woman prime minister Israel has had.

MAY 3, 1898–DECEMBER 8, 1978
UKRAINE ➡ UNITED STATES OF AMERICA AND ISRAEL

ILLUSTRATION BY
DECUE WU

"IT ISN'T REALLY IMPORTANT
TO DECIDE...EXACTLY WHAT
YOU WANT TO BECOME WHEN
YOU GROW UP. IT IS MUCH MORE
IMPORTANT TO DECIDE ON THE
WAY YOU WANT TO LIVE."
—GOLDA MEIR

HANNAH ARENDT

PHILOSOPHER AND POLITICAL THEORIST

Once there was a girl with a brilliant mind who wasn't afraid to ask puzzling questions. Her name was Hannah, and by the time she was a teenager, Hannah knew ancient Greek, had read many classic books, and had memorized many German and French poems.

Hannah went to a university where she learned how to think big and ask hard questions. She studied a subject called philosophy, which is the study of knowledge, right and wrong, and the way people think. In 1929, Hannah earned her PhD in philosophy and wanted to become a professor so she could help other people become deep thinkers too.

But in 1933, Hannah was thrown into prison. She had been researching the Nazi Party and their plans to harm Jewish people. When Nazi officials found out, they arrested her.

After she was released, Hannah escaped to France and then **immigrated** to New York City as a **refugee**. She eventually became a professor and taught at some of the top American universities. Hannah wrote political philosophy books that examined topics such as the struggle between good and evil. One of her most important theories attempted to explain how ordinary people can get swept up in governments and political systems that do evil things. It was something she had tried to understand in her own country as she watched her fellow Germans join the Nazis. Hannah's deep thinking and writing made her one of the most important philosophers of the century.

OCTOBER 14, 1906–DECEMBER 4, 1975

GERMANY ➜ FRANCE AND UNITED STATES OF AMERICA

ILLUSTRATION BY
ALESSANDRA
DE CRISTOFARO

"THE SAD TRUTH IS THAT
MOST EVIL IS DONE BY
PEOPLE WHO NEVER MAKE
UP THEIR MINDS TO BE
GOOD OR EVIL."
—HANNAH ARENDT

HAZEL SCOTT

MUSICIAN AND ACTIVIST

Once upon a time, there was a girl named Hazel with a special gift for music. Hazel's mother was a pianist and a music teacher, and whenever one of her students hit a wrong note, Hazel would scream as if she were hurt.

One day, when she was three years old, Hazel climbed up on the piano bench and tapped out a favorite song on the keys, without ever being taught. It turned out she had a perfect ear for music and couldn't stand to hear a note played wrong.

Soon she moved with her mother and grandmother from their home in Trinidad to New York City in search of more opportunities. When she auditioned at the Juilliard School, one of the world's most famous music schools, the professor who heard her play said she was a genius. He even gave her a special scholarship. Juilliard didn't usually take students until they were 16—and Hazel was only eight!

Jazz, blues, classical: Hazel could sing and play it all. She soon became famous, and used her celebrity to fight back against the **discrimination** that black people faced. When she was asked to appear in Hollywood movies, she refused to do roles or wear costumes that were demeaning to black women. When she toured, she refused to play for **segregated** audiences.

"Why would anyone come to hear me...and refuse to sit beside someone just like me?" she said. Newspapers said she had "a style all her own."

JUNE 11, 1920–OCTOBER 2, 1981
TRINIDAD → UNITED STATES OF AMERICA

ILLUSTRATION BY
SABRENA KHADIJA

"WHO EVER WALKED
BEHIND ANYONE TO
FREEDOM? IF WE CAN'T
GO HAND IN HAND,
I DON'T WANT TO GO."
—HAZEL SCOTT

ILHAN OMAR

POLITICIAN

Once there was a small girl in Somalia whose grandfather told her a secret: she had the spirit of a mighty queen, like Somalia's legendary Queen Arawelo. This made the girl, Ilhan, feel proud.

When Ilhan was about eight years old, a war broke out in Somalia. Rockets flew near her home, and a few even hit her house. Her family fled to a **refugee** camp in Kenya, and four years later, they found **asylum** in a new country: the United States. There, Ilhan and her family settled in Minnesota. Ilhan was different from many of the kids at her school because she was black, and a refugee, and Muslim.

Ilhan's grandfather explained to her that America was a democratic country, which meant that everyone could have a voice in their government, no matter their differences. She was fascinated by the way politics could change people's lives for the better.

Ilhan became an American **citizen** when she was 17 years old. After she graduated from college, she worked on political campaigns before deciding to run for office herself. In 2016, she won a seat in Minnesota's state government. Two years later, she ran for US Congress—and won. Ilhan became the first Somali American woman to serve as a US representative. When she flew to Washington, DC, to be sworn in, she landed at the same airport where she'd arrived as a refugee.

Though some people criticize Ilhan's ideas, she isn't afraid to speak up for what she believes is right. Thanks to her, many more people have their voice represented in America's democracy.

BORN OCTOBER 4, 1982

SOMALIA ➔ KENYA AND UNITED STATES OF AMERICA

ILLUSTRATION BY
ALESSANDRA
DE CRISTOFARO

"THE FLOOR
OF CONGRESS
IS GOING TO LOOK
LIKE AMERICA."
—ILHAN OMAR

INDRA DEVI

YOGI

Eugenie was a girl who felt at home everywhere in the world. Her father was from Sweden, and her mother was from Russia. She was born in Latvia, and when she was a young woman, she moved to Germany, where she became an actor and dancer.

But one place called to her more than anywhere else: India. She was fascinated by the country's poetry, its **culture**, and, most of all, yoga, a spiritual practice that involved meditation, breathing exercises, and poses that calmed a person's body and mind. At the time, yoga was mainly practiced in India. In the Soviet Union, it was even banned. Eugenie wanted to know more about it.

In 1927, she sailed to India, and three years later she met a famous guru, or teacher, named Sri Tirumalai Krishnamacharya. The first time she asked him to teach her yoga, he said no. Mostly men practiced yoga, and he wouldn't teach a woman. But she persisted, and eventually he agreed. Eugenie decided to adopt a new name in her new home: Indra Devi.

It did not take long for Sri Krishnamacharya to see that Indra was a special student who could share yoga with the world. She moved all over—to China, to the United States, to Mexico, and eventually to her adopted home of Argentina.

Indra called yoga the "art and science of living." Her many admirers around the world called her *mataji*, which means "mother" in Hindi.

MAY 12, 1899–APRIL 25, 2002

LATVIA ➜ INDIA AND ARGENTINA

"IN MEDITATION,
YOU ASK FOR NOTHING.
YOU JUST CONTEMPLATE."
—INDRA DEVI

ILLUSTRATION BY
JOSEFINA SCHARGORODSKY

JAWAHIR JEWELS ROBLE

REFEREE

Once there was a girl in London who played soccer every chance she had. Never mind the skirts and hijab she wore, or her parents' disapproval—she knew she belonged on the soccer field. Jawahir—known as JJ—had learned to play soccer on the streets of Mogadishu, where she sometimes used a potato as a soccer ball. When JJ's family fled Somalia because of civil war and moved to England, her love of soccer was one thing in her life that didn't change.

As a teenager, JJ's love of soccer led to an unexpected opportunity. One day, she was asked to referee for a junior league soccer game. JJ loved the challenge so much that she decided to make it her career.

In soccer, as in most sports, referees need to be quick thinkers and confident. As the first female Muslim soccer referee in the United Kingdom, JJ also had to overcome **prejudice** and **racism**. Players were often surprised to see that their referee was a small Somali woman wearing a hijab. "I don't let that stop me from doing my work," JJ said. "Refereeing is a tough job, there is a lot of pressure, you have to be focused and make quick decisions, so I don't have time to think about what people think of me."

JJ quickly advanced from refereeing youth games to adult games. She won awards for her work and has used her influence to encourage other Muslim girls to play soccer. She has set a goal for herself to be a referee at the 2023 Women's World Cup. "It would be a dream come true," JJ said.

BORN CIRCA 1994

SOMALIA ➜ UNITED KINGDOM

ILLUSTRATION BY
VERONICA RUFFATO

"IT'S GOOD TO STRETCH YOURSELF,
TO TEST YOURSELF. DECISION-MAKING,
BEING STRONG: YOU LEARN SO MANY
VALUES FROM BEING A REF."
—JAWAHIR JEWELS ROBLE

JOSEPHINE BAKER

SCAN TO HEAR MORE

ENTERTAINER AND ACTIVIST

Once there was a girl who dazzled audiences in Paris with her jeweled skirts and spectacular dancing.

As a young black girl growing up in the United States, Josephine cleaned houses and babysat to earn money, and she was sometimes treated with cruelty and ignorance by the white people she worked for. Eventually she joined a vaudeville troupe and toured the country as an entertainer. Then when she was 19 years old, Josephine left for France, where her amazing career as a singer, dancer, and actor took off. She officially became a French **citizen** in 1937.

During World War II, Josephine used her fame and talents to help fight the Nazis. She charmed German officials, passed information to the **Allies**, and carried private messages for the **resistance** in invisible ink on her music sheets. The French government later made her a knight of the Legion of Honor, its highest award for bravery.

After the war, Josephine visited the United States. She was angry to see that black people there still faced the same **discrimination** she had as a girl. She stood alongside Martin Luther King Jr. and made a speech to a spellbound audience before the March on Washington in 1963.

"I have walked into the palaces of kings and queens and into the houses of presidents...," she said. "But I could not walk into a hotel in America and get a cup of coffee, and that made me mad. And when I get mad, you know that I open my big mouth. And then look out, 'cause when Josephine opens her mouth, they hear it all over the world."

JUNE 3, 1906–APRIL 12, 1975
UNITED STATES OF AMERICA ➞ FRANCE

ILLUSTRATION BY
TYLA MASON

"WHEN I SCREAMED LOUD ENOUGH,
THEY STARTED TO OPEN THAT DOOR
JUST A LITTLE BIT, AND WE ALL STARTED
TO BE ABLE TO SQUEEZE THROUGH IT."
—JOSEPHINE BAKER

JUDY CASSAB

PAINTER

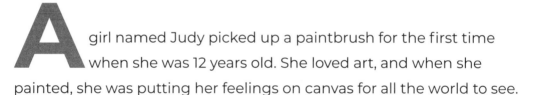

A girl named Judy picked up a paintbrush for the first time when she was 12 years old. She loved art, and when she painted, she was putting her feelings on canvas for all the world to see.

But then World War II came to Europe, and Judy's family's life was in danger because they were Jewish. Judy had to leave art school and live under a false identity to avoid being captured. When the war was over, she was saddened by the destruction she saw around her. She wanted to paint only beautiful things.

In 1951, Judy and her husband, Jancsi Kampfner, moved with their two young sons to Australia. The family lived in a crowded boarding house with many other immigrants, and it was hard to find work. But Judy was determined to make art. She started painting portraits of businesspeople and their families in Australia. When word of her talent spread, she started traveling around the world to paint portraits of royals and other famous people.

Judy painted beautiful landscapes and abstract images, but she also loved portraying people. When people came to her studio to sit for a portrait, she asked them questions about themselves. She wanted to know what they were like on the inside as well as the outside.

In 1967, Judy became the first woman artist to twice win Australia's top prize for portraiture.

AUGUST 15, 1920–NOVEMBER 3, 2015

AUSTRIA ➡ AUSTRALIA

"THE EYES ARE WHERE I RETURN ALWAYS, LIKE A SHIP TO THE LIGHTHOUSE."
—JUDY CASSAB

ILLUSTRATION BY CECILIA PUGLESI

JULIETA LANTERI

PHYSICIAN AND POLITICIAN

Once there was a girl who believed that women and men were equal, even when laws said they were not. Julieta's family **emigrated** from Italy to Argentina when she was young, and Julieta quickly discovered that her new country had just as many challenges as her old one.

Julieta was smart and determined. She was the first girl to enroll in her postsecondary school and later went to college *and* medical school. However, she was told that women shouldn't have careers, and she couldn't participate in some of the activities in medical school classes. She was also discriminated against because she was an immigrant.

After Julieta became a doctor, she applied to be a professor at the medical school, but she was rejected because she wasn't a citizen. In order to apply for citizenship in Argentina, a woman usually had to be married. And even once Julieta was married and became a **citizen** in 1911, she was not allowed to vote.

Julieta worked hard to change unfair laws. As a doctor, she helped people who didn't have access to medicine and people who had mental illnesses. She also became a politician and boldly spoke up for women's **suffrage** and other causes. She even started her own political party—the National Feminist Union. Sadly, Julieta died in a car accident in 1932. Fifteen years later, women got the right to vote in Argentina, and when they did, it was thanks to the work of brave women like Dr. Julieta Lanteri.

MARCH 22, 1873–FEBRUARY 25, 1932
ITALY ➞ ARGENTINA

ILLUSTRATION BY
KIKI LJUNG

VOTE

"WOMEN MUST FIGHT
TO ACHIEVE THE REALIZATION
OF THEIR RIGHTS."
—JULIETA LANTERI

KAREN CORR

BILLIARDS PLAYER

Once upon a time, there was a girl who wanted a spot at a certain kind of table. Karen liked to tag along with her father when he went to the local pub in their town in Northern Ireland. When they got there, Karen's eyes always went to a green table in the corner. It was a table for snooker, a game similar to billiards, or pool.

When Karen was eight, her family moved to England. Her brother and her father joined a local snooker club. By the time she was 14, Karen didn't want to just stand on the sidelines and watch anymore. She was ready to learn to play and insisted she be allowed to join the club too.

As it turned out, Karen was good at snooker—very good. She loved its quiet power, how a single quick movement of the cue stick sent balls spinning in many different directions.

She entered her first professional tournament less than a year later and made it to the final rounds. When she was 21, she won the World Ladies Snooker Championship, then won it two more times in the coming years.

It was hard to earn a living playing snooker in the UK, even as one of the best players in the world. So Karen switched her game to pool and moved to the United States, where professional pool players could earn much bigger prizes. Within a few years, Karen was ranked as the number one women's pool player in the world. In 2012, Karen, whose nickname became the Irish Invader, was named to the Billiard Congress of America Hall of Fame.

BORN NOVEMBER 10, 1969
UNITED KINGDOM ➔ UNITED STATES OF AMERICA

ILLUSTRATION BY
AKVILE MAGICDUST

"WHEN I WON THE NATIONALS,
I WAS SO HAPPY THAT I JUMPED
ON TOP OF THE POOL TABLE
AND DID AN IRISH JIG!"
—KAREN CORR

KAREN HORNEY

PSYCHOANALYST

Women had only been legally allowed to attend university in parts of Germany for six years when Karen announced in 1906 that she was going to medical school. Her parents hated the idea—medical school was no place for a proper young woman! Karen didn't care.

While at university, Karen gave birth to her first child and both her parents died within a year. It was a lot to deal with at once. Throughout this difficult time, Karen received psychological counseling, which sparked her interest in psychoanalysis—mental health treatment where doctors help patients explore their thoughts, emotions, and fears.

Eventually, Karen taught psychoanalysis and treated patients in Berlin. The most famous psychoanalyst at that time was a man named Sigmund Freud, but he misunderstood women, saying they were just jealous that they couldn't be more like men!

Karen thought this was ridiculous. Women were human beings with feelings of their own. In her writing, Karen focused on how the **cultures** people grew up in could affect the way they thought about themselves—something that was true for men and women alike.

By the early 1930s, Karen was at odds with Freud and his followers in Germany, and worried by the Nazi Party's rise to power. She **immigrated** to the United States and found a home in New York City. Today she is recognized as a trailblazer in feminine psychology.

SEPTEMBER 16, 1885–DECEMBER 4, 1952

GERMANY ➞ UNITED STATES OF AMERICA

ILLUSTRATION BY
LUISA RIVERA

"LIKE ALL SCIENCES
AND ALL VALUATIONS,
THE PSYCHOLOGY
OF WOMEN HAS HITHERTO
BEEN CONSIDERED ONLY
FROM THE POINT
OF VIEW OF MEN."
—KAREN HORNEY

KARIN SCHMIDT

MUSHER AND VETERINARIAN

O nce upon a time, there was a girl who loved animals. Karin took care of anything her mother would let her keep in the house: dogs and cats, of course, but also mice, snakes, ducks—even bugs! Some parents wouldn't allow a small zoo in their home, but Karin's parents were very supportive.

Karin had been born in Germany. Before she was five years old, her family moved: first to Canada, then to the United States, where they bounced around from state to state. Karin ran around outdoors, camped, and cared for animals wherever they went. By six years old, Karin knew exactly what she wanted to do when she grew up. She would become a veterinarian.

After she graduated from veterinary school in 1981, Karin was ready for adventure. She packed up her van and drove to Fairbanks, Alaska, to take a job as a vet. She also discovered a popular local sport: dogsledding.

Karin built her own sled out of boards and skis, and got a big Saint Bernard mix to pull it. She loved the feeling of racing across the snow with her dog. For a person who loved being outdoors and being with animals, it was a perfect fit for her. She officially became a dog musher and got a better sled—and more dogs! She volunteered as a race veterinarian too, caring for dogs as they ran hundreds of miles in cold and icy conditions, making sure they didn't get injured or overworked. Eventually, she became the head veterinarian for the Iditarod, the most famous sled dog race in the world.

BIRTHDATE UNKNOWN

GERMANY ➔ CANADA AND UNITED STATES OF AMERICA

ILLUSTRATION BY
ELENIA BERETTA

"THERE ARE THOSE OF US WHO
REALLY CARE. THERE ARE PEOPLE
SETTING VERY HIGH STANDARDS
FOR DOG CARE."
—KARIN SCHMIDT

KEIKO FUKUDA

JUDOKA

As a girl growing up in Japan, Keiko studied calligraphy, flower arranging, and tea ceremony like other proper young women. One day, she decided she was going to learn **judo** too.

Keiko was no ordinary student. Her grandfather was a samurai and a jujitsu master, and her judo teacher was one of her grandfather's best students. He had invented this new martial art where opponents use balance and strength to pin each other to the mat. He sent Keiko a special invitation to train with him.

At first, Keiko was shocked to see women judoka—judo athletes—being aggressive and physical. But a person didn't have to be big to succeed at judo. They just had to be smart, strong, and willing to work hard.

When Keiko found out that she would have to give up judo to go through with an arranged marriage, she made a decision. She would not marry. Her fellow judoka would be her family instead.

Before he died, Keiko's teacher asked his students to go teach judo around the world. So that's what Keiko did. She moved to the United States to teach this new sport, and all the while, she rose higher in judo's ranks. By 2006, she was a ninth-degree black belt and the highest-ranking female judoka in the world. Just one step remained to judo's highest rank—a position no woman had ever achieved before.

In 2011, at the age of 98, Keiko was promoted to tenth-degree black belt by USA Judo. She was the first woman to earn judo's highest honor.

APRIL 12, 1913–FEBRUARY 9, 2013
JAPAN ➜ UNITED STATES OF AMERICA

ILLUSTRATION BY
HELEN LI

"BE STRONG, BE GENTLE,
BE BEAUTIFUL."
—KEIKO FUKUDA

LASKARINA "BOUBOULINA" PINOTSIS

NAVAL COMMANDER

Once upon a time, there was a girl named Laskarina, and she was born to be a rebel. Her father, a Greek sea captain, was thrown in jail for helping to plan a rebellion against the Ottomans, who ruled Greece at the time. Laskarina was born inside a prison within the Ottoman Empire, in a country that is now known as Turkey, during one of her mother's visits to her father. It was the first time she would take people by surprise—but not the last.

After her first husband died, Laskarina married a rich trader who commanded many ships. When he died too, Laskarina took over his boats and his business, and ordered several new ships of her own. She named the largest one *Agamemnon*, after the king in Greek mythology.

With her fleet of ships, Laskarina joined a secret organization working to end the Ottoman Empire's rule. The organization's only woman, she used her own money to buy weapons and pay soldiers who would fight under her command to free Greece. When the day of the uprising came at last, Laskarina sailed into battle as a commander, directing her ships to go wherever her fellow rebels needed them most.

Under her command, Laskarina's ships stopped supplies from reaching their enemies, and her soldiers captured fortresses and saved Greek towns from destruction. She also saved innocent people from being killed.

Laskarina died in 1825, a few years before her dream of an independent Greece came true.

CIRCA MAY 1771–MAY 22, 1825

TURKEY → GREECE

ILLUSTRATION BY
ALICE PIAGGIO

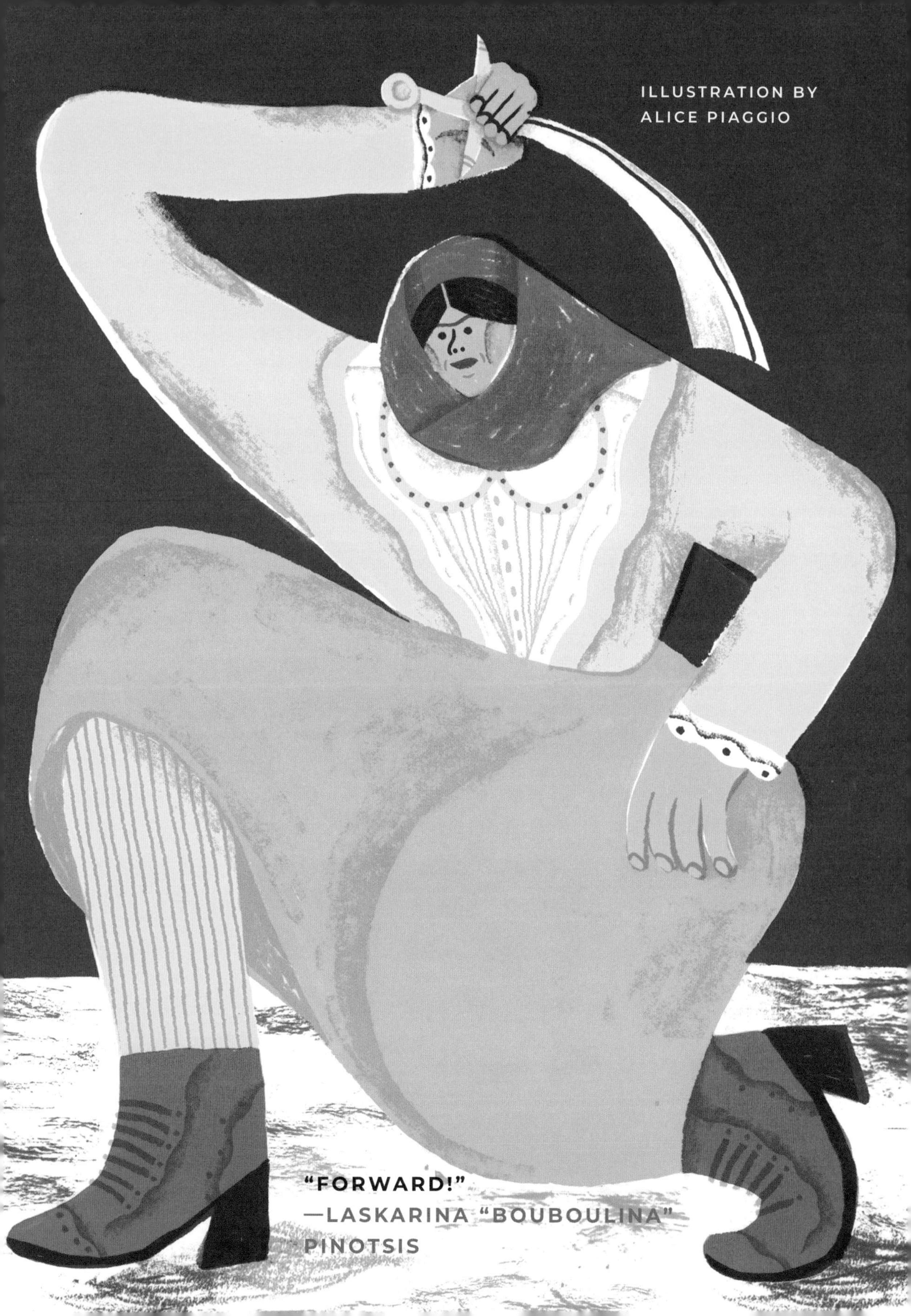

"FORWARD!"
—LASKARINA "BOUBOULINA"
PINOTSIS

LINA BO BARDI

ARCHITECT

Once there was a girl who loved to draw houses, but she didn't want her drawings to stay on paper. She wanted to bring them to life. When Achillina Bo (known as Lina) told her father she wanted to be an architect, he was doubtful. Very few women chose architecture as a career. But Lina went to architecture school anyway.

Lina opened her own architecture studio in Milan when she was 28. With World War II thundering through Europe, business was slow. Later, her studio was destroyed by bombs and never rebuilt. Eventually, Lina left Italy with her new husband, an art critic named Pietro Maria Bardi. In 1947, Pietro was asked to establish an art museum in São Paulo, Brazil. After they arrived in South America, Lina reopened her studio and designed one of her first Brazilian projects: their house.

Lina called it Casa de Vidro, or "Glass House." It looked like a greenhouse hanging in the rainforest canopy. Casa de Vidro was good practice for Lina's next big project: designing the new home of the São Paulo art museum. The Museu de Arte de São Paulo is also a modern building. It looks like a glass box suspended above the ground, and is considered to be one of Lina's most important works. Perhaps because she was a foreign-born woman, Lina's architectural skill was often overshadowed by Brazilian-born men. But today many consider Lina to be one of the best—and most overlooked—architects of the twentieth century.

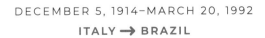

DECEMBER 5, 1914–MARCH 20, 1992
ITALY ➡ BRAZIL

ILLUSTRATION BY
ABELLE HAYFORD

"I AM CURIOUS
AND THIS QUALITY
BROADENS MY
HORIZONS."
—LINA BO BARDI

LISA STHALEKAR

CRICKET CHAMPION AND COMMENTATOR

Once upon a time, there was a girl who was adopted by a loving family who supported her dreams. Lisa spent the first three weeks of her life in an orphanage in India. One day, a family came to the orphanage—a man, a woman, and a little girl—and as soon as they saw Lisa, they knew she was meant to be their daughter and sister. They adopted Lisa and brought her home to Michigan.

Lisa's family moved to Kenya before settling in Australia when she was four years old. From the beginning, Lisa took after her father. She shared his love of stamp collecting, classical music, and, most important, his love of cricket. Lisa's father was from India too, and cricket was the most popular sport in the country.

Growing up, Lisa spent a lot of time playing cricket in the backyard, usually with boys. She didn't know that girls or women played cricket until her father took her to watch a women's match. It wasn't long before Lisa was a professional player herself. By the time she was 18, Lisa was playing for the Women's National Cricket League. She later became one of the top women cricketers in Australia, playing for two of the country's World Cup–winning teams.

In 2013, she retired from the sport and became a cricket commentator. She also started using her influence to encourage people to adopt, so other children could have the same opportunities she had. "My story is a really positive one," Lisa said. "Kids deserve to have a permanent, loving, and safe home available to them."

BORN AUGUST 13, 1979

INDIA ➜ UNITED STATES OF AMERICA, KENYA, AND AUSTRALIA

"SPORT HAS SUCH A UNIQUE CAPACITY TO BRING DIFFERENT CULTURES TOGETHER."
—LISA STHALEKAR

ILLUSTRATION BY
KARINA COCQ

LIZ CLAIBORNE

· · · · · · · · · · · · · · · · · · · ·

FASHION DESIGNER AND CEO

Anne Elisabeth Claiborne was born in Belgium to American parents. Her father didn't think it was important for her to graduate from school, so Liz took up painting instead. When her family moved to the United States in 1939, she was on her way to becoming a professional artist.

Liz started to dream of being a fashion designer after she sketched a high-collared coat that won a contest. With 50 dollars in her pocket, she moved to New York and got a job as a sketch artist for a women's clothing designer. For the next 20 years or so, she worked behind the scenes in the fashion industry.

But Liz didn't want to be like other fashion designers. Instead of creating glamorous clothing for high-priced boutiques, she wanted to design inexpensive styles for everyday life. Most business clothing for women was a little boring, and Liz thought women should be able to look stylish and professional but still be comfortable.

Liz launched her fashion line in 1976, and by the end of the decade, women were wearing her imaginative designs everywhere. Her affordable mix-and-match fashions flew off the shelves, and soon her company was making millions of dollars a year. It eventually became one of the first companies founded by a woman to make the Fortune 500, an annual list of the most financially successful companies in the United States.

· ·

MARCH 31, 1929–JUNE 26, 2007

BELGIUM ➝ UNITED STATES OF AMERICA

"I WANTED TO DRESS BUSY
AND ACTIVE WOMEN LIKE
MYSELF—WOMEN WHO
DRESS IN A RUSH AND WHO
WEREN'T PERFECT."
—LIZ CLAIBORNE

LORELLA PRAELI

ACTIVIST

Once there was a girl who dreamed of becoming an American **citizen** and helping others become citizens too. Lorella was two years old when she visited the United States for the first time. Back home in Peru, she had been hit by a car and lost one of her legs. Her parents brought her to a special hospital in the US. "My parents were determined that I would reach my full potential and not be limited by my disability," Lorella said.

Lorella and her parents made so many trips to the American hospital that, when she was 10 years old, Lorella's family moved to Connecticut. She didn't know that she and her family were **undocumented** immigrants until she filled out college applications. This meant they didn't have the same protection and opportunities as legal citizens. She worried that her family would be forced to leave.

When she was in college, Lorella learned about United We Dream, a network of young people working on behalf of immigrant rights. She met undocumented people who weren't afraid of their status, and it gave her courage. Lorella volunteered with United We Dream, became their director of advocacy and policy, and later worked for political campaigns.

Lorella has devoted her life to immigration reform. Along the way, she's shared her own story and challenged politicians to take action. She became a US citizen in 2015, but her work is not done. "I feel even more committed to continue to fight," Lorella said.

BORN AUGUST 18, 1988

PERU → UNITED STATES OF AMERICA

"I CAN NO LONGER
JUST SIT AND WAIT
FOR SOMETHING
TO HAPPEN."
—LORELLA PRAELI

ILLUSTRATION BY
JEANNE DETALLANTE

LUPE GONZALO

MIGRANT FARMER AND
LABOR ORGANIZER

Every mile of the long, difficult journey from Guatemala to the United States, Lupe thought of her children back home. She missed them terribly but hoped that the money she would earn as a migrant worker in the United States could give them a better life.

Lupe found work picking fruits and vegetables in Immokalee, Florida. She spent hours in the fields lugging heavy baskets of tomatoes and peppers in temperatures well over 100 degrees. But even after filling baskets all day, she earned only enough to pay for food and a bed in a crowded trailer.

Worse than the labor was the way she and other women workers were treated. Sometimes employers refused to pay them. Sometimes they touched Lupe and her fellow workers in ways that made them angry, afraid, and uncomfortable. They said ugly things to them and abused them. Lupe knew she and the other workers deserved to be treated with respect. One day, she decided she could be silent no longer.

Lupe joined a group called the Coalition of Immokalee Workers. She helped start a project called the Fair Food Program. This program asked grocery stores and restaurants to buy food only from farms that paid workers fairly and gave them safe and healthy working conditions. Thanks to Lupe and her fellow organizers, some of the biggest food companies in the world have committed to the Fair Food Program, and countless workers' lives are better.

BORN CIRCA 1980
GUATEMALA ➜ UNITED STATES OF AMERICA

"WE ARE HUMAN BEINGS, WE ARE WOMEN, AND NOBODY IS GOING TO KEEP STEPPING ON OUR DIGNITY."
—LUPE GONZALO

ILLUSTRATION BY SALLY CAULWELL

LUPITA AMONDI NYONG'O

ACTRESS

Lupita Nyong'o was an adult when she finally had the courage to admit she wanted to be an actor. She had a college degree and an office job, but she left that behind to fly back to Kenya for other opportunities and to plan for her future. Almost six years later, Lupita won her first Oscar.

Lupita's parents had left their home in Kenya for political reasons, so Lupita was born in Mexico and given a Spanish name. Her family returned to Kenya when Lupita was about a year old, but she never forgot the country where she was born. When she was a teenager, Lupita lived in Mexico for a few months to learn Spanish. Today she has both Kenyan and Mexican citizenship and speaks four languages: Luo, Spanish, English, and Swahili.

Lupita was a star from the start of her career as an actor. She was nominated for a Golden Globe and won an Oscar for her first major role. She has starred in many more movies since then.

But not all of Lupita's work happens in Hollywood. She also uses her influence to bring attention to issues that are close to her heart. She has even written a children's book about a young Kenyan girl named Sulwe, who has the darkest skin in her family. Like Lupita herself, Sulwe learns to see her own beauty and accept herself for who she is.

BORN MARCH 1, 1983

MEXICO → KENYA AND UNITED STATES OF AMERICA

ILLUSTRATION BY
MONICA AHANONU

"NO MATTER WHERE YOU'RE FROM,
YOUR DREAMS ARE VALID."
—LUPITA AMONDI NYONG'O

MADELEINE ALBRIGHT

POLITICIAN

When she was a little girl, Madeleine's family fled their home in Czechoslovakia, which is now known as the Czech Republic. Her parents said they left for political reasons. But more than 50 years later, Madeleine learned the truth: her family was Jewish. They left the country and became Catholic to be safe from the Nazis. After World War II, her family returned, but they didn't stay long. In 1948, 11-year-old Madeleine crossed the Atlantic on a huge ship to start a new life in America.

In Europe, Madeleine's father had been a **diplomat**. In the United States, he taught political science at a university. Madeleine shared her father's enthusiasm for politics and global issues. After marrying Joseph Albright and having three daughters, Madeleine earned her PhD in public law and government.

After working in politics for many years, Madeleine became the first woman to ever be US secretary of state. She was a foreign policy expert and a champion for human rights. But she also became known for something surprising: her pin collection. Madeleine often wore pins—a coiled snake, an eagle, a heart—to communicate her thoughts without words. The pins were a way to start conversation or make people smile. When asked about her favorite diplomatic accessory, Madeleine said: "In order to get through a lot of complicated issues, it helps to have a little bit of humor."

BORN MAY 15, 1937

CZECH REPUBLIC ➜ UNITED STATES OF AMERICA

ILLUSTRATION BY
BARBARA DZIADOSZ

"IT TOOK ME QUITE A LONG
TIME TO DEVELOP A VOICE,
AND NOW THAT I HAVE IT,
I AM NOT GOING TO BE SILENT."
—MADELEINE ALBRIGHT

MALIKA OUFKIR

AUTHOR

Once there was a girl who lived like royalty. Malika's father was an adviser to King Hassan II of Morocco, and she spent much of her childhood roaming the vast halls of the king's palaces.

Unfortunately, Malika's fairy-tale life was disrupted when her father tried to overthrow the king. As punishment, the king had her father killed and ordered 19-year-old Malika, her five brothers and sisters, and her mother thrown into a secret prison in the desert.

For 14 years, Malika was held in isolated prisons with little food and terrible conditions. When she and her family members were kept apart from one another, one of Malika's brothers managed to set up a secret network between the cells so they could still hear one another speak. When the guards were not listening, Malika entertained her family with stories she had invented to keep their strength and spirits up.

Then came her daring escape. Though she was weak from lack of food, she and two of her siblings managed to dig a secret tunnel with makeshift tools including a spoon and the lid of a sardine can. Malika was worried they'd get caught but even more scared to stay in that prison any longer. When the moment was right, they crawled through the tunnel and ran toward freedom.

Eventually, Malika moved to France and wrote the story of what happened to her family. Because she spoke up about their experience, readers all over the world came to understand what political prisoners endured in Morocco—and the strength it took for them to survive.

BORN APRIL 2, 1953

MOROCCO ➔ FRANCE

"HOWEVER POWERFUL HE WAS,
HOWEVER UNTOUCHABLE HE WAS...
ONE WOMAN WITH NO WEAPONS,
NO POWER, NOTHING, SUCCEEDED
IN DEFEATING HIM."
—MALIKA OUFKIR

MARCELA CONTRERAS

HEMATOLOGIST

Once upon a time, a young woman named Marcela knew she wanted to be a doctor, just like her father was. She began her studies at the University of Chile, where she became interested in something everyone on earth has in common: blood.

Marcela graduated with honors after studying hematology, which is the study of blood, and immunology, which is the study of how bodies defend themselves from illness.

In 1972, Marcela won a scholarship to study and work in the United Kingdom. People were worried about the instability of the government in Chile, so Marcela and her husband decided to move to London with their two children.

At the time, the blood centers in the UK weren't connected to one another, making it hard to send spare donations where they were needed. If the UK had one system for the whole country, it would save countless lives. Marcela was asked to take charge of this special project.

Marcela's leadership made sure that donated blood was always available to people who needed it after surgery, illness, or accidents, no matter where they lived.

Based on the success of this system in the UK, Marcela went on to direct an organization that worked to make sure there was a sufficient supply of safe blood in countries around the world—including her native Chile.

BORN JANUARY 4, 1942

CHILE ➡ UNITED KINGDOM

ILLUSTRATION BY
KARINA COCQ

"EVERYTHING IS POSSIBLE
IN THIS LIFE. IT'S ALL A MATTER
OF HARD WORK AND DETERMINATION.
YOU SHOULD NEVER FEEL LESS
THAN ANYONE BECAUSE YOU'RE
SO FAR AWAY IN THE WORLD."
—MARCELA CONTRERAS

MARIA GOEPPERT MAYER

THEORETICAL PHYSICIST

Maria was destined to become a professor—just like her father, and his father, grandfather, and so on, for many generations! But because Maria's **ancestors** were men, her path would be a little different.

Maria's specialty was physics. She married an American physicist named Joseph and moved to the United States when Joseph got a job at Johns Hopkins University. But even though Maria was also qualified, the university refused to hire her as professor. It was the Great Depression, a time when there were very few jobs to be had in the US, and people thought that men deserved jobs more than women did.

Maria wasn't about to give up her work. She did her research in an empty office on campus, publishing papers and a scientific book without a paycheck or a title. She did the same thing at Columbia University when Joseph got a job there. And when he found a job at the University of Chicago, the school said Maria could work as a professor too—as long as they didn't have to pay her!

All the while, Maria continued her important work in science, including nuclear physics. With her research partners, she figured out why some atoms were more stable than others. This was a breakthrough—a big one. In 1963, Maria won the Nobel Prize for her discoveries. She was the second woman, after Marie Curie, to win the prize in physics.

JUNE 28, 1906–FEBRUARY 20, 1972

POLAND ➔ UNITED STATES OF AMERICA

"WINNING THE PRIZE WASN'T HALF AS EXCITING AS DOING THE WORK ITSELF."
—MARIA GOEPPERT MAYER

ILLUSTRATION BY
ANNALISA VENTURA

MARJANE SATRAPI

GRAPHIC NOVELIST

Once there was a girl who used her art to stand up against an unjust government. When Marjane was young, big changes happened in Iran. It started with a **revolution** and a war with Iraq. At first, some people thought the revolution might be a good thing. There were big celebrations in the streets the day it happened.

Marjane and her parents were Muslim like the new government leaders were, but they disagreed with their politics. After the revolution, Iran had a strict religious government. Each time the government created a new rule, Marjane would bend it. When it said all women must wear veils, Marjane let her hair show. When it created a dress code, she wore forbidden sneakers and a denim jacket. When certain music was banned, she secretly bought cassette tapes of it. And when her teachers praised Iran's leaders, she asked brave questions.

Marjane's parents were proud of their daughter, but they were scared too. She could go to jail for her behavior. Her parents eventually sent her to boarding school in Austria, where she'd be safer.

After high school, Marjane moved to France to study art. She had always loved comics, so she created some of her own. Using simple black-and-white drawings, she told the story of her childhood in Iran. A publisher bought her graphic novel, *Persepolis*, and it became an international best seller. Later, Marjane helped turn the book into an Oscar-nominated film. Since settling in France, Marjane continues to use art to tell stories about the home she left behind.

BORN NOVEMBER 22, 1969

IRAN → FRANCE

"ONE ISN'T BORN COURAGEOUS.
ONE BECOMES IT."
—MARJANE SATRAPI

ILLUSTRATION BY
ELENA DE SANTI

MARTA EMPINOTTI

BASE JUMPER

Once there was a girl who dreamed of flying. The first time Marta went skydiving, she was only a teenager. She fell in love with the feeling of weightlessness, of soaring above the world like a bird.

Her family taught her to always be independent and never be tied down. Marta loved her parents and three sisters in Brazil, but there was so much of the world to see. She went traveling, and her first stop was the United States, where there was lots of skydiving—and something else exciting too: BASE jumping. She decided to make the US her new home.

Instead of leaping from a plane, BASE jumpers use their parachutes to leap from places high above the earth, like bridges, cliffs, or tall buildings. It can be very dangerous, but Marta always made sure to be professionally strapped into her parachute. Marta loved the feeling of jumping better than anything else in the world.

Marta has made more than 1,600 jumps and is one of the sport's most respected athletes. She has traveled all over the world in search of new adventures, and has jumped from skyscrapers in Malaysia, waterfalls in Venezuela, and many places in between. BASE jumping has enabled her to see the world in a whole new way.

"When I'm high above the ground, maybe 600 or 800 feet up, the feeling is very spiritual," Marta said. "On the horizon, the sun is rising, turning the clouds pink and yellow. It's so peaceful; it's like paradise…. It's just me and nature. Then I jump and feel the thrill. When I land, I see the sunrise again. How many people watch the sunrise twice in one day?"

BORN DECEMBER 18, 1964

BRAZIL ➡ UNITED STATES OF AMERICA

"YOU NEED TO CHOOSE WHAT MAKES YOU HAPPY, AND THIS DECISION MIGHT NOT BE THE EASIEST, BUT IT IS DEFINITELY THE RIGHT ONE."
—MARTA EMPINOTTI

ILLUSTRATION BY SARAH LOULENDO

MERLENE JOYCE OTTEY

SPRINTER

Once there was a girl who could run like the wind. Her name was Merlene. Merlene lived in Jamaica and ran everywhere she could. Her family did not have much money, and she often had to race barefoot when she and her schoolmates competed against one another. She still ran faster than almost everyone else. Sometimes when she crossed the finish line, she was surprised to see how many runners were still on the track trying to finish the race!

When Merlene was 16 years old, she heard that a Jamaican man had won the gold medal in the men's 200-meter dash at the Olympic Games, and she wondered how far racing could take her too.

Four years later, it was Merlene's turn in Moscow, Russia. She took home the bronze medal in the women's 200-meter dash—the first Olympic medal ever won by a Caribbean woman.

Merlene competed in the Olympics six times after that—more than any other track-and-field athlete—and won eight more Olympic medals.

At an age when many runners retire, Merlene moved to Slovenia and decided to compete for her new home country. In 2004, she ran in her seventh Olympics, advancing to the semifinals over runners half her age.

In 2014, Merlene moved again—this time to Switzerland. She still holds the world record for the women's indoor 200-meter sprint.

BORN MAY 10, 1960

JAMAICA → SLOVENIA AND SWITZERLAND

ILLUSTRATION BY
LUISA RIVERA

531

"I JUST LOVE RUNNING.
ONCE YOU LOVE SOMETHING,
YOU CAN PUT UP WITH ALL
THE TORTURE."
—MERLENE JOYCE OTTEY

MIN JIN LEE

AUTHOR

Min looked nervously around her classroom in New York City. It was 1976, and seven-year-old Min had just moved from South Korea with her sisters and parents. All around her, children chatted away in English, a language Min did not know. When she tried to say new words, classmates laughed at her. Being laughed at hurt, so she didn't speak often.

As a teenager, Min traveled two hours each way by train to her high school. Though the trip was long, Min never felt alone. She loved to read, and she always brought a book with her on her journeys. As the trains rumbled across bridges and under streets throughout New York City, she lost herself in new worlds and characters.

Min went to law school and became a lawyer, but she never stopped believing in the power of storytelling. She wanted to become a writer and tell stories that she understood from her own life and those of the people around her—people who had moved away from their first countries and settled all around the world, carving new lives for themselves in societies that often ignored or belittled their experiences.

Min's first novel, *Free Food for Millionaires*, was published in 2007. She then moved to Tokyo for four years to write the epic story of a Korean family living in Japan—it was called *Pachinko*. When *Pachinko* was published in 2017, it earned recognition as a National Book Award finalist, a number of other honors, and the admiration of readers all over the world who fell in love with the stories and characters Min created.

BORN NOVEMBER 11, 1968

SOUTH KOREA → UNITED STATES OF AMERICA

ILLUSTRATION BY
EVA RUST

"MY FAMILY NEVER WENT
ANYWHERE. BUT I'D READ SO
MANY NOVELS THAT, IN MY MIND,
I'D SORT OF BEEN EVERYWHERE."
—MIN JIN LEE

MIN MEHTA

ORTHOPEDIC SURGEON

Sit up straight! When she was 11 years old, Min heard that from more adults than she could count. Then one day, a family friend who was also a nurse said something that changed her life. She revealed that Min couldn't sit up straight because she had scoliosis—a curve in her spine.

Although she was born in Iran, Min grew up in India in the 1930s, when there wasn't much that doctors could do to help children with scoliosis. Min wanted to change that. She had known since she was six years old that she wanted to be a doctor when she grew up. By the time she finished medical school in India, she knew exactly what kind of doctor she wanted to be: a surgeon.

Min decided to move to the UK to continue her medical training. There were hardly any women working as surgeons at that time, so when Min was offered an interview in London, the other doctors were shocked when she walked in the room—they had thought *Min* was a man's name!

Min became one of the most respected **orthopedic** surgeons in the UK for her study of scoliosis in children. She realized that in many cases, if a child's back could be held in the correct position for enough time, starting when they were very small, the extra curve in their spine would straighten naturally as the child grew. Min taught other surgeons how to use a special plaster cast, now called a Mehta cast, to correct children's spines without surgery.

Doctors today still use Mehta casts to treat scoliosis in children.

NOVEMBER 1, 1926–AUGUST 23, 2017
IRAN ➜ INDIA AND UNITED KINGDOM

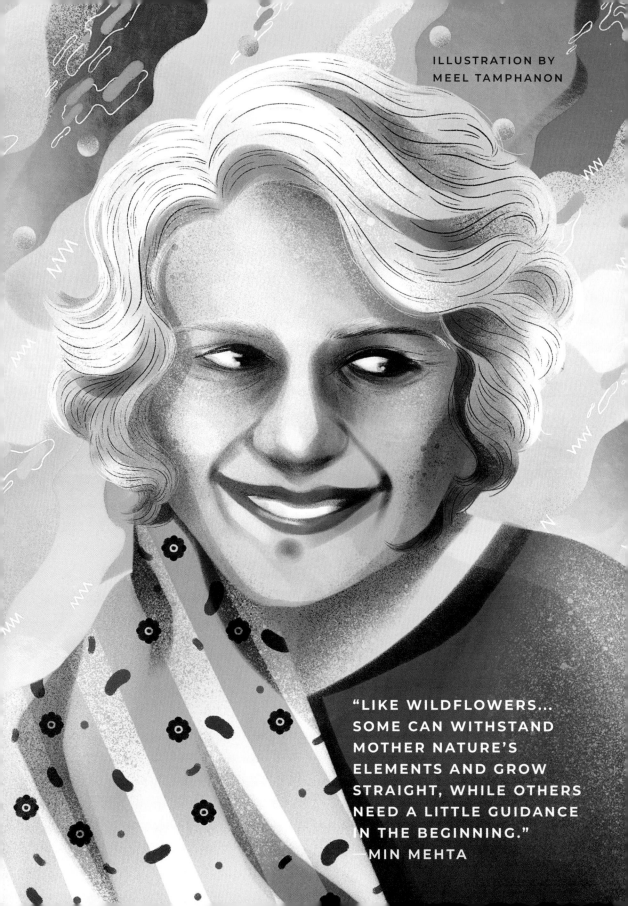

ILLUSTRATION BY
MEEL TAMPHANON

"LIKE WILDFLOWERS...
SOME CAN WITHSTAND
MOTHER NATURE'S
ELEMENTS AND GROW
STRAIGHT, WHILE OTHERS
NEED A LITTLE GUIDANCE
IN THE BEGINNING."
—MIN MEHTA

MUZOON ALMELLEHAN

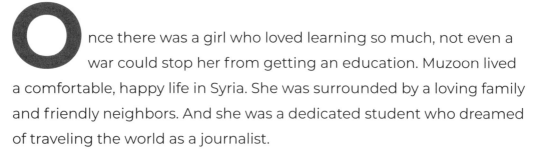

ACTIVIST

Once there was a girl who loved learning so much, not even a war could stop her from getting an education. Muzoon lived a comfortable, happy life in Syria. She was surrounded by a loving family and friendly neighbors. And she was a dedicated student who dreamed of traveling the world as a journalist.

But when Muzoon was around 11 years old, a war overtook her country, and her parents were forced to leave Syria. Muzoon could pack just one bag, and she filled it with her most prized possessions: her schoolbooks. Her father told her to pack less, but Muzoon insisted, "These books are my power. These books are my future."

Muzoon and her family lived in a **refugee** camp for the next few years, sharing a single tent with no electricity. The camp had schools, but Muzoon discovered that many children—especially girls—didn't attend. She walked through the camp, encouraging parents to send their daughters to school.

In 2015, Muzoon and her family finally settled in England. Their new home welcomed them, and she made many friends. But Muzoon couldn't forget her fellow refugees. In 2017, she became a Goodwill Ambassador for UNICEF, the youngest person to ever be chosen for the role at the time. At university, Muzoon continues to campaign for girls' education. And her homeland has never been far from her heart. "I believe in the Syrian people, especially in the Syrian children," she said. "I believe we are strong enough to rebuild our country."

BORN CIRCA APRIL 1998

SYRIA ➡ UNITED KINGDOM

"IN THE MIDDLE OF THE DARKNESS, LEARNING GIVES YOU LIGHT."

ILLUSTRATION BY
MALIHA ABIDI

NADINE BURKE HARRIS

PEDIATRICIAN

Once there was a girl who wanted to be a pediatrician so she could help children be healthy. With a father who was a scientist and a mother who was a nurse, Nadine knew from an early age how science could help people.

After moving from Jamaica to California as a kid, Nadine often felt out of place because there were few immigrants or children of color in her school. At first, she spoke English using a Jamaican dialect called patois. This made it difficult for classmates and teachers to understand her. But these challenges didn't stop Nadine from excelling in school.

Nadine studied medicine for a long time and eventually became a pediatrician. She opened a pediatric clinic in one of the poorest and most underserved neighborhoods in San Francisco. Over time, Nadine noticed that her most unhealthy patients had something in common: they had a lot of stress and difficulties in their lives. Rather than simply treating her young patients' symptoms, Nadine wanted to treat the cause. She created an organization to research childhood trauma. "I was inspired to make sure that every child has an equal opportunity to grow up healthy," Nadine said.

In 2019, Nadine was asked to be California's first-ever surgeon general—a leading spokesperson for medical issues. In her new role, Nadine continued to help children who have experienced toxic stress. According to Nadine, the sooner doctors understand their patients' problems, the sooner their patients can be healed.

BORN OCTOBER 9, 1975
JAMAICA UNITED STATES OF AMERICA

ILLUSTRATION BY
VERONICA CARRATELLO

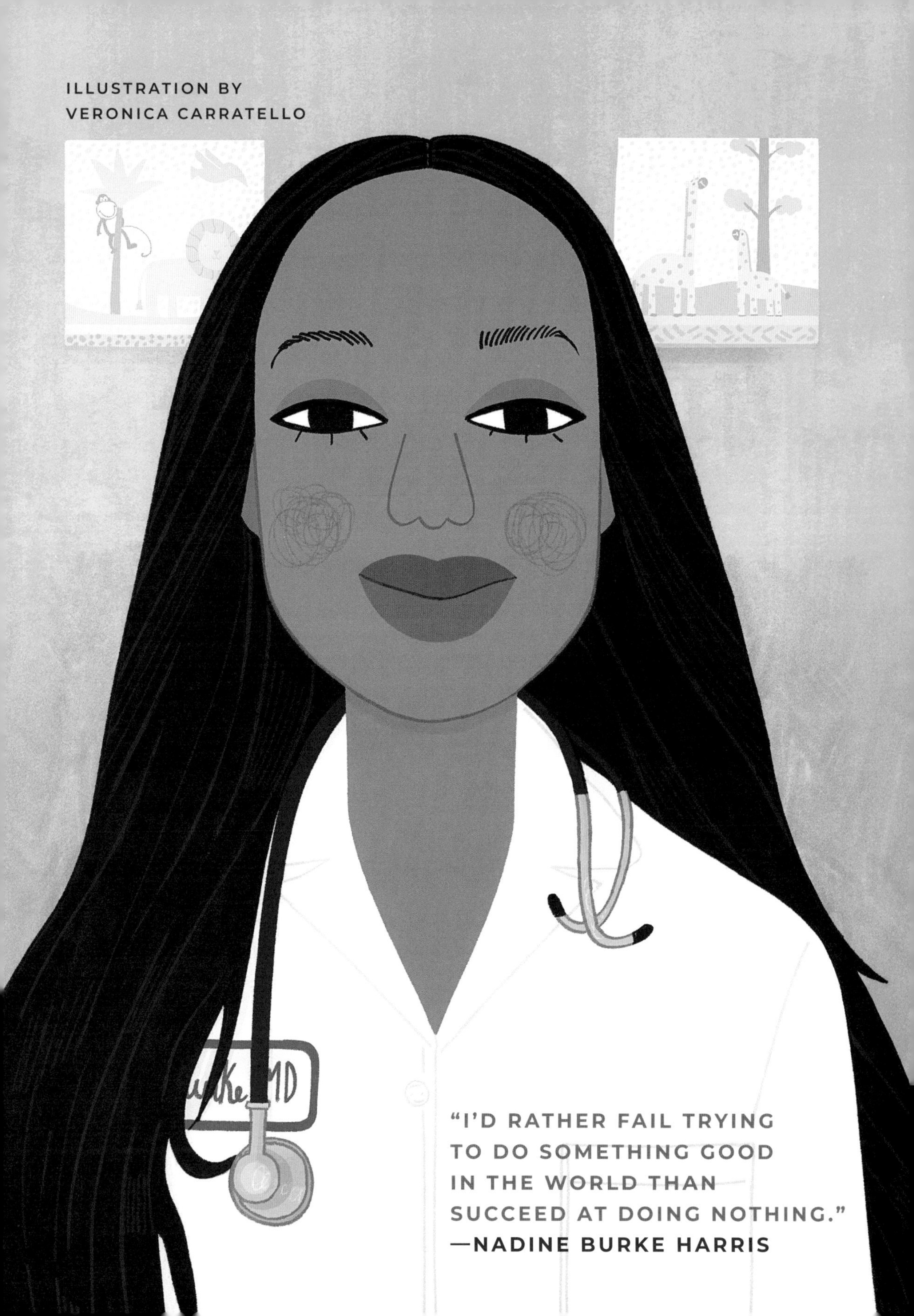

"I'D RATHER FAIL TRYING
TO DO SOMETHING GOOD
IN THE WORLD THAN
SUCCEED AT DOING NOTHING."
—NADINE BURKE HARRIS

NAMI AND REN HAYAKAWA

Nami stood still and strong as a statue, the string of her bow pulled tight. With a sound like a whisper, she let go. Her arrow shot through the air and plunged straight into the center of the target. Another bull's-eye.

Nami wasn't the only girl from South Korea who loved archery. Every four years, the country watched spellbound as the South Korean national team—the finest in the world—competed in the Olympics, taking most of the gold medals home with them.

Nami's sister, Ren, also took up archery after watching Nami practice the sport. Both girls eventually followed their mother to Japan, where she'd moved several years earlier.

In 2008, Nami competed in archery in the Beijing Olympics for Japan, but lost in the quarterfinal. Ren went to college in Japan on an archery scholarship but didn't think she was strong enough to compete in the Olympics. Nami encouraged her to try anyway. At the trials, Ren didn't just do well—she earned a spot on the team!

At the 2012 Olympics in London, a reporter asked Ren what her goal for the competition was. "I want to give everything I have so that after it's all over, I can look back on it and become satisfied with myself," she said. And that's what she did. Together with her teammates, Ren earned a bronze medal in the team competition, the first women's archery medal brought home to Japan.

NAMI, BORN OCTOBER 6, 1984 • REN, BORN AUGUST 24, 1987

SOUTH KOREA ➜ JAPAN

ILLUSTRATION BY
YASMINE GATEAU

"SINCE WE WON A MEDAL
AT THE OLYMPIC GAMES,
I HOPE THIS WILL HELP MAKE
ARCHERY MORE POPULAR
IN JAPAN AMONG CHILDREN."
—REN HAYAKAWA

NIKI YANG

ANIMATOR AND VOICE ACTOR

Once there was a girl who wanted to share her wild imagination with the world. Niki grew up in South Korea, where she went to school, practiced the violin, and learned to run a household. The first time Niki picked up a comic book, however, she discovered a new world. The colorful illustrations and stories fascinated her. One day she decided she wanted to create characters and worlds of her own.

Niki's traditional family had other plans. Her mother wanted Niki to marry a doctor or lawyer. No one expected a young woman like her to pursue a career of her own. But that's exactly what she did. Niki eventually moved to the US to study animation at the California Institute of the Arts. Then she worked at a few animation studios and became a storyboard artist and writer. The animated shows she helped create became very popular and opened new doors for Niki's career.

One of Niki's biggest challenges during her first years in America was learning to speak English. But her accent and ability to speak Korean led to a surprising opportunity. One of her friends was creating an animated series called *Adventure Time* and needed a voice actor who spoke Korean. Niki auditioned for the part and was hired! Shortly afterward, she was also hired for an English-speaking part on the show.

Niki has continued to work as an animator and voice actor, and to branch out into new areas of filmmaking. After years of working on other successful shows, Niki even started developing a pilot for her own animated series.

BORN SEPTEMBER 19, 1982
SOUTH KOREA → UNITED STATES OF AMERICA

"DON'T FORGET TO HAVE FUN WITH WHAT YOU DO! THAT'S WHERE TRUE CREATIVITY COMES FROM."
—NIKI YANG

ILLUSTRATION BY DECUE WU

NOOR INAYAT KHAN

SCAN TO HEAR MORE

SPY

Once upon a time, there was a girl named Noor whose mother was an American poet and whose father was a musician and Indian prince who believed in tolerance and nonviolence. Her family moved frequently, from Moscow to London to Paris, until her father died unexpectedly. Although Noor was only 13, she took care of her brothers, her sister, and her heartbroken mother.

When World War II began in Europe, Noor fled with her family to England, where she became a radio operator. Because she could speak French, the British government chose Noor to join a special group of spies in France sending secret wireless messages between British and French agents. Some of her bosses weren't sure if she could handle the job because of her childlike nature. Beneath her gentle exterior, though, was a brave spirit.

As a spy, Noor pretended to be a children's nurse named Jeanne-Marie. In reality, she was one of the sharpest and most skilled radio operators in the **resistance**. When other agents in her network were found out and arrested, Noor took over their tasks, until she was doing the work of six operators at once.

Eventually, Noor was captured and killed by the Nazis. Her last word was *"liberté"*—freedom. Noor was awarded the George Cross and the French Croix de Guerre after her death, the highest award for bravery outside of combat.

JANUARY 1, 1914–SEPTEMBER 13, 1944

RUSSIA ➡ UNITED KINGDOM AND FRANCE

"THE PATH OF THE HEART IS THORNY, / WHICH LEADS IN THE END TO BLISS."
—NOOR INAYAT KHAN

ILLUSTRATION BY
YEVHENIA HAIDAMAKA

OLGA KORBUT

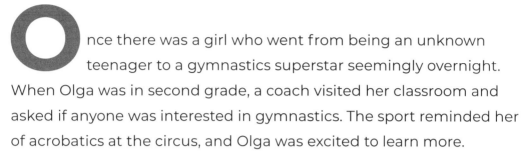

GYMNAST

Once there was a girl who went from being an unknown teenager to a gymnastics superstar seemingly overnight. When Olga was in second grade, a coach visited her classroom and asked if anyone was interested in gymnastics. The sport reminded her of acrobatics at the circus, and Olga was excited to learn more.

After her first few lessons, Olga began to train more formally. By 1972, she earned a spot on the Soviet Union's Olympic team! She was one of the youngest and smallest members, but at the Summer Games in Munich, Olga surprised everyone.

Gymnasts were usually known for their elegance, but Olga was a different kind of gymnast. She wowed the judges with technical skills and acrobatics that had never been seen before. A new kind of backflip was later named after her: the Korbut flip. Olga also freely showed her emotions. She cried after her mistakes and grinned when she did well. Her fearlessness and spunky personality made her a fan favorite.

At her first Olympics, Olga won four medals—three gold and one silver. Around the world, girls signed up for gymnastics and wrote letters to their new hero. Olga received so much fan mail—20,000 letters a year—that her hometown hired a postal worker just for her. In 1988, she was the first person to be inducted into the International Gymnastics Hall of Fame. A few years later, Olga moved to the United States, where she still teaches gymnastics to young athletes today.

BORN MAY 16, 1955

BELARUS → UNITED STATES OF AMERICA

ILLUSTRATION BY
JENNIFER POTTER

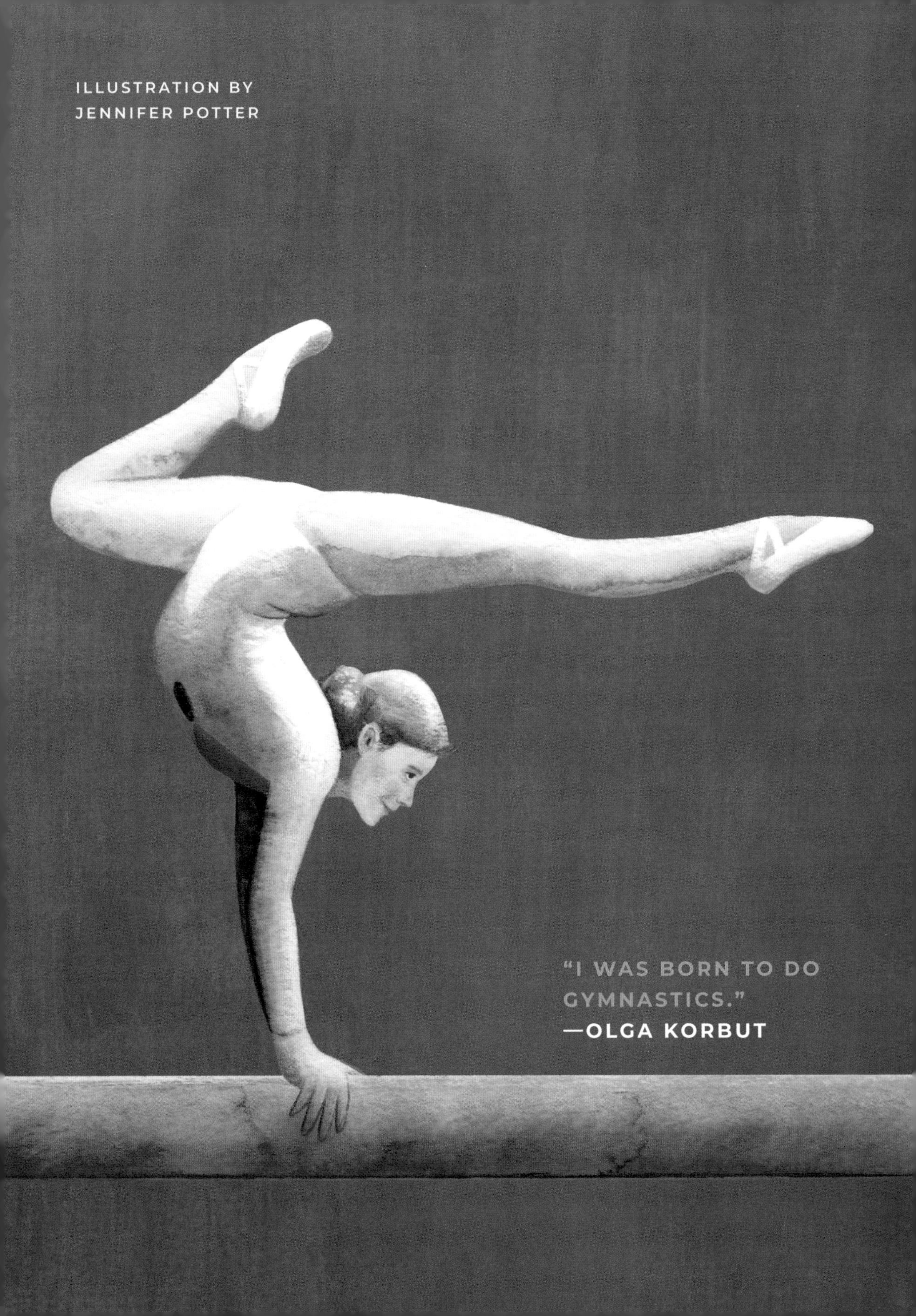

"I WAS BORN TO DO GYMNASTICS."
—OLGA KORBUT

PAULA NEWBY-FRASER

TRIATHLETE

Once there was a girl who was good at swimming and running. Paula was born in Zimbabwe and moved with her family to South Africa when she was four years old. When Paula was 22, she heard about an upcoming local triathlon: a race where competitors have to swim, cycle, and run.

Paula knew she could do two of those sports, but she had never tried cycling before. Still, she bought a bike, entered the race—and won the women's event! Shortly after, she became the women's triathlon champion in South Africa. She decided to train as a professional triathlete and moved to the United States.

The biggest triathlon of all was the Ironman World Championship, held in Kona, Hawaii. Competitors had to swim for 2.4 miles, bike for 112 miles, and run 26.2 miles, one right after the other.

Paula entered the race in 1986 and was the first woman to ever finish in under 10 hours. In 1988, she smashed the women's course record. She won five of the next six Ironman World Championships. People called her the Queen of Kona. Then in 1995, with less than a mile to go in the race, her body broke down. She finished fourth, feeling sad and disappointed. She decided she would do the race again, but this time she would train a different way than her competitors did—and she would run just for her own enjoyment. She did it—and won her eighth Ironman!

Paula has more Ironman championship wins than any triathlete ever. The world record time she set in 1992 stood for 17 years.

BORN JUNE 2, 1962

ZIMBABWE → SOUTH AFRICA AND UNITED STATES OF AMERICA

ILLUSTRATION BY
JEANNE DETALLANTE

"TO ME THE GREATEST
LESSON AS AN ATHLETE
AND IN TRAINING IS
JUST DON'T GET GREEDY
KNOW THAT YOU HAVE
TO GET UP AND GO AGAIN
THE NEXT DAY."
—PAULA NEWBY-FRASER

PEARL TRAN AND THU GETKA

DENTISTS

Thu was 17 and Pearl just 12 when their lives changed forever. A war between their country, South Vietnam, and neighboring North Vietnam was coming to a close. Many people, Thu's and Pearl's families included, chose to flee rather than risk violence at home.

Both of their families moved to the United States. Thu's family settled in Virginia, Pearl's in Georgia. There, they began new lives.

Though they didn't know each other, Thu's and Pearl's careers began to follow surprisingly similar paths. Both were good students who excelled in science and biology. Thu went to dental school, and Pearl—after first trying medical school, where she couldn't stand the long hours—did the same. They even became the same kind of dentist: a periodontist, who specializes in caring for people's gums.

Pearl eventually decided to become a dentist for the US Navy. She was assigned to a residency at the National Naval Medical Center in Bethesda, Maryland. Shortly after her arrival, a new periodontist came to the center to be Pearl's mentor. It was Thu! She had also joined the US Navy. In fact, she was the first Vietnamese American woman to be promoted to the rank of captain in the US Navy.

The two women were stunned to realize how similar their lives had been. Leaving their homes in Vietnam and becoming **refugees** had been a scary experience, but Pearl and Thu both built new lives and went on to use their talents to serve the country they adopted as their own.

PEARL TRAN, BORN CIRCA 1963 • THU GETKA, BORN CIRCA 1958
VIETNAM ➞ UNITED STATES OF AMERICA

"AS A KID IN SAIGON, I DIDN'T UNDERSTAND A LOT OF THINGS THAT WERE GOING ON BEFORE I LEFT VIETNAM."
—PEARL TRAN

ILLUSTRATION BY VALENCIA SPATES

PNINA TAMANO-SHATA

LAWYER AND LAWMAKER

O nce there was a Jewish girl named Pnina who was born in Ethiopia. The government made it hard for people like Pnina's family to practice their religion, and during a time of civil war and famine, they fled to a **refugee** camp in Sudan before immigrating to Israel.

Even though Pnina had lived in Israel since she was three years old, she was given a hard time by other children at school. Her parents found jobs as cleaners and worked hard to provide for her and her siblings, but because they didn't speak Hebrew, Pnina had to speak for them at school, the doctor's, and the social work office. She understood how hard life was for people who were different and who did not have a voice.

When she got to college, Pnina led protests against **racism**, her voice carrying clear and strong. After graduating, she went to work as a television journalist. When her bosses asked her to cover a protest of Ethiopian Israelis, Pnina realized that she could not simply stand to the side. She put down her microphone and joined the **protesters** herself!

Pnina decided to become a lawyer and fight against **discrimination**. In 2013, she became a member of the Knesset, Israel's parliament—the first Ethiopian-born woman to represent her community there.

"My experiences growing up as an Ethiopian in Israel had prepared me well to help others too," she said. "I felt like I had a responsibility toward Israeli society to make things better."

BORN NOVEMBER 1, 1981

ETHIOPIA ➝ ISRAEL

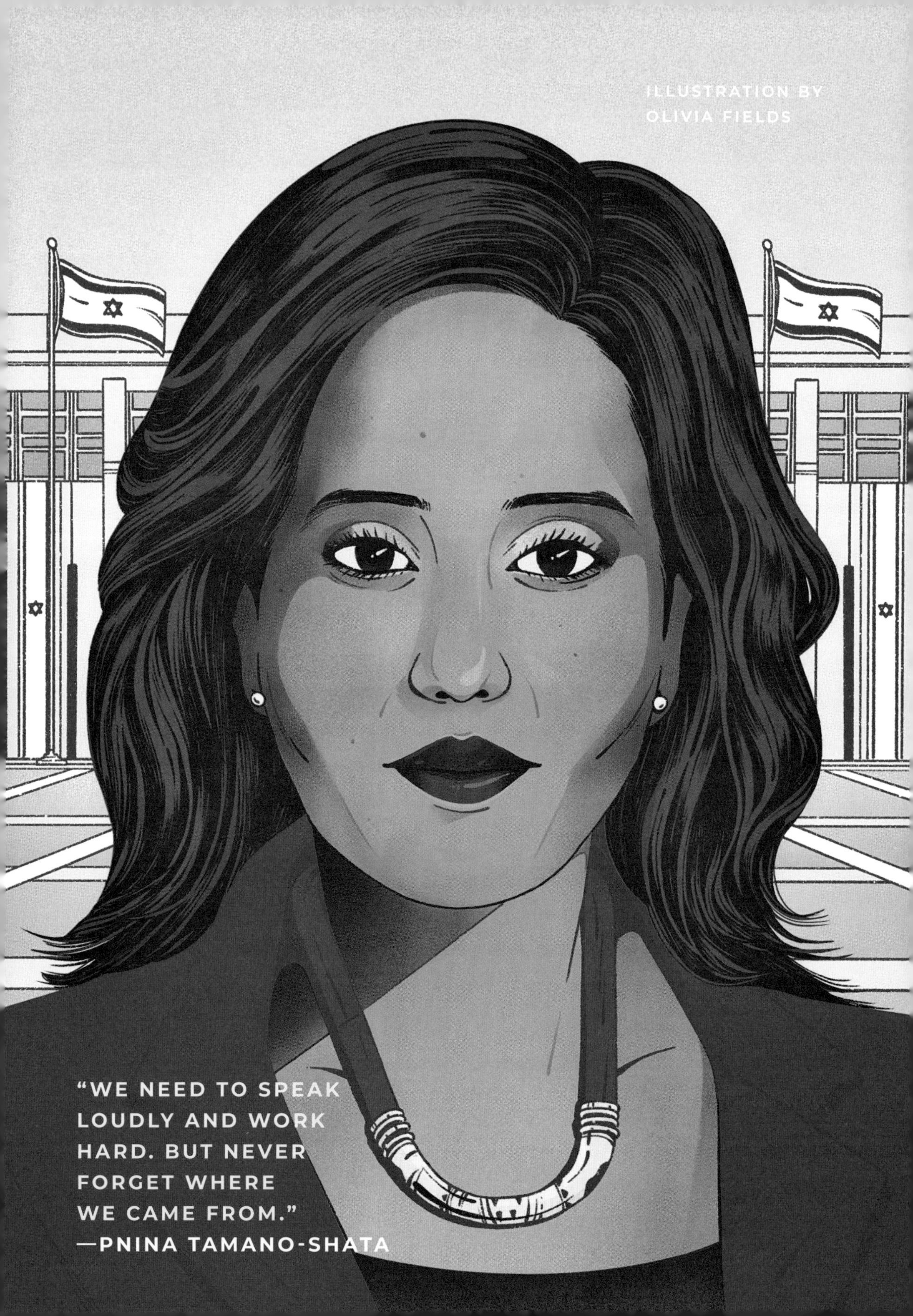

ILLUSTRATION BY
OLIVIA FIELDS
“WE NEED TO SPEAK
LOUDLY AND WORK
HARD. BUT NEVER
FORGET WHERE
WE CAME FROM.”
—PNINA TAMANO-SHATA

RAPELANG RABANA

COMPUTER SCIENTIST AND ENTREPRENEUR

Once there was a girl who wanted an education more than anything. But when she was a teenager, Rapelang worried she wouldn't be able to take her final high school exams.

Rapelang's family had moved to South Africa from nearby Botswana. Her parents worked hard to send her to boarding school, but it was expensive. If they couldn't pay, Rapelang couldn't continue her studies. Faced with a tricky problem, Rapelang earned a scholarship for her final term—and passed her exams with honors.

Rapelang then went to the University of Cape Town in South Africa and studied computer science. She liked how coding let her create new things from her own imagination. When she graduated, she knew she didn't want to go work for a big business that would tell her what to do all day. She wanted to go her own way.

Before most smartphones existed, Rapelang and a friend started a company called Yeigo that let people speak over the internet, instead of over expensive phone lines. Their company was a huge success as it made that personal connection more affordable.

For her next big project, Rapelang returned to her love of education. She started an online business called Rekindle Learning to help people of all ages do better in school and work, wherever they lived.

Rapelang is one of the world's most exciting young entrepreneurs. "The opportunities to be whoever you want to be have never been more accessible to those who pursue their dreams," she said.

BORN NOVEMBER 5, 1983

BOTSWANA ➡ SOUTH AFRICA AND UNITED STATES OF AMERICA

"TRUE SUCCESS COMES FROM OPERATING FROM AN AUTHENTIC SPACE AND BEING TRUE TO YOUR OWN GOALS AND ASPIRATIONS."
—RAPELANG RABANA

ILLUSTRATION BY MICHELLE D'URBANO

REYNA DUONG

CHEF

Once there was a girl who believed all people should be treated with respect, no matter their abilities. Before Reyna turned three, her family left Vietnam as **refugees** and moved to the United States, where her little brother, Sang, was born.

Sang was born with Down syndrome, and Reyna did her best to look out for him. Their childhood was not easy, but Reyna's happiest times were helping her mother in the kitchen. Her mother made meals from scratch, including broth, which took two whole days.

When their parents passed away, Reyna became Sang's guardian. To help her and her brother feel less sad, Reyna cooked familiar meals that reminded them of their mother. The experience inspired Reyna to open a sandwich shop in their mother's honor.

Reyna filled the menu with delicious banh mi, but sharing good food wasn't her only purpose. Reyna wanted to run a business where she and Sang could work together. She wanted to show her community that people with Down syndrome deserve the opportunity to work just like everyone else.

Today Sang and many other people with differing abilities work in Reyna's restaurant. And once a year, on World Down Syndrome Day, the restaurant throws a big party. For Reyna, it's a celebration of the brother she loves and the hope she has for a more welcoming world.

BORN MAY 30, 1977

VIETNAM ➜ UNITED STATES OF AMERICA

"BONDING OVER A MEAL TOGETHER
IS A UNIVERSAL LANGUAGE."
—REYNA DUONG

RIHANNA

ENTREPRENEUR AND SINGER

Once there was a girl who wanted her music to be heard all over the world. When Rihanna was a teenager, she auditioned for a record label. The producers were so impressed, they encouraged Rihanna to move to the United States. Even though she loved Barbados and her family, she wasn't afraid to leave it all behind. "I wanted to do what I had to do, even if it meant moving to America," Rihanna said.

Not long after she arrived in the US, the label offered her a contract, and her career took off. Her songs played on the radio and fans lined up to see her onstage. Yet it took a while for Rihanna to find her true voice. In Barbadian **culture**, Rihanna said, being quiet was considered polite. But in the US, her quietness was seen as rude. "You mean well, and it can come across in a different way in a different culture," Rihanna said.

Rihanna has built a reputation as an artist and entrepreneur who's true to herself. She's won nine Grammys and is one of the best-selling music artists of all time. Her musical success also opened doors into areas she never expected, including business. In 2017, Rihanna launched Fenty Beauty, a cosmetics brand that focused on inclusivity. She and her team spent two years developing foundation that came in a huge variety of skin tones—more than 40 shades. Her company's emphasis on diversity has inspired other cosmetics brands to do the same. Then in 2019, Rihanna created her own luxury fashion line. "The thing that keeps me alive and passionate is being creative," Rihanna said.

BORN FEBRUARY 20, 1988

BARBADOS → UNITED STATES OF AMERICA

"MUSIC HAD LED ME TO THESE OTHER OUTLETS, AND TO THINGS I GENUINELY LOVE."
—RIHANNA

ILLUSTRATION BY JESTENIA SOUTHERLAND

ROJA MAYA LIMBU AND SUJANA RANA

UNION ORGANIZERS

Roja was around 19 years old when she left her home in Nepal and moved to Lebanon. She had trained to be a teacher, but she wanted a better life for herself and was ready to work hard to get it. Eventually she found a job helping an elderly lady in her home, and for more than four years, she worked every single day with no time off.

After several years in Lebanon, Roja met Sujana, who was also from Nepal. Sujana, too, worked long, hard hours as a domestic worker with few rights. Sujana and Roja had sometimes felt isolated and afraid in their jobs. Together, they realized they were not alone.

There were more than 250,000 immigrants in Lebanon who worked as housekeepers, nannies, and caregivers. Some of them were abused by the people they worked for. Sometimes their bosses stole their money or refused time off and kept them confined.

Sujana and Roja wanted to change things for workers like themselves, so along with the others, they decided to form a union.

There were laws to protect workers in Lebanon, but those laws didn't apply to migrant workers like Sujana and Roja, and the government did not approve of the union. In 2016, both Sujana and Roja were arrested and forced to leave Lebanon and return to Nepal. But the work they started continues. Today people in Lebanon are still fighting for fair treatment for domestic workers.

ROJA, BORN AUGUST 6, 1985 • SUJANA, BORN SEPTEMBER 9, 1971

NEPAL ➞ LEBANON

"THEY SAID THAT MY CRIME WAS HELPING THE VICTIM GIRLS.... I HAD DONE THAT, AND IF IT WAS A CRIME, THEN THERE COULD BE NOTHING BETTER THAN THAT."
—SUJANA RANA

ILLUSTRATION BY ALINE ZALKO

ROSALIE ABELLA

JUDGE

Once upon a time, there was a girl named Rosalie who knew how important it was for laws to treat everyone with the same respect. Her parents were Polish Jewish people who had survived World War II, and Rosalie was born in a **displaced persons** camp.

Rosalie's family moved to Canada when she was small, and although her father had been a lawyer in Germany, he was not allowed to practice law in Canada because he was not a **citizen**.

Only four years after Rosalie became a lawyer herself, she was asked to serve as a judge in Canada's family court. She was the first Jewish woman to become a judge in Canada and one of the youngest judges in the country's history. She was also the first person in Canada to become a judge while pregnant!

Every day she saw people struggling in a system that treated them unfairly because of their gender, disability, or skin color. Rosalie tried her best to listen with an open mind and be fair in her decisions.

"I learned to see law from the experiences of the people who were before me...," Rosalie said later. "Looking at the law and justice from their eyes taught me how to be a judge."

Around 1984, Rosalie was put in charge of a huge job: to figure out how to make workplaces in Canada more equal to all workers. Her report was used in other countries to make their workplaces fairer too.

In 2004, Rosalie became the first Jewish woman to serve on Canada's Supreme Court.

BORN JULY 1, 1946
GERMANY ➔ CANADA

ILLUSTRATION BY
SASHA KOLESNIK

"WHEN YOU ARE AN
IMMIGRANT, YOU NEVER
THINK IN TERMS
OF ENTITLEMENT.
YOU THINK IN TERMS
OF OPPORTUNITIES
AND WORKING
REALLY HARD."
—ROSALIE ABELLA

ROSE FORTUNE

ENTREPRENEUR AND POLICE OFFICER

Once upon a time, the waterfront in the town of Annapolis Royal, Canada, was a busy place. There were boxes and parcels everywhere, and travelers, sailors, and fishermen came and went at all hours of the night. Some people looked at the waterfront and saw chaos. Rose saw opportunity.

Rose's parents were enslaved when she was born, but they wanted their daughter to grow up free. During the American Revolution, British forces promised Rose's father that he and his family would be freed from slavery if he fought on their side and won. When the American rebels triumphed, Rose's family and many other black families who had sided with the British left the United States and moved to Canada.

Eventually, Rose looked for ways to earn a living at the waterfront.

Using wheelbarrows, she started a business carrying luggage and goods to and from the ships—a business that her family went on to run for more than 100 years. Rose would even go directly to the inn where her customers were staying and make sure they didn't miss their ship. In the days before alarm clocks or telephones, this was very helpful!

Rose knew everyone on the docks, and she made sure that people obeyed its rules. Wearing heavy boots and a man's coat over her dress and apron, Rose patrolled the waterfront on foot and sent troublemakers running.

She is now recognized as Canada's first female police officer.

MARCH 13, 1774–FEBRUARY 20, 1864

UNITED STATES OF AMERICA ➞ CANADA

ILLUSTRATION BY
SABRENA KHADIJA

ROSELI OCAMPO-FRIEDMANN

MICROBIOLOGIST

Once there was a girl growing up in the Philippines who was fascinated by plants that lived in odd places: moss growing on the sides of buildings, flowers blooming on balconies, tiny weeds curling up through cracks in the sidewalk. Her name was Roseli, and when she went to college at the University of the Philippines, she got a degree in botany, the study of plants.

To continue her education, Roseli moved to Israel to get a graduate degree from Hebrew University. There, she met a scientist named Imre Friedmann. Imre had discovered tiny blue-green algae inside and on the underside of rocks. They mostly grew in deserts or hard-to-reach places, so they were very hard to study. But Roseli was able to grow them in the laboratory. People joked that she had a "blue-green" thumb!

Roseli and Imre got married, settled in the United States, and traveled the world seeking out life-forms that grew in places too cold, hot, dry, or unusual for most other plants. Together, they discovered extremely small living microorganisms within rocks in Antarctica's deserts and frozen into the earth in Siberia. With her amazing talent for growing things, Roseli took tiny samples of these microbes home and grew more of them in her lab so scientists could study them.

After NASA landed the Viking probe on Mars in 1976, scientists studied the research Roseli contributed to to learn more about the kinds of life that might exist on a planet with such a harsh environment.

NOVEMBER 23, 1937–SEPTEMBER 4, 2005
PHILIPPINES ➡ UNITED STATES OF AMERICA

"DRY VALLEYS ARE REGARDED AS THE CLOSEST TERRESTRIAL ANALOG TO MARTIAN OR OTHER EXTRATERRESTRIAL PLANETARY ENVIRONMENTS."
—ROSELI OCAMPO-FRIEDMANN

ILLUSTRATION BY SALLY CAULWELL

SAMANTHA POWER

DIPLOMAT

Nine-year-old Samantha felt nervous as she sat at her desk in her new school in the United States. She looked down at her clothes. She felt out of place in the dark-green cardigan and plaid skirt she'd worn at her Catholic school in Ireland. She made an effort to fit in, even practicing an American accent and learning baseball stats.

Samantha was afraid of how people would treat her if they thought she was different. But the longer she stayed in her new home, the more Samantha adjusted. She also noticed—and loved—that all sorts of people were able to live together peacefully in the US.

When Samantha was 22, she decided to become a journalist. There was a terrible war happening in the southeastern European country of Bosnia. Samantha went there and wrote about the suffering she saw. It made her angry that countries, including the United States, didn't do more to stop the fighting and help people. She wrote a book about the way the world reacts when people kill other people because of their religion or **ethnicity**. The book won the Pulitzer Prize.

Years later, when Barack Obama became president, he remembered Samantha's book. He asked her to be the US **ambassador** to the United Nations and help decide how the US should act abroad. The choices were hard, but Samantha always tried to argue for what she believed would make the world a better place.

Today Samantha is a professor at Harvard University, where she teaches students the lessons she learned as a writer and **diplomat**.

BORN SEPTEMBER 21, 1970

IRELAND ➜ UNITED STATES OF AMERICA

"PEOPLE WHO CARE, ACT, AND REFUSE TO GIVE UP MAY NOT CHANGE *THE* WORLD, BUT THEY CAN CHANGE MANY INDIVIDUAL WORLDS."
—SAMANTHA POWER

ILLUSTRATION BY SARAH LOULENDO

SANDRA CAUFFMAN

ELECTRICAL ENGINEER

Once upon a time, there was a girl who dreamed of working for NASA. On a summer night in Costa Rica, Sandra watched the first moon landing on her neighbors' TV. The living room was packed with people, but as Neil Armstrong's boot touched the moon's surface, no one said a word. They were too amazed. "I walked home that night and looked at the moon so far away," Sandra said, "and I knew then that I wanted to be part of that adventure."

Sandra shared her dream with her mother right away. Sandra's family was poor, and her mother raised her family alone, working long hours at difficult jobs. But she saw the light in her daughter's eyes and encouraged her to work hard.

Sandra *did* work hard. She excelled in school and enrolled in a Costa Rican university. She wanted to study electrical engineering, but a professor told her it wasn't "ladylike," so she studied industrial engineering instead. In the middle of college, Sandra's family moved to the US. There, she was able to study electrical engineering (and physics), like she'd always wanted to, and earned her degree.

A few years later, Sandra achieved her childhood dream—she was hired by NASA. She became a NASA engineer, focusing on designing satellites and on space exploration—including missions to Mars! "I just finished launching a satellite to Mars," Sandra said in 2015. "It is just incredible that a little piece of me and a little piece of Costa Rica has traveled to Mars and is now orbiting the Red Planet."

BORN MAY 10, 1962

COSTA RICA ➜ UNITED STATES OF AMERICA

ILLUSTRATION BY
MAÏTÉ FRANCHI

"WHEN I WAS SEVEN YEARS OLD,
I WANTED TO GO TO THE MOON.
LOOK WHERE I AM TODAY.
I HAVE LANDED AMONG THE STARS."
—SANDRA CAUFFMAN

SARA MAZROUEI

PLANETARY GEOLOGIST

Once there was a girl in Iran who wanted to blaze her own trail like a comet in the night sky. Sara spent her childhood marveling at outer space and reading books about brave girls who weren't afraid to be different. It was good training for what was to come.

When Sara was 13, her family moved to Canada so she and her sisters could study and be whatever they wanted. Things *were* different in Canada, but not all doors were open the way they'd hoped.

Sara dreamed of being a NASA scientist. While working on her PhD, she was chosen for a NASA internship, but a few weeks after she arrived, Sara received unexpected news: she didn't have security clearance to be at NASA because she had been born in Iran. The officials even questioned how she had gotten the internship. Sara was frustrated— she had been honest about her birthplace from the beginning.

Nevertheless, Sara's sense of adventure and her love of math and science propelled her to finish her internship, get her PhD, and become a planetary scientist. She went on to teach others about space and to study things including the history of asteroids and the best landing locations for future lunar missions. She also spoke out for equality. She believed that people should be free to be leaders in STEM careers, no matter their gender or where they're from. "I wonder how much more I could've achieved," Sara said, "if I didn't have to spend half of my time defending the fact that I belong where I am."

BORN NOVEMBER 3, 1987
IRAN → CANADA

"WHY DOES IT MATTER WHERE YOU WERE BORN WHEN YOU'RE TRYING TO STUDY THINGS OUT OF THIS WORLD?"
—SARA MAZROUEI

ILLUSTRATION BY
EVA RUST

SARA MCLAGAN

NEWSPAPER EDITOR

Sara was only a toddler when her family moved from Northern Ireland to Canada. Her father had been sent by the British government to take up a job there as an engineer.

Sara started working as a switchboard operator when she was about 13 years old, and soon Western Union put her in charge of connecting all the messages that passed between her station in Matsqui, British Columbia, and the United States. Thick calluses grew on her fingertips from tapping out messages in Morse code, but Sara didn't care. She liked being part of the system that brought people information—and she was good at it. She eventually became an office manager, a job that few women held.

When Sara got married, her husband, John, wanted to start a brand-new newspaper: the *Vancouver Daily World*. He knew Sara was the perfect person to help.

Sadly, around 1901, John became very sick and died. Sara didn't want to see the paper shut down. Instead, she decided to run it herself. She managed the staff, wrote stories, and read over the pages to check for mistakes before they went to the printer. She also made sure that the paper ran articles on things that would be helpful to women who worked hard to care for their homes and families. She oversaw stories on topics such as health, child care, and nutrition. By taking on this important role, Sara became Canada's first-ever female newspaper publisher of a major daily paper.

CIRCA 1856–MARCH 20, 1924

IRELAND ➡ CANADA

ILLUSTRATION BY
BARBARA DZIADOSZ

SAU LAN WU

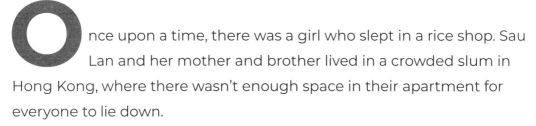

PHYSICIST

O nce upon a time, there was a girl who slept in a rice shop. Sau Lan and her mother and brother lived in a crowded slum in Hong Kong, where there wasn't enough space in their apartment for everyone to lie down.

Growing up, Sau Lan first dreamed of becoming a painter. Then one day, she read a book about the great physicist and chemist Marie Curie, and changed her mind. She would become a scientist instead and search for a different kind of beauty in her work.

When it came time to go to university, Sau Lan knew her family could not afford to pay her tuition. Then she got a letter from Vassar College in New York. It offered her a full scholarship to study there.

After Vassar, Sau Lan went on to get a PhD in physics at Harvard University. She was fascinated by the tiny particles that made up atoms, which in turn made up everything else in the universe. Because they were so small, they were also very hard to study.

In 1974, Sau Lan's research team discovered a particle called J/psi, which helped scientists understand more about how matter works. Soon after, she helped discover gluon, a particle that holds parts of an atom together. Then she tackled one of the most important challenges in all of physics: the discovery of the Higgs boson, a particle so hard to find that many scientists were not even sure it existed. In 2012, Sau Lan's team found evidence that the Higgs boson was real— and to Sau Lan, it was beautiful.

BORN CIRCA 1941

HONG KONG ➝ UNITED STATES OF AMERICA

"TRY TO INNOVATE. NOTHING WILL BE EASY. BUT IT IS ALL WORTH IT TO DISCOVER SOMETHING NEW."
—SAU LAN WU

ILLUSTRATION BY ADRIANA BELLET

SURYA BONALY

FIGURE SKATER

Once upon a time, a figure skater glided onto the ice in a beautiful, sparkling costume for a performance no one would ever forget. It was the 1998 Olympic Games in Nagano, Japan, and there had never been a skater like Surya. She could do things on the ice that hardly anyone else could: cartwheels, giant leaps, even a backflip. She won the French national championships nine times, the European championships five times (once with a broken toe), and three silver medals in the world championships. When Surya skated, she felt like she was making art on the ice.

Surya's most famous move—the backflip—was banned from the Olympics. Skaters weren't allowed to do flips in competition. But Nagano would be her last Olympic performance, and she didn't expect to win, so Surya didn't care what the judges said. She wanted to do something big and brave.

As the music soared, Surya did a backflip and landed on one foot! No skater in history had ever done that before—or since. The crowd went wild. They hurled flowers onto the ice. When the music stopped, Surya turned away from the judges, ignoring her scores, and bowed to the audience instead.

After the Olympics, Surya became a professional figure skater and coach, and eventually moved to the United States. Some estimated that she had done more than 500 backflips in shows around the world. It was her signature move, and she was unstoppable.

BORN DECEMBER 15, 1973

FRANCE ➤ UNITED STATES OF AMERICA

ILLUSTRATION BY
JULIETTE LÉVEILLÉ

"I DID MY BEST, BUT
I CAN ALWAYS DO BETTER."
—SURYA BONALY

SUSAN FRANCIA

ROWER

Once there was a girl born in Hungary who grew so tall and strong that everyone thought she must be a star athlete. The coaches at Susan's high school in the United States—from basketball to field hockey—all wanted the six-foot-two student to join their teams. But her athletic ability was just average. In basketball, she spent most of her time sitting on the bench. "I was really good at cheering for my teammates," Susan said. In fact, the only athletic award she won her senior year was Most Spirited. After her high school experience, no one could've imagined that Susan would one day be an Olympic gold medalist.

During her sophomore year of college, Susan joined her university's rowing team on a whim. She missed playing sports, and rowing was one of the only teams at her school that let anyone try out. Susan had never even held an oar. Yet when she and her teammates pulled the boat through the water, it felt like something she'd been born to do. Over the next few years, Susan became a powerful and determined rower. "For the first time, I didn't just have 'potential,'" Susan said. "I was actually excelling!"

Some of Susan's coaches encouraged her to try out for the Olympic team. After she graduated from college, that's exactly what she did. She not only made the Olympic team for the 2008 Beijing Summer Games but Susan and her teammates also won a gold medal! Four years later, at the Summer Olympics in London, she won a gold medal again. Afterward, Susan used her Olympic journey to inspire others.

BORN NOVEMBER 8, 1982

HUNGARY ➡ UNITED STATES OF AMERICA

ILLUSTRATION BY
KATHRIN HONESTA

"IT WAS AWESOME
TO FIND SOMETHING
WHERE I COULD
FINALLY LIVE UP
TO MY POTENTIAL."
—SUSAN FRANCIA

SUSAN POLGAR

CHESS CHAMPION

One day in Budapest, a little girl named Susan walked into a neighborhood chess club with her father. The men in the room were surprised to see the girl, but one of the men agreed to play her in a match. Later, the room was even more surprised when she won!

Susan was only four years old, but she was already training to be a chess champion. Her father, László, was a psychologist who studied child prodigies. He thought that any child could become a "genius" in a subject they put their mind to. Rather than send Susan and her sisters to school, László taught them at home, training them to be expert chess players. The sisters studied chess for six hours a day!

In the 1970s, the world's best chess players were men. Some people thought this was proof that the female brain was unable to understand the game. But Susan and her sisters proved them wrong, winning matches against both women *and* men. By 15, Susan was the best female chess player in the world. In 1986, she became the first woman to qualify for the Men's World Chess Championship. She wasn't allowed to play that year, but the rules were later changed to allow women competitors.

Susan was a world-champion chess player four times, won 10 medals in the Chess Olympiad, and was the first woman to earn the title of Grandmaster—the highest honor in chess—the same way men did. After moving to the US in 1994, she founded her own chess training center to teach the next generation of players.

BORN APRIL 19, 1969
HUNGARY ➔ UNITED STATES OF AMERICA

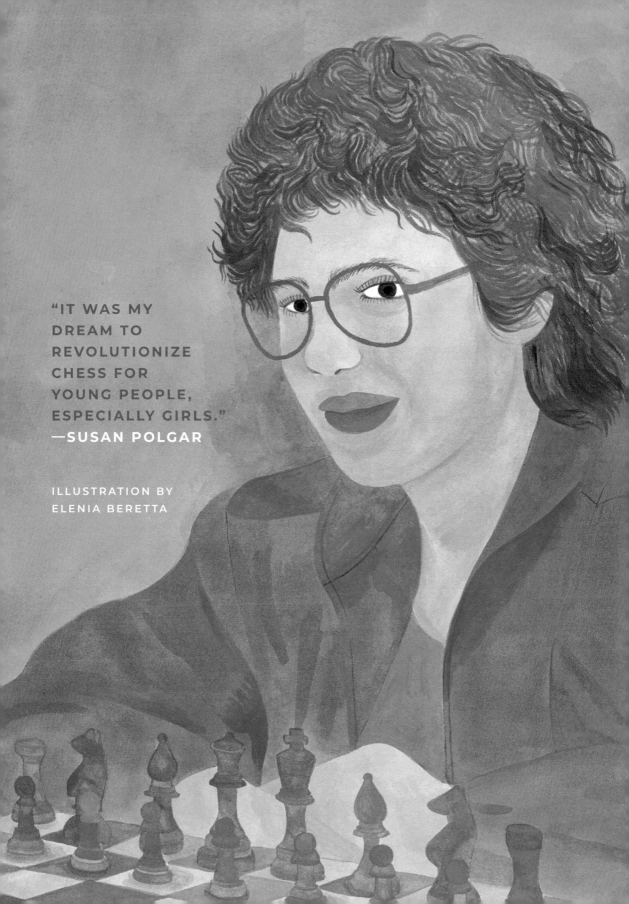

"IT WAS MY DREAM TO REVOLUTIONIZE CHESS FOR YOUNG PEOPLE, ESPECIALLY GIRLS."
—SUSAN POLGAR

ILLUSTRATION BY ELENIA BERETTA

TEREZA LEE

ACTIVIST

Once there was a girl whose dream of a better life sparked hope for others. Tereza was born in Brazil to Korean parents but moved to the United States as a toddler. When Tereza was still young, her father told her a secret: they were **undocumented** immigrants and not legal **citizens**.

Her family's secret made Tereza feel afraid all the time. Chicago was the only home she had ever known. But if the US government found out about her family, they could send them back to Brazil or South Korea.

Tereza channeled her energy into music and spent hours alone practicing the piano. Music gave her hope, and when she was in high school, she played Tchaikovsky Piano Concerto with the Chicago Symphony Orchestra.

When a teacher encouraged her to apply for college, Tereza shared her secret. They contacted their senator, Dick Durbin, who wrote a bill just for Tereza that would allow her to attend college. Soon other undocumented students heard about it and asked for help too. Senator Durbin drafted a new bill called the DREAM Act. It would create a way for people who had arrived in the US as children to become citizens.

The bill was on its way to becoming law when the terrorist attacks of September 11, 2001, stopped it in its tracks. Today thousands of people are still working to pass the DREAM Act. What started as one girl's dream became a movement that helped others find their voice.

BORN JANUARY 12, 1983
BRAZIL ➡ UNITED STATES OF AMERICA

ILLUSTRATION BY
SOPHIE CUNNINGHAM

"KEEP GOING OUT, KEEP
DOING THIS, KEEP FIGHTING,
BECAUSE IT ONLY MAKES YOU
STRONGER. THIS IS THE ONLY
WAY WE CAN LET PEOPLE
KNOW THIS IS WHO WE ARE."
—TEREZA LEE

TIMNIT GEBRU

COMPUTER SCIENTIST

O nce there was a girl who lived in a home filled with people who loved numbers and science. In Timnit's house in Ethiopia, when you encountered a problem, you found a way to fix it.

When Timnit was a teenager, war broke out between Ethiopia and Eritrea. People of Eritrean descent, like Timnit and her family, were being forced to flee. Her family left the country and found **asylum** in the United States.

When Timnit started high school in Massachusetts, she tried to enroll in the hardest math and science classes. To Timnit's confusion, the teacher discouraged her. This teacher didn't think a student from Africa could do high-level work. Timnit couldn't believe how ridiculous that was. She graduated as soon as she could and enrolled at Stanford University. By the time she left Stanford, she had a PhD in electrical engineering!

During her graduate studies, Timnit got interested in artificial intelligence. She saw that many computer programs came built-in with **prejudices** and biases. Those that recognized faces, for example, didn't work as well on people of color. If artificial intelligence was going to change the world for the better, Timnit realized, it had to be fair. The people who built these tools should look like the people who used them, so Timnit started programs to encourage women and people of color to study engineering.

Today Timnit works for Google to create ethical artificial intelligence programs.

ILLUSTRATION BY
AURÉLIA DURAND

"THERE IS NO SUCH THING AS A MATH
PERSON VERSUS NOT A MATH PERSON.
THAT'S SOCIETY TELLING YOU THERE IS
ONLY ONE TYPE OF PERSON FOR ONE FIELD."
—TIMNIT GEBRU

TURIA PITT

Once there was a girl who was determined to overcome any obstacle in her path. Turia was born in Tahiti and grew up on a cliff overlooking the Pacific Ocean in Australia. Nearly every day before and after school, she'd surf the blue waves or run along the beach. She loved exploring the Australian landscape.

When it was time to choose a career, one option stood out: mining engineer. Turia loved science, math, and the outdoors. She was a problem solver and liked the idea of working in the remote Australian outback.

After she got her first engineering job, Turia ran an ultramarathon—100 kilometers through the outback. A few hours into the race, she was suddenly surrounded by a raging grassfire. Amazingly, Turia survived, but most of her body and face had been burned, and she lost several fingers. She was in the hospital for a long time.

Doctors told her she would never run again, but Turia didn't give up. Over the next two years, she relearned to walk, talk, and feed herself. Then she set bigger goals—and achieved those too. After her accident, Turia completed two Ironman triathlons, hiked the Kokoda Trek, sailed around French Polynesia (the region where she was born), became a motivational speaker, launched a business, wrote three books, and became a mother. "I've rebuilt my life," Turia said, "and defied every expectation placed on me."

BORN JULY 25, 1987

TAHITI ➜ AUSTRALIA

ILLUSTRATION BY LÉA TAILLEFERT ROLLAND

"YOU ARE NOT LIMITED BY WHAT OTHER PEOPLE THINK OF YOU, OR BY WHAT YOU THINK OF YOURSELF!"
—TURIA PITT

VELMA SCANTLEBURY

TRANSPLANT SURGEON

Once there was a girl who wanted to be a doctor—but she faced so many challenges that she almost gave up. Velma was born in Barbados. As a child, she loved to visit the beach with her dad, ride the open-air bus to school, and play sports with her friends. She also dreamed about her future.

When she was 15, Velma and her family moved to the United States. It was a very difficult time. At her new school in Brooklyn, Velma was teased about her hair, her accent, and her clothes. Even her school guidance counselor treated Velma differently from the other students. She told Velma that college wasn't for her and that she should get a job instead. "To her, I had no promising future," Velma said. "The darkness of my skin blinded her."

But Velma did get into college—and was awarded a full scholarship! She earned a biology degree and later attended medical school. Velma continued to face **discrimination**, but with the friendship and guidance of a female professor, she persevered. She also realized that she loved learning about surgery. In 1989, Velma became the first female African American transplant surgeon.

Velma has performed more than 2,000 transplant surgeries and has won many awards for her work. She has also written a book and taught in order to share her knowledge with others. Velma works hard to address inequality in the medical field and to encourage girls to become surgeons even when it seems difficult.

BORN OCTOBER 6, 1955

BARBADOS → UNITED STATES OF AMERICA

"SURROUND YOURSELF
WITH POSITIVE PEOPLE WHO
ARE GOING TO LIFT YOU UP."
—VELMA SCANTLEBURY

XIYE BASTIDA

ACTIVIST

Once upon a time, a terrible drought gripped Xiye's hometown of San Pedro Tultepec, Mexico. The land was parched. The lake dried up. Crops died. After two years, the rain finally came—but it wasn't a normal storm. It poured and poured until the land flooded.

Xiye belonged to the Otomi Toltec, a nation of Indigenous people. Her community understood the importance of living in balance with the environment and caring for the earth. When Xiye moved with her family to New York City, she saw the damage left by Hurricane Sandy and realized the balance was dangerously off. The climate was in crisis. She had to do something to make it right.

In March 2019, when she was 17 years old, Xiye organized a strike at her high school in New York. Under her leadership, around 600 students walked out of class to demand that governments take action to stop climate change and protect the planet. Months later, Xiye and other young activists around the world led a week of global strikes and protests for climate change and Indigenous rights.

To make time for her activism, Xiye had to give up gymnastics and other activities she loved. But the earth was worth it.

"Indigenous people have been taking care of the earth for thousands of years because that is their **culture**," Xiye said. "For me, being an environmental activist and a climate justice **activist** is not a hobby. It's a way of life."

BORN APRIL 18, 2002

MEXICO ➜ UNITED STATES OF AMERICA

"EARTH IS OUR HOME. IT GIVES YOU AIR, WATER, AND SHELTER. EVERYTHING WE NEED. ALL IT ASKS IS THAT WE PROTECT IT."
—XIYE BASTIDA

ILLUSTRATION BY SALLY DENG

YOKY MATSUOKA

ROBOTICS ENGINEER

Once upon a time, there was a girl who dreamed with the intensity of a machine. In the beginning, she wanted to become a professional tennis player when she grew up. She moved to the United States at the age of 16 and hoped to make it as a pro.

Unfortunately, Yoky suffered injury after injury and decided that a tennis career wasn't for her. Instead she found herself daydreaming: what if she built a robot that could play tennis with her whenever she wanted?

So Yoky went to the University of California, Berkeley, and studied robotics. She wanted to know how robots could help people. Yoky became a pioneer in the field of neurorobotics, studying the relationship between computers and the central nervous system.

Yoky eventually built mechanical arms that could help people learn to use their muscles again after a stroke. Her work was so creative, she received a prize called the MacArthur Fellowship—sometimes known as the genius grant.

Yoky wasn't the type of scientist to focus on just one project, though. She wanted to help people "become better versions of who they've always wanted to be." She was one of the first people to work at Google X, a top secret research department dedicated to solving hard problems. Then she helped start a company called Nest Labs and built a smart home thermostat. She went on to work for Google Health, which aims to use technology to change and save people's lives, and Panasonic.

BORN CIRCA 1972

JAPAN ➜ UNITED STATES OF AMERICA

"LIFE IS SHORT AND THERE ARE A LOT OF PEOPLE'S LIVES I WANT TO IMPROVE BECAUSE OF THINGS I CAN CONTRIBUTE IN A WAY THAT'S DIFFERENT FROM OTHERS."
—YOKY MATSUOKA

ILLUSTRATION BY LISA LANOË

YOSHIKO CHUMA

CHOREOGRAPHER AND PERFORMANCE ARTIST

When Yoshiko danced, wild things happened. She would leap around and stomp her boots on the floor. She left the stage and walked around the theater, or grabbed a chair and swung it over her head. Her performances were always different from anything audiences had seen before.

Yoshiko never took formal dance classes. As a girl in Osaka, Japan, Yoshiko had an elementary school teacher who taught students modern dance, and she was encouraged to learn more about the world outside their community. By the time Yoshiko went to university, she longed to travel.

A friend told her about a place that drew artists from all over the world: New York City. That's where Yoshiko decided to go. She did not speak English, but when she danced, she felt like she was communicating with her body.

Yoshiko's performances were a mix of modern dance and performance art. Sometimes audiences were confused. Yoshiko liked it that way. She started her own dance company named the School of Hard Knocks. That means learning things out in the real world, the way that Yoshiko did, instead of safely inside a classroom.

Yoshiko and her dance company have won many Bessie Awards, the highest honor for independent dancers in New York City. She has traveled to more than 40 countries and worked with more than 2,000 people to create her unique works of art.

BORN DECEMBER 25, 1950

JAPAN ➡ UNITED STATES OF AMERICA

ILLUSTRATION BY
ELENI DEBO

"I WISH MY AUDIENCE
WOULD NOT HAVE
EXPECTATIONS OR
PRECONCEPTIONS.
THEY LIMIT THE
IMAGINATION."
—YOSHIKO CHUMA

YOUNG JEAN LEE

PLAYWRIGHT

Once there was a girl who spent her childhood playing with dollhouses, moving the plastic people around like actors on a stage. Young Jean and her parents had left South Korea for the United States, eventually settling in a small town in Washington when she was just two years old. The town was an unfriendly place for Asian Americans. Throughout her childhood, Young Jean remembers being ashamed of her **culture**, even hiding the food they ate.

But her life changed when Young Jean moved to California for college. For the first time, she was surrounded by other Asian Americans. She had found a place where she could belong. Young Jean majored in English and spent years studying Shakespeare. She was fascinated by Shakespeare's plays and over-the-top characters. Young Jean soon realized something important: she didn't want to just study plays—she wanted to write them.

Young Jean started to read all the plays she could get her hands on. She even wrote to a well-known playwright for advice. She wanted to write plays for experimental theater, productions that didn't follow the typical rules and had unexpected elements. Young Jean began writing, attended graduate school, and later founded her own theater company to produce her work. To this day, she has continued to write plays that explore challenging topics such as race, identity, and politics.

In 2018, she became the first Asian American woman to have a play produced on Broadway.

BORN MAY 30, 1974

SOUTH KOREA → UNITED STATES OF AMERICA

ILLUSTRATION BY
SALINI PERERA

"I'M CONTINUALLY TRYING
TO CHALLENGE MYSELF...
TO ACTUALLY FACE THINGS THAT
MAKE ME UNCOMFORTABLE."
—YOUNG JEAN LEE

YUAN YUAN TAN

BALLERINA

Yuan Yuan was a girl who loved music. Whenever she heard a song on the radio or television in her family's Shanghai apartment, her body would sway, and she'd find herself dancing in time with the rhythm. Her mother wanted to send her to ballet school.

"Absolutely not!" her father said. He wanted Yuan Yuan to become a doctor. Ballet was a distraction, he thought.

"We'll flip a coin," her mother said firmly.

Ten-year-old Yuan Yuan held her breath as the silver-colored five-cent coin tumbled through the air. When it landed, her mother's side was facing up. She was going to learn ballet!

Yuan Yuan eventually won many prizes at international ballet competitions for her graceful, elegant style. When she was 18, the artistic director of the San Francisco Ballet invited her to the United States to dance as a guest star at the company's 1995 opening night gala. Afterward, that director asked her to stay and join the ballet company permanently.

Yuan Yuan soon became a principal dancer, one of the company's most senior and special ballerinas. She was the youngest principal dancer in the company's history and the first to come from Asia.

Yuan Yuan has danced the lead in the world's most famous ballets, including *Giselle*, *Swan Lake*, and *The Nutcracker*. In 2015, she celebrated her twentieth anniversary with the San Francisco Ballet with a special tour of performances in China—the place where her life as a ballerina began, all thanks to the flip of a coin.

BORN FEBRUARY 14, 1977

CHINA ➡ UNITED STATES OF AMERICA

ILLUSTRATION BY
PETRA BRAUN

"TO BE PERFECT IS IMPOSSIBLE,
BUT TO BE BETTER IS POSSIBLE.
WHEN I LOOK BACK AND SEE THAT
I'M BETTER THAN YESTERDAY,
THEN IT'S GOOD ENOUGH."
—YUAN YUAN TAN

ZAINAB SALBI

ACTIVIST

Once there was a girl who understood the joy of love—and the pain of war. Growing up in Iraq, Zainab was surrounded by laughter. But Iraq was controlled by a **dictator** named Saddam Hussein, and her parents eventually became worried for her safety. When she was only 19, they arranged for her to marry an Iraqi American man who lived in the United States.

This man turned out to be cruel. Zainab was all alone in an unfamiliar country. She could not go back to Iraq, but she also would not stay with a person who treated her badly.

Zainab escaped from her abusive husband. She took any job she could to support herself and studied for her university degree. In college, Zainab learned how war affected women all over the world, forcing them from their homes and endangering their lives. Now that she was safe, she wanted to help women who weren't.

When she was 23, Zainab founded Women for Women International, a humanitarian organization that helps women survivors of war rebuild their lives. Zainab led this group for 20 years before she was ready for a new challenge. Stories could change people's lives, she thought. What if she helped women tell their own?

Zainab travels the world to interview female lawmakers, **activists**, and leaders. Her books, television shows, and documentaries encourage people to understand one another and have compassion for one another's experiences.

BORN SEPTEMBER 24, 1969

IRAQ UNITED STATES OF AMERICA

ILLUSTRATION BY
NOA DENMON

"NOT TO BE LIKE ANY MAN
BUT TO BE MYSELF. THAT'S
WHAT FEMINISM IS TO ME."
—ZAINAB SALBI

WRITE YOUR STORY

Once upon a time, _____

_____

_____

_____

_____

_____

_____

_____

_____

_____

_____

_____

_____

_____

_____

_____

_____

_____

_____

_____

_____

_____

_____

_____

_____

_____

_____

_____

DRAW YOUR PORTRAIT

GLOSSARY

ABOLITIONIST (noun) – a person who wants to end slavery

ACTIVIST (noun) – a person who campaigns to create social or political change

ALLIES (noun) – the group of countries that came together to oppose the Axis powers (Germany, Italy, Japan) during World War II

AMBASSADOR (noun) – a person sent to another country as a representative of their government

ANCESTOR (noun) – a person who was part of one's family several generations ago

ASYLUM (noun) – protection granted by a nation

CITIZEN (noun) – a native or naturalized member of a state or nation

CULTURE (noun) – the shared characteristics of a society or group of people, including food, clothing, language, customs, beliefs, and religion

DICTATOR (noun) – a single ruler who has complete authority over a country

DIPLOMAT (noun) – a person whose job is to keep good relations between the governments of different countries

DISCRIMINATION (noun) – the unfair treatment of a person or group in a certain category, especially based on race, age, gender, or religion

DISPLACED PERSON (noun) – a person who is forced to leave their home and/or country

EMIGRATE (verb) – to leave one's country in order to permanently live in another

ETHNICITY (noun) – identity with a certain racial, national, or cultural group

HOLOCAUST (noun) – the massacre of civilians on a large scale, especially Jewish people, that took place during World War II

JUDO (noun) – a martial art of unarmed combat intended to train the body and mind; a modified form of jujitsu (a Japanese method of defending oneself by using strength and weight instead of weapons); the word combines the Japanese characters *jū*, meaning "gentleness," and *do*, meaning "art"

IMMIGRATE (verb) – the act of coming to a country to live there permanently

LEGACY (noun) – something handed down from the past; a person's mark on the world that lives on after they stop working or pass away

ORTHOPEDIC (adjective) – a word used to describe treatment of muscles, bones, or joints

PHILANTHROPY (noun) – the act of helping others on a large scale

PREJUDICE (noun) – a judgment of someone based on external characteristics before knowing anything about them

PROTESTERS (noun) – a group of people who publicly demonstrate that they are opposed to something (for example, a law)

RACISM (noun) – a belief that certain racial groups possess qualities that make them superior or inferior to others

REFUGEE (noun) – a person who is forced to leave their country because of war, exile, or natural disaster

RESISTANCE (noun) – a group of people within the same country, such as the French Resistance and the Dutch Resistance, who joined forces to work against Nazi rule during World War II

REVOLUTION (noun) – when people attempt to overthrow a government

SEGREGATION (noun) – the act of isolating or separating a race, class, or group from others

SUFFRAGE (noun) – the right to vote in an election

UNDOCUMENTED (adjective) – lacking the appropriate immigration or working papers

YIDDISH (noun) – a language written in Hebrew characters used by Jewish people of central and eastern European origin

ILLUSTRATORS

· · · · · · · · · · · · · · · · · ·

Seventy extraordinary women and nonbinary artists from all over the world created the portraits of the trailblazing Rebels in this book. Here they are.

MALIHA ABIDI, UK, 134

MONICA AHANONU, USA, 48, 114

AMALTEIA, PORTUGAL, 32

MARIAN BAILEY, USA, 58

ADRIANA BELLET, SWEDEN, 174

ELENIA BERETTA, ITALY, 98, 180

FANNY BLANC, FRANCE, 18, 42

PETRA BRAUN, AUSTRIA, 46, 198

VERONICA CARRATELLO, ITALY, 136

SALLY CAULWELL, IRELAND, 112, 164

KARINA COCQ, CHILE, 106, 120

MAGGIE COLE, USA, 6

SOPHIE CUNNINGHAM, UK, 182

MICHELLE D'URBANO, ZAMBIA, 152

ALESSANDRA DE CRISTOFARO, ITALY, 78, 82

CAMILLE DE CUSSAC, FRANCE, 2

ELENA DE SANTI, SPAIN, 124

ELENI DEBO, ITALY, 62, 194

SALLY DENG, USA, 190

NOA DENMON, USA, 28, 200

JEANNE DETALLANTE, BELGIUM, 110, 146

AURÉLIA DURAND, FRANCE, 184

BARBARA DZIADOSZ, GERMANY, 116, 172

CINDY ECHEVARRIA, USA, 40

OLIVIA FIELDS, USA, 150

MAÏTÉ FRANCHI, FRANCE, 24, 168

YASMINE GATEAU, FRANCE, 138

MARTA GIUNIPERO, ITALY, 72

YEVHENIA HAIDAMAKA, UKRAINE, 142

ABELLE HAYFORD, USA, 104

GOSIA HERBA, POLAND, 66, 108

KATHRIN HONESTA, INDONESIA, 178

BODIL JANE, THE NETHERLANDS , 60

LACI JORDAN, USA, 64

SABRENA KHADIJA, USA, 80, 162

SASHA KOLESNIK, RUSSIA, 160

LISA LANOË, UK, 34, 192

NAN LAWSON, USA, 74

SONIA LAZO, EL SALVADOR, 26

JULIETTE LÉVEILLÉ, FRANCE, 176

HELEN LI, POLAND, 4, 100

KIKI LJUNG, SPAIN, 92

SARAH LOULENDO, FRANCE, 126, 166

AKVILE MAGICDUST, LITHUANIA, 94

CRISTINA MARTÍN, SPAIN, 52

TYLA MASON, SOUTH AFRICA, 88

JENNY MEILIHOVE, ISRAEL, 8

NICOLE MILES, THE BAHAMAS, 36, 118

D'ARA NAZARYAN, USA, 30, 68

SALINI PERERA, CANADA, 196

ALICE PIAGGIO, SWITZERLAND, 12, 102

JENNIFER POTTER, USA, 56, 144

LISTEN TO MORE EMPOWERING STORIES ON THE REBEL GIRLS APP!

Download the app to listen to beloved Rebel Girls stories, as well as brand-new tales of extraordinary women. Filled with the adventures and accomplishments of women from around the world and throughout history, the Rebel Girls app is designed to entertain, inspire, and build confidence in listeners everywhere.

ACKNOWLEDGMENTS

This book would not exist without my team at Rebel Girls. Thank you Michon, Giulia, Ele, Pam, Maithy, Grace, Cesar, Lisa, Annalisa, Karen, Emilio, Jes, Mel, Ashley, Rachel, Kristen, Lauren, Montse, Marina, and Megan. You all made this book possible by believing in me and in our shared mission. Thank you too, to Corinne, Andrea, Christine, Elizabeth, Ariana, and Marisa. I will be forever grateful.

To the Rebel Girls who continue to read and share our stories—now in nearly 50 languages!—and to the Rebel moms, dads, aunts, uncles, cousins, teachers, librarians, and friends who read along with them: you are the reason I started this movement in the first place. You inspire me to push toward a more just world every day.

To my parents, Angelo and Lucia, improbable and irresistible, and always united when it counts. To my friends, thank you for never hesitating. You have made me stronger and freer. To my all-star D.C. team, Lin, Mandy, and Deneen: you're my heroes!

To all the people who have helped me along my journey as an immigrant in the United States: thank you for making this land, my land.

ABOUT THE AUTHOR

ELENA FAVILLI is a *New York Times* bestselling author, journalist, and breaker of glass ceilings. She is the cofounder of Rebel Girls and serves on the board, leading all impact initiatives. In 2016, she cowrote and published the most crowdfunded literary project in history, *Good Night Stories for Rebel Girls*, now translated into nearly 50 languages. Elena has written for the *Guardian, Vogue, ELLE, COLORS magazine, McSweeney's, RAI, Il Post,* and *La Repubblica*, in addition to authoring four books within the Rebel Girls series.

REBEL GIRLS is a global, multi-platform empowerment brand dedicated to helping raise the most inspired and confident global generation of girls through content, experiences, products, and community. Originating from an international best-selling children's book, Rebel Girls amplifies stories of real-life women throughout history, geography, and field of excellence. With a growing community of nearly 20 million self-identified Rebel Girls spanning more than 100 countries, the brand engages with Generation Alpha through its book series, award-winning podcast, events, and merchandise. With the 2021 launch of the Rebel Girls app, the company has created a flagship destination for girls to explore a wondrous world filled with inspiring true stories of extraordinary women.

Rebel Girls' books and podcast have won awards, including:

- 2021 People's Choice Podcast Award, #1 in Kids & Family
- 2020 Discover Pods Award, Best Kids & Family Podcast
- 2020 Webby Award, Best Kids & Family Podcast
- 2020 New York Festivals Radio Award, Gold in Education Podcasts
- 2020 Corporate Content Award, Best Use of Content in a Social Context
- 2019 People's Choice Podcast Award, #1 in Education
- 2018 Australian Book Industry Award, International Book
- 2018 Publishers Weekly Star Watch Superstar
- 2017 Blackwell's, Book of the Year
- 2017 Foyles, Book of the Year

Join the Rebel Girls' community on:

Facebook: facebook.com/rebelgirls

Instagram: @rebelgirls

Twitter: @rebelgirlsbook

Web: rebelgirls.com

App: rebelgirls.com/app

If you liked this book, please take a moment to review it wherever you prefer!

MORE FROM REBEL GIRLS

Let the stories of more real-life women entertain and inspire you!
Each volume in the Good Night Stories series includes 100 tales
of extraordinary women.

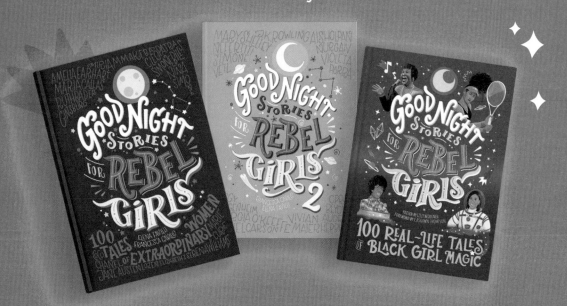

Check out these mini books too! Each one contains 25 tales of
talented women, along with a quiz and some engaging activities.

Dig deeper into the lives of these five real-life heroines with the Rebel Girls chapter book series!

Uncover the groundbreaking inventions of Ada Lovelace, one of the world's first computer programmers.

Explore the thrilling adventures of Junko Tabei, the first female climber to summit Mount Everest.

Learn the exciting business of Madam C. J. Walker, the hair care industry pioneer and first female self-made millionaire in the US.

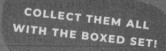

Discover the inspiring story of Dr. Wangari Maathai, the Nobel Peace Prize–winning environmental activist from Kenya.

Follow the awe-inspiring career of Alicia Alonso, a world-renowned prima ballerina from Cuba.

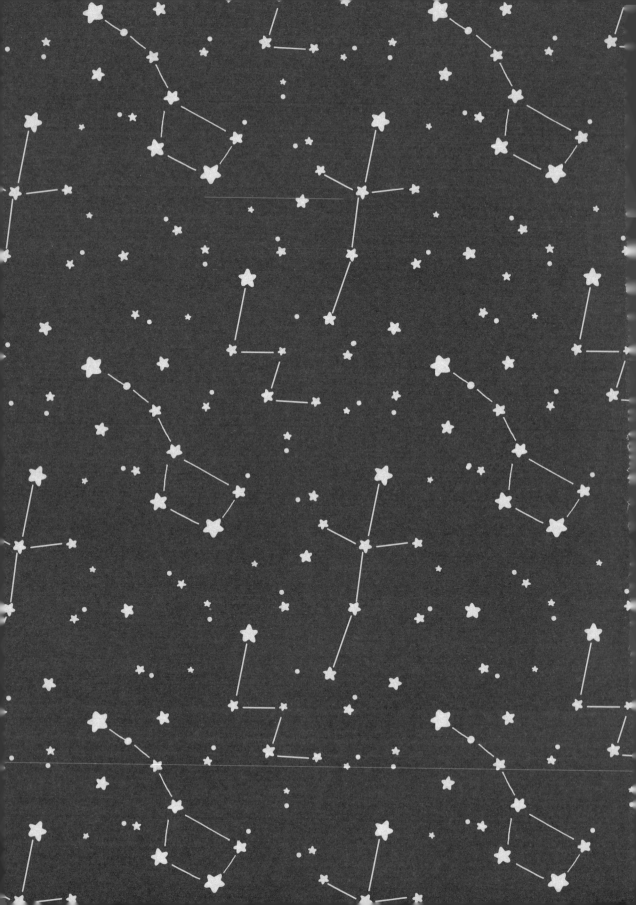

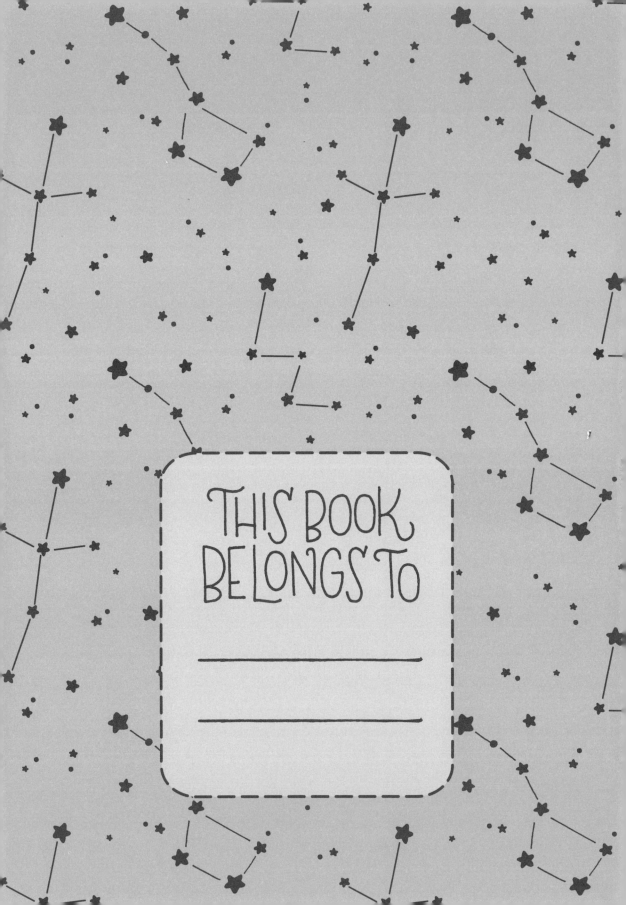

THIS BOOK
BELONGS TO

_____

_____

Good Night Stories for Rebel Girls 2

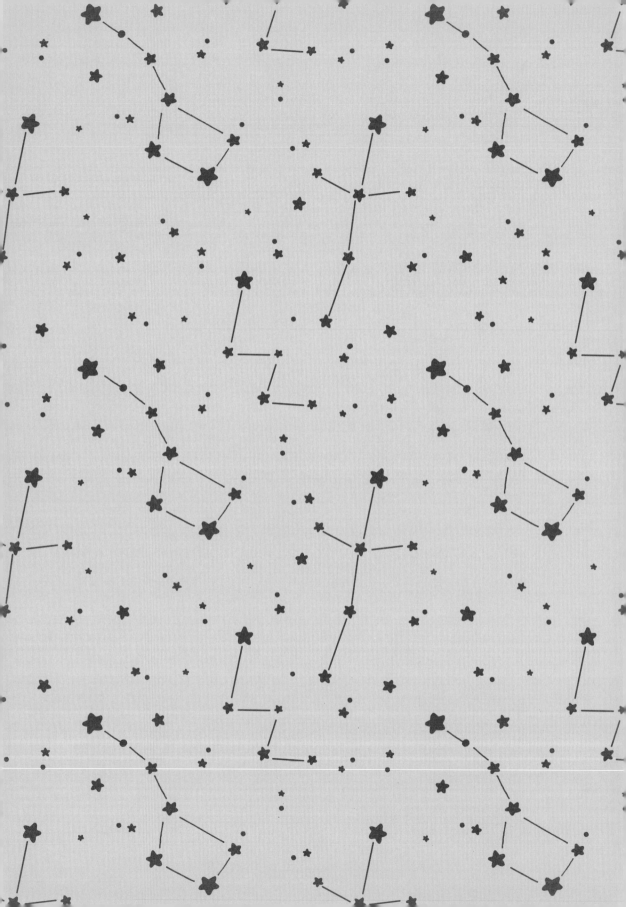

GOOD NIGHT STORIES FOR REBEL GIRLS 2

FRANCESCA CAVALLO AND **ELENA FAVILLI**

REBEL GIRLS®

Good Night Stories for Rebel Girls and all other Rebel Girls titles are available for bulk purchase for sales promotions, premiums, fundraising, and educational needs.
For details, write to sales@rebelgirls.com.

This is a work of creative nonfiction. It is a collection of heartwarming and thought-provoking bedtime stories inspired by the life and adventures of 100 heroic women. It is not an encyclopedic account of the events and accomplishments of their lives.

www.rebelgirls.com

Editorial direction and art direction by Francesca Cavallo and Elena Favilli

Cover design by Pemberley Pond
Graphic design by Giulia Flamini

Editor: Anita Roy
Research editor: Arianna Giorgia Bonazzi

Printed in China, 2021
10 9 8 7 6

Good Night Stories for Rebel Girls 2 is FSC® certified.

ISBN: 978-0-997-89582-7

TO THE REBEL GIRLS OF THE WORLD:

YOU ARE THE PROMISE.
YOU ARE THE FORCE.

DON'T STEP BACK,
AND EVERYONE WILL MOVE FORWARD.

OTHER BOOKS FROM REBEL GIRLS

Good Night Stories for Rebel Girls

Good Night Stories for Rebel Girls:
100 Immigrant Women Who Changed the World

Good Night Stories for Rebel Girls:
100 Real-Life Tales of Black Girl Magic

Good Night Stories for Rebel Girls:
The Chapter Book Collection

I Am a Rebel Girl: A Journal to Start Revolutions

Rebel Girls Champions

Rebel Girls Climate Warriors

Rebel Girls Lead

Rebel Girls Powerful Pairs

Questions for Rebel Girls

CONTENTS

BONUS! AUDIO STORIES!

Download the Rebel Girls app to hear longer stories about some of the extraordinary women in this book. You will also unlock creative activities and discover stories of other trailblazing women. Whenever you come across a bookmark icon, just scan the code, and you'll be whisked away on an audio adventure.

SCAN TO HEAR MORE!

PREFACE

Dear Rebels,

As you read this letter, the first volume of *Good Night Stories for Rebel Girls* is on the nightstands of millions of people. All over the world, children and grown-ups are talking about their favorite Rebel Girl. Teachers are designing lessons around these pioneers. Politicians are reading these stories at political conventions, young women are opening the book to cheer up after a bad day, and soon-to-be dads are buying it to welcome their daughters into this world.

Good Night Stories for Rebel Girls has been translated into more than 40 languages, and every day we can almost hear your voices in the messages you send us via social media. When we see pictures of this book in your homes, it's a lot like looking at a family album. A family made up of people of every religion, every nationality, every color, every age, every kind—a global family whose members come from small villages (like the ones we grew up in) and big cities.

In 2016, in our small Los Angeles apartment, we started a little fire. A fire we could gather around to tell each other new kinds of stories.

You joined us. You invited your friends and brought more firewood. You came, bringing your hopes and your frustrations, your courage and your fear, your weakness and your strength. You came to listen, but you also came to speak. The fire got bigger. The family grew.

And this is what *Good Night Stories for Rebel Girls 2* is about. It's about the stories you told us by that fire. It's about the Southeast Asian American female firefighter in New York City whom Christine told us about. It's about the first all-female anti-poaching unit in South Africa that Rita told us about on Snapchat. It's about the Irish pilot who built herself a plane.

Aidan told us about her at a signing event.

Some say stories can't change the world. But we disagree.

Time and again, you messaged us to say you had discovered a story in our book. The fact is that *Good Night Stories for Rebel Girls* is training hundreds of thousands of people to see stories they couldn't see before. It's inspiring them to look for talent where they thought there was none. It's making it easier to find potential in unpredictable places.

When we tap into the talent of an entire population—instead of just half of it—endless possibilities open up.

When we see one another for who we are, free of harmful stereotypes, we create real progress.

When we recognize oppression and take action to end it, we all become stronger.

As you rest your head on your pillow after reading one or three of these stories—whether it's after an exhausting day of play or a long day at work, whether you're in Cape Town or Aotearoa, whether someone read you the story or you read it by yourself—know that you've just sat by a fire with hundreds of thousands of fellow Rebels who, just like you, are on a journey.

The Good Night Stories for Rebel Girls series is a small part of a conversation that is bigger than each of us. Bigger than our individual hopes. Certainly bigger than our fears.

Thank you for sitting with us by this fire.

Now let's get started.

Francesca Cavallo
Elena Favilli

Good Night Stories for Rebel Girls 2

AGATHA CHRISTIE

AUTHOR

Once upon a time, there was a girl who loved to write. Poems, love stories, mysteries, letters—she tried them all. Agatha wanted to be a professional writer more than anything. She talked about her dream with her dog, George Washington, during their daily walks. Each new place she and George visited, Agatha looked at as a setting for a story, and every time she met someone, she wondered if that person could be one of her characters.

Agatha sent her stories to magazines but got turned down. The rejection letters kept piling up, but Agatha didn't let that stop her. She was an avid reader and especially loved murder mysteries.

So she wrote her own detective novel.

The Mysterious Affair at Styles featured Hercule Poirot, a Belgian detective with a glorious mustache. Many publishers turned down Agatha's manuscript, but finally one said yes.

When the novel was published, it was a huge success and marked the beginning of an unbelievable career. Agatha's books have sold more than a billion copies and have been translated into more than 100 different languages, making her the best-selling novelist of all time.

Hercule Poirot with his pointy mustache and Miss Marple with her cute hats became two of the most popular literary detectives ever. They appeared in TV shows and movies, and kept millions of people guessing as they figured out whodunit.

Through her remarkable career, Agatha wrote 66 detective novels, 14 short story collections, and the world's longest-running play, *The Mousetrap.*

SEPTEMBER 15, 1890–JANUARY 12, 1976
UNITED KINGDOM

· 2 ·

ILLUSTRATION BY
GIULIA TOMAI

"THE BEST TIME FOR
PLANNING A BOOK IS
WHILE YOU'RE DOING
THE DISHES."
—AGATHA CHRISTIE

AISHOLPAN NURGAIV

SCAN TO
HEAR MORE

EAGLE HUNTER

Once there was a 13-year-old girl named Aisholpan who lived in the icy-cold Altai Mountains. For seven generations, the men in her tribe had hunted with golden eagles to provide their families with food and fur.

Golden eagles are big, fierce creatures with sharp claws and curved beaks that can be extremely dangerous. But to Aisholpan, they were simply beautiful. She longed to train an eagle of her own, so one day she said to her father, *Dad, I know that no girls have ever done this, but if you teach me, I'll be good.* Her father, who was a great eagle hunter, paused to think. Then he said, *You are strong. You are not afraid. You can do it.*

Her heart sang with joy.

Aisholpan and her dad rode their horses high into the snowy mountains. Finding an eaglet to train wasn't easy. Aisholpan reached a nest with a rope tied around her waist, trying not to slip on the sharp rocks. In the nest, she found a tiny golden eagle, all alone.

She covered the bird's head with a blanket to calm her down, then brought her home. Aisholpan sang and told stories so the eaglet would recognize her voice. She fed her small chunks of meat and taught her how to land on her gloved arm. "I treat her with respect, because if she trusts me, she won't fly away. We will be a team for a few years. Then I'll return her to the wild. The circle of life must continue."

Aisholpan became the first woman to enter the Golden Eagle Festival in Ölgii, Mongolia. After her, three more girls started training to become eagle hunters.

BORN 2001
MONGOLIA

ILLUSTRATION BY
SALLY NIXON

"I PLAN TO TEACH
MY YOUNGER SISTER
EAGLE HUNTING."
—AISHOLPAN NURGAIV

ALICE BALL

CHEMIST

SCAN TO HEAR MORE

Once upon a time, there was no cure for leprosy, a disease that attacks the body and can leave victims terribly disfigured. Because there was no treatment and people believed leprosy was very contagious, sufferers used to be isolated in leper colonies with nothing to do but wait for death—or for a cure to be found.

In search of that cure, an incredibly talented young Hawaiian chemist named Alice was studying the properties of an oil extracted from the chaulmoogra tree. This oil was used in traditional Chinese and Indian medicine to treat skin diseases, and it also had been used for leprosy, with mixed results. Sometimes it worked, and sometimes it didn't.

Why? was Alice's burning question. Why doesn't it work *every* time?

She teamed up with an assistant surgeon at a Honolulu hospital to try to find the answer to that question. She developed a way to separate out the active elements of chaulmoogra oil and created a new extract that could be injected directly into a patient's bloodstream—with amazing results.

Unfortunately, Alice died before she was able to publish her findings. So the University of Hawaii did it for her—without giving her credit! The president of the university even called the extraction technique the Dean Method, as if he had invented it himself.

Many years later, Alice's amazing contribution was finally recognized. Now, every four years on February 29, Hawaii celebrates Alice Ball Day.

She was the first Black American and the first woman to teach chemistry and graduate with a master's degree at the University of Hawaii.

JULY 24, 1892–DECEMBER 31, 1916
UNITED STATES OF AMERICA

ILLUSTRATION BY
MARTINA PAUKOVA

ANDRÉE PEEL

FRENCH RESISTANCE FIGHTER

Once upon a time, there was a young woman who ran a beauty parlor. Andrée was smart and stylish, and she always had a bright smile for her customers. *Bonjour, madame,* she would call out. *How would you like your hair cut today?*

Then World War II broke out, and everything changed.

When Hitler invaded her country, Andrée joined the French Resistance, a network of ordinary people who worked in secret against the Nazis. She helped distribute underground newspapers to other members of the Resistance. It was risky and dangerous work. Andrée was soon promoted to sergeant and given the code name Agent Rose.

Many times she risked her life. She would sneak out at night and line up a row of flaming torches to signal to Allied planes as they crossed enemy lines. The pilots looked for these bright spots and knew that they could land safely there, thanks to Agent Rose. She helped save more than 100 British pilots from being captured by the Nazis before she herself was captured and sent to a concentration camp.

Sick, starving, and dressed in blue-and-white-striped pajamas, Andrée was lined up with other prisoners in front of a firing squad, about to be shot, when Allied troops arrived and saved them.

Andrée was hailed as a hero. The president of the United States and the British prime minister both sent her letters to thank her for everything she had done. She went on to live a long life—but she always kept a scrap of that blue-and-white material to remind her of those terrible days and to confirm that, as she said, "Miracles do happen!"

FEBRUARY 3, 1905–MARCH 5, 2010
FRANCE

ILLUSTRATION BY
ZOSIA DZIERŻAWSKA

"I WAS DESTINED ALWAYS TO BE A FIGHTER."
—ANDRÉE PEEL

ANGELA MERKEL

CHANCELLOR

Once upon a time, in Templin, Germany, there lived a seven-year-old girl named Angela. One Sunday, she was listening to her father's sermon in church when her mother started to cry.

What's the matter? Angela asked.

They are going to build a wall, her mother said. *They want to seal off the border between East Germany and West Germany.*

Angela was stunned. *Why would they build a wall?* she thought. *People should be free to go wherever they like.* Not only would East Germans be stopped from going to the West, but they would be barred from listening to the news coming from the other side.

Every day, Angela hid in the school bathroom with a little radio. It was illegal to listen to stations from the West. But she didn't care. She wanted to know what was happening in her country!

When Angela grew up, she studied **quantum chemistry** and wanted to become a university professor. But the government had a special force known as the secret police. They told Angela that she would be promoted, but only if she spied on others. Angela refused. She never became a professor.

She was working as a researcher in a lab when the Berlin Wall was demolished. She called her mom and said, *I think we're free to go to the West.* Indeed, they were.

Angela would go on to become chancellor of Germany—a determined leader who knew the pain walls could cause and never wanted her people to be divided again.

BORN JULY 17, 1954

GERMANY

"THAT IS WHAT WE SEEK AND FOR WHICH WE STRIVE—HARMONY AMONG NATIONS. THAT WAS AND ALSO REMAINS THE GREATEST GOAL OF EUROPEAN UNITY."
—ANGELA MERKEL

ANITA GARIBALDI

REVOLUTIONARY

Once upon a time, there was a skilled horsewoman who loved freedom. Her name was Anita. Her country—Brazil—was going through a difficult time. An emperor ruled the country, and a group of rebels, called Ragamuffins, had started an uprising to replace him with politicians who would be voted in by ordinary Brazilians.

Anita believed in democracy, so even though she knew that the Ragamuffins had little chance of beating the mighty imperial army, she joined their fight.

One day, a bearded Italian man called Giuseppe Garibaldi walked into a café. Anita and Giuseppe looked at each other, fell instantly in love, and decided to travel together to wherever the battle was bloodiest.

Anita was seven months pregnant when things got ugly for the rebels. Giuseppe ordered a retreat, but Anita kept fighting, even after her horse was killed. Total chaos broke out, and the two lost sight of each other.

Anita was captured and told by imperial troops that Giuseppe was dead. Heartbroken, she asked permission to cross back into enemy territory, on foot, to look for his body. When she couldn't find him, she stole a horse and escaped, crossing a raging river by hanging on to the horse's tail so she wouldn't be swept away. She traveled for days until, exhausted, she reached a farm—and there she found Giuseppe!

The two hugged and kissed, ecstatic to be together for the birth of their first son, Menotti. The Ragamuffin War was just the first in a series of battles Anita and Giuseppe fought together. Eventually, her name came to symbolize freedom and courage all over the world.

AUGUST 30, 1821–AUGUST 4, 1849
BRAZIL

ILLUSTRATION BY
SARAH MAZZETTI

ANNE BONNY

PIRATE

SCAN TO
HEAR MORE

Anne was a girl with wild red hair. She was scruffy and tough, and she used to hang out with pirates at the port taverns. When she grew up, she even married one named James Bonny.

Together they sailed to the Bahamas, but when James started spying on his fellow pirates for the British government, Anne left him and ran away with a pirate captain named John Rackham. Calico Jack, as he was known, was famous for wearing flamboyant trousers made from striped **calico cloth**.

Anne's best friend was a dressmaker called Pierre. One day, they decided to rob a French merchant vessel that was passing by. They splashed blood on their sails, the ship's deck, and themselves. They put one of Pierre's dresses on a mannequin and splashed that with blood too.

By the light of the full moon, they sailed silently toward the French ship. When they were close enough for the other crew to see, Anne appeared next to the mannequin brandishing an ax.

Terrified, the sailors abandoned ship without a fight!

Anne also became friends with another woman pirate named Mary Read. Disguised as a man, Mary was part of the crew on a ship that Anne and Calico Jack had captured. Anne and Mary took charge of the ship. They dressed sometimes as men and sometimes as women, and they became inseparable.

When the British navy ordered the crew of the ship to surrender, Anne and Mary fought back fiercely, but because their fellow sailors were drunk, they were quickly captured.

CIRCA 1700–CIRCA 1782

IRELAND

AUDREY HEPBURN

~~~

ACTOR AND HUMANITARIAN

Once upon a time, there was a little girl named Audrey who ate tulips. It wasn't because she loved flowers, though—it was because she was so hungry. Life in the Netherlands during World War II was hard. There was never enough food on the table, and Audrey often felt the pangs of hunger in her empty stomach. Tulip bulbs didn't taste good, but they kept her from starving.

When Audrey was older, she moved to England and became a film actor. She was admired the world over for her elegance and luminous beauty. Famous fashion designers flocked to her, and she became a style icon, known for her little black dress, long gloves, and diamond tiara. After her most famous film, *Breakfast at Tiffany's*, was released, the "Hepburn look" became so popular that women used to dress just like her. They would even visit the famous jewelry store in New York City to stand on the same spot she did in the movie.

But Audrey wanted to do more than just star in films and be admired for her clothes. She wanted to help others, especially poor and hungry children—children who were as hungry as she had once been. She dedicated her life to serving UNICEF (United Nations Children's Emergency Fund), the same charity that had helped her when she was a girl during the war. She believed that no child should ever be so hungry they would have to eat flower bulbs.

When Audrey died, a new pure white tulip was named in her honor, to celebrate the wonderful work she did for UNICEF.

~~~

MAY 4, 1929–JANUARY 20, 1993

BELGIUM, THE NETHERLANDS, AND UNITED KINGDOM

ILLUSTRATION BY
MARTA SIGNORI

"THE BEST THING TO HOLD ONTO
IN LIFE IS EACH OTHER."
—AUDREY HEPBURN

BEATRICE VIO

FENCER

Once upon a time, there was an Italian girl who was a formidable fencer. Her name was Beatrice, but everyone called her Bebe.

While she was in middle school, Bebe became very ill. By the time her parents got her to the hospital, she was fighting for her life. She had contracted meningitis, a severe illness that attacks the brain and spinal cord. To save her, the doctors had to amputate her forearms and her legs below the knee.

Bebe was in the hospital for more than 100 days. When she recovered from the surgery, she had one goal in mind: to go back to fencing. Nearly everyone told her it was impossible. But Bebe had a plan.

First, she relearned how to walk, shower, open windows, and brush her teeth. She even taught her classmates how to use her brand-new artificial limbs! Then she strapped her foil, a type of sword, to her arm and started training again. As the only fencer in the world without arms and legs, Bebe had to invent a technique that would work for her. After a while, she was ready to try competing again.

In a few years, with the help of two of the most famous fencing teachers in Italy, she became a champion. She won the World Cup in Canada, the European Championships in Italy, the World Championship in Hungary, and the gold medal at the Paralympics in Rio de Janeiro.

"To be special," Bebe says, "you need to turn your weakness into the thing you're most proud of."

BORN MARCH 4, 1997

ITALY

ILLUSTRATION BY
CRISTINA PORTOLANO

"I TELL MYSELF I'M THE
ONE THAT HAS TO BE AN
EXAMPLE TO OTHERS."
—BEATRICE VIO

BEATRIX POTTER

Once upon a time in London, there lived a girl who loved to paint animals. Beatrix spent all year looking forward to the summer, when she and her little brother could escape the drab gray city streets for the wild Highlands of Scotland.

As soon as she had unpacked her bags, Beatrix would gather up her paints and brushes, pull on her boots, and head outside. She sat so quietly that field mice would scamper past her and rabbits would hop up and nibble the grass at her feet. The squirrels got quite used to her sitting at the edge of the woods as they chased one another through the branches above her head.

When she was old enough, Beatrix left the city and moved to the countryside. One day, she sent a letter to a young friend of hers, a little boy called Noel. In the letter, she made up a story about a naughty rabbit in a smart blue jacket who steals vegetables from the garden next door and is chased by the farmer. Beatrix named him Peter, after her own pet rabbit. Noel loved the story and wanted more, so Beatrix kept writing to him and even included pictures of Peter and his three siblings, Flopsy, Mopsy, and Cottontail. Eventually, she published the story as an illustrated book.

Millions of children came to love Beatrix Potter's books and her unforgettable characters, including Mrs. Tiggy-winkle, Squirrel Nutkin, and the two naughty mice, Tom Thumb and Hunca Munca. Her very first book, *The Tale of Peter Rabbit*, became one of the most popular children's stories of all time.

JULY 28, 1866–DECEMBER 22, 1943

UNITED KINGDOM

ILLUSTRATION BY
BARBARA DZIADOSZ

"I CANNOT REST, I MUST
DRAW, HOWEVER POOR
THE RESULT, AND WHEN
I HAVE A BAD TIME COME
OVER ME, IT IS A STRONGER
DESIRE THAN EVER."
—BEATRIX POTTER

BEYONCÉ

SINGER, SONGWRITER,
AND BUSINESSWOMAN

Beyoncé was six years old when her dad started selling people tickets to go to their house and see her sing and dance. When Beyoncé told her mom she wanted to create a band with her friends, her mom said, *Okay. I'll make your costumes.* And so Destiny's Child was born.

Beyoncé was the queen of the band. She was driven, focused, and interested in learning as much as possible about every aspect of the music business.

At first, her dad was her manager. But when she decided she wanted to be in control of her career, Beyoncé asked him to step aside. Beyoncé didn't *just* want to be a popular singer—she wanted to be a powerhouse. And that's what she became.

One song at a time, one album at a time, one concert at a time, Beyoncé forged her own path and became an inspiration to people around the world. She sang about freedom, about love, about independence, and about pain: both personal pain and social injustice. She inspired millions of Black women to be proud of their culture, of their origins, of their own unique style.

When Beyoncé performed during the half-time show of Super Bowl XLVII, the biggest annual sporting event in the United States, she entered the stadium leading an army of female dancers all dressed in black. With her compelling song "Formation," she dropped a Black power anthem in front of 100 million viewers.

Today, she is the most influential living pop star in the whole world.

BORN SEPTEMBER 4, 1981
UNITED STATES OF AMERICA

ILLUSTRATION BY
ELINE VAN DAM

"WE ALL HAVE THE
CONFIDENCE IN US
TO TAKE CHANCES AND
BET ON OURSELVES."
—BEYONCÉ

BILLIE JEAN KING

TENNIS PLAYER

SCAN TO HEAR MORE

Once there was a formidable tennis player named Billie Jean. She was a great champion who won all the most important tennis tournaments of her day. But there was something she found profoundly bothersome. At the time, female players earned only a fraction of the prize money that male players made.

Why should women put up with being paid less? Billie Jean asked. *We sell the same number of tickets.*

That's just how it is, the tournament organizers replied.

Do something about it, she said, *or I will* **boycott** *your tournament.*

The tournament organizers laughed at her, but she wasn't joking. She got together with nine other female tennis players, and they created their own circuit with 19 tournaments and many big sponsors.

The battle for equality in tennis had just begun.

A woman's place is in the kitchen, proclaimed Bobby Riggs, a male tennis player who strongly believed that women were worth less than men.

Oh yeah? said Billie Jean. *I'll show you.*

They played each other in a historic match called the Battle of the Sexes. Thirty thousand people in the stadium and 90 million television viewers around the world watched Billie Jean beat Bobby in straight sets.

Organizers of the US Open finally met her demand, making it the first major tennis tournament to offer equal prize money to men and women. Thanks to Billie Jean, today tennis is one of the few sports where female and male athletes have achieved equal pay in all the biggest tournaments.

BORN NOVEMBER 22, 1943

UNITED STATES OF AMERICA

"BE AHEAD OF YOUR TIME."
—BILLIE JEAN KING

THE BLACK MAMBAS

One day, a park warden named Craig put together an all-female team of rangers to stop poachers in the South African savanna. He called them the Black Mambas.

He recruited high school graduates from the communities surrounding the wildlife park. *It's important to protect the rhinos,* he explained, *so future generations will see them for real and not just on posters!* He gave the women uniforms and set up a training program.

The Black Mambas learned how to survive in the savanna, how to spot animal traps, and what to do when they encountered lions, elephants, buffaloes, and hyenas. They learned how to track poachers and patrol the park's perimeter fence—armed with only pepper spray and handcuffs.

"This war on poaching is bigger than guns and bullets," declared Nomutu Magakene, one of the Mambas. Another, Felicia Mogahane, said, "The Mambas are the eyes and ears of the reserve."

The Black Mambas took great pride in their work. They talked to people about the importance of rhinos in their communities and about how lucky they were to live in one of the most biodiverse countries in the world. They gave presentations in schools and taught children that it was wrong to cooperate with poachers and lay traps in the park.

It took only a year of Black Mamba patrols for the traps and snares to disappear almost completely and the rhino killings to stop entirely.

The Black Mambas became heroes.

FORMED IN 2013
SOUTH AFRICA

"WE ARE FIGHTING FOR OUR ANIMALS AND SHOWING PEOPLE THAT WOMEN CAN BE BEAUTIFUL AND STRONG."
—LEITAH MKHEBELA

ILLUSTRATION BY
ALICE BENIERO

BOUDICCA

Once upon a time, there was a fearless warrior queen who spearheaded a rebellion against the Romans.

Boudicca led her tribe, the Iceni, into battle. Her husband, the king, had died and left his kingdom to their daughters. But the Roman emperor Nero decided that no woman could rule an area under Roman control, and he sent his troops to enslave the Britons. The noble Iceni were killed or imprisoned, and Boudicca and her daughters were whipped.

To defend her family, Boudicca gathered together a tribal army and led an attack against the mighty Roman Empire. With her long red hair flying and her sword held high over her head, she struck fear into the hearts of her enemies. Her army stormed the city of Colchester, in what is now southeastern England, destroying the temple of Claudius, the former Roman emperor, and killing thousands of Romans and their supporters.

Even more Britons joined Boudicca, and by the time she reached the mart of Londinium, or present-day London, her army was 100,000 people strong—all of them loyal to the rebel queen. But despite being heavily outnumbered, the Romans, who had better weapons, won and Boudicca died fighting.

Her name comes from the Celtic word *bouda*, meaning "victory." For her bravery and her strength, she came to symbolize the fighting spirit of the British. Today, near Westminster Bridge in London, you can see a huge bronze statue of Boudicca and her daughters, driving a magnificent horse-drawn carriage.

CIRCA 30–61 CE
UNITED KINGDOM

ILLUSTRATION BY
MONICA GARWOOD

"I AM NOT FIGHTING
FOR MY KINGDOM
AND WEALTH NOW.
I AM FIGHTING AS AN
ORDINARY PERSON FOR
MY LOST FREEDOM, MY
BRUISED BODY, AND MY
OUTRAGED DAUGHTERS."
—BOUDICCA

BRENDA MILNER

NEUROPSYCHOLOGIST

Brenda wanted to understand how the brain works, so she studied psychology. After college, she moved to Canada and pursued her PhD at the Montreal Neurological Institute-Hospital. She was such a good student that she was offered a position as a professor at McGill University. Much to everyone's astonishment, she turned it down.

Her colleagues told her, *You're a psychologist in a neurological institute. This is no place to build your career.* And Brenda answered, simply, *I like it here.*

Shortly after, she was asked to work with a special patient who had undergone surgery to remove the temporal lobes on both sides of his brain, making it impossible for him to create new long-term memories.

Every day, Brenda would sit with the man, running different tests and taking detailed notes. Eventually, she started to notice something strange: each morning, her patient showed improvement on all the tests, even though he had no memory of doing them the day before. It was a groundbreaking discovery! Brenda realized that the brain has at least two different memory systems: one that handles names, faces, and experiences, and a second that handles motor skills, such as swimming or playing the piano.

"I knew very well I was witnessing something important," she recalled.

Brenda would sit with patients, talk to them, and write down every tiny detail they told her. In this way, she was able to detect specific brain injuries.

Brenda is considered the founder of neuropsychology and one of the world's leading experts on memory.

BORN JULY 15, 1918
UNITED KINGDOM

"I AM INCREDIBLY CURIOUS ABOUT THE LITTLE THINGS I SEE AROUND ME."
—BRENDA MILNER

ILLUSTRATION BY MARYLOU FAURE

BUFFALO CALF ROAD WOMAN

Once upon a time, a brave Cheyenne warrior saved her brother during a battle. Her name was Buffalo Calf Road Woman.

At the time, settlers and US government soldiers were determined to steal the land from the Native Americans who were its original inhabitants and wipe out the Indigenous nations. As General George Crook led his troops across the Great Plains toward her village, Buffalo Calf Road Woman took her gun, leaped onto her horse, and joined the Cheyenne men to fight back. Some of them protested, saying that because she was a woman she couldn't take part in the fight, but she had already pushed her horse into a gallop, a cloud of dust billowing behind her.

The battle was raging when she suddenly spotted her brother, Comes in Sight, trapped in a gully and surrounded by Crook's soldiers. Fearlessly, Buffalo Calf Road Woman sprinted down into the ditch with bullets flying all around. She pulled her brother onto her horse, and they galloped off together to safety. It was a breathtaking rescue.

The other warriors couldn't believe their eyes. They hadn't been nearly as daring as Buffalo Calf Road Woman. If it hadn't been for her, Comes in Sight would have been killed.

They felt diminished by her courage and didn't want anyone to know what had happened, so they agreed never to talk about her feat. But one valiant warrior called Wooden Leg spoke up. It's because of him that today we know the thrilling story of one of the bravest warriors in the West, Buffalo Calf Road Woman.

CIRCA 1850s–1879

UNITED STATES OF AMERICA

CARMEN AMAYA

DANCER

The night Carmen came into the world, Barcelona, Spain was lashed by a terrible storm. Thunder boomed, lightning crashed, and the rain turned the narrow lanes into raging streams of filthy water.

Carmen's family were Romani, and flamenco dancing was in their blood. When Carmen's father first saw her dance, he wondered if something of that storm had entered his daughter's veins when she was born.

Carmen learned flamenco steps from her aunt, who was herself a great dancer. But the little girl never played by the rules: she made up her own. To earn money, she danced barefoot in the *tavernas* down by the waterfront. She gained the respect of even the toughest sailors, who nicknamed her La Capitana—the Captain.

Soon she began to perform in big theaters. She earned enough money for her family to move out of the shack where she was born and into a decent apartment. They could afford to eat ham sandwiches instead of sardines.

Onstage, Carmen preferred tight-fitting trousers and a high-cut bolero jacket to the *traje de flamenca*, the traditional dress worn by female dancers. When she first appeared like that, the audience was in an uproar. How dare this woman wear men's clothing! But when she began to dance, Carmen silenced them all. Stamping out lightning-fast rhythms on the stage, she sometimes broke the floorboards. Her footwork was so ferocious, one member of the audience said her dancing "seemed like something supernatural."

CIRCA 1918–NOVEMBER 19, 1963

SPAIN

"TROUSERS ARE UNFORGIVING: THEY SHOW EVERY MISTAKE AND THEY GIVE YOU NOTHING TO TAKE HOLD OF."
—CARMEN AMAYA

ILLUSTRATION BY ANA JUAN

CELIA CRUZ

SINGER

In the poor quarter of Havana, Cuba, a young girl used to sing her brothers and sisters to sleep. *What an incredible voice!* said the neighbors. *She sings like an angel.*

When Celia was older, her cousin entered her in a singing competition on a local radio station. She came first—and won a cake as a prize!

Celia loved to sing **Santería** songs in the Yoruba language of West Africa. Her father disapproved of her singing and wanted her to become a teacher. But music, and especially the bewitching rhythms of **salsa**, ran through Celia's veins.

She joined the National Conservatory of Music and started to make recordings. One day, a popular salsa band called La Sonora Matancera needed a new singer. This was Celia's big break! She leapt at the chance.

But soon after, a revolution broke out in Cuba, and many musicians fled to the United States. Celia was one of them. Still, she never forgot where she came from.

One day, when she was at a café in Miami, a waiter asked her if she took her coffee with or without sugar. *Are you crazy?* She laughed. *I'm Cuban! We always have azúcar!* From then on, whenever she was onstage, she would cry out, *Azúcar!*—"Sugar!"—and the crowd would go wild.

With her flamboyant personality, her amazing voice, and her infectious rhythms, Celia helped to make salsa music hugely popular in the US. She recorded more than 80 albums, won seven Grammy Awards, earned a Recording Academy Lifetime Achievement Award, and was the undisputed Queen of Salsa for 40 years.

OCTOBER 21, 1925–JULY 16, 2003

CUBA

ILLUSTRATION BY
PING ZHU

"WHEN PEOPLE HEAR ME
SING, I WANT THEM TO BE
HAPPY, HAPPY, HAPPY."
—CELIA CRUZ

CHIMAMANDA NGOZI ADICHIE

AUTHOR

Once upon a time in Nigeria, there was a little girl called Chimamanda who loved books. She read all the books she could find, and when she was seven years old, she started to write her own stories.

Chimamanda had always lived in Nigeria. She snacked on mangoes and played in the sun all year long. Still, all the characters in her stories were white: they had blue eyes, ate apples, and played in the snow. *I didn't think people with chocolate-colored skin could be in books*, she said.

One day, Chimamanda realized that was a silly thought and started to look for African books with African people in them. Even though she lived in Africa, these were harder to find than European or American books full of white people. But when she did, she thought it was great to see people who looked like her as characters in books. She wanted to see more of them.

Chimamanda became an exceptional writer. She traveled the world and told stories about Nigeria and the United States, about women and men, about migration and hair salons, about fashion and war.

She had a witty sense of humor and an amazing gift for explaining complicated things clearly. People loved her books and her speeches. They shared videos of her lectures with one another to feel inspired and empowered.

Chimamanda became a passionate advocate for gender equality. "Some people will say a woman is subordinate to men because it's our culture," she said. "But culture is constantly changing . . . Culture does not make people. People make culture."

BORN SEPTEMBER 15, 1977
NIGERIA

"RACISM SHOULD NEVER HAVE HAPPENED AND SO YOU DON'T GET A COOKIE FOR REDUCING IT."
—CHIMAMANDA NGOZI ADICHIE

ILLUSTRATION BY
PALESA MONARENG

CHRISTINA OF SWEDEN

QUEEN

Once upon a time, there was a six-year-old queen. Her name was Christina, and she had succeeded her father on the throne at the time of his death.

Christina was smart and fiercely independent. Because she had a lot of responsibility on her shoulders, she knew she had to grow up fast, so she studied philosophy, art, foreign languages—and even ballet, to be able to move as gracefully as a queen.

When Christina turned 18, everyone expected her to marry a suitable man from a noble family—someone to increase her power. But she was in love with one of her ladies-in-waiting, a young and beautiful woman called Ebba Sparre, and she had no interest in marriage.

After reigning for 10 years, Christina shocked everyone by giving up the throne and moving to Rome, Italy. There, she had a wonderful time, making friends with artists, writers, scientists, and musicians from all over Europe. She realized that she missed being queen, however, and plotted to seize control of the Kingdom of Naples. Her plan quickly fell apart.

Pope Alexander VII called her "a queen without a realm, a Christian without faith, and a woman without shame," and he was right. Christina was never ashamed to show the world who she really was, even in the face of criticism. She was unconventional, and she loved it. Thanks to her free spirit, she became one of the most influential women of her time.

In Rome, Christina formed the literary circle that gave rise to the Academy of Arcadia, an institute for literature and philosophy that exists to this day.

DECEMBER 8, 1626–APRIL 19, 1689

SWEDEN

ILLUSTRATION BY
ELENI KALORKOTI

"IT IS A FAR GREATER HAPPINESS
TO OBEY NO ONE THAN TO RULE
THE WHOLE WORLD."
—CHRISTINA OF SWEDEN

CLARA ROCKMORE

SCAN TO HEAR MORE

MUSICIAN

One day, in Russia, a four-year-old girl stood on a table and started playing the violin. Her name was Clara, and she was auditioning for the St. Petersburg Conservatory. Clara was a child prodigy, and she had her heart set on becoming a famous violinist.

After the Russian Revolution, though, Clara's parents decided to flee the country. They undertook a difficult and dangerous journey that was partly paid for by concerts given by Clara and her sister along the way. By the time they reached New York City, Clara had developed a weakness in her arm that forced her to abandon the violin. She was heartbroken.

Before long, however, Clara saw something miraculous: an instrument that could be played without being touched at all! The performer would stand in front of an electronic deck and wave their hands between two antennas. The movements would be picked up by the device and transmitted as music, like a magician casting a spell. This strange new instrument was called a theremin, after its inventor, Leon Theremin.

I can play in the air, thought Clara. *It is so beautiful!*

The theremin was hard to play, but she was a natural. She became a pioneer of electronic music and the world's most famous thereminist. Her hands floated over the theremin, and the sweetest, most enchanting melodies materialized in the air.

Leon Theremin fell in love with Clara. He made her a birthday cake that spun and lit up as soon as she got close to it. Though he proposed to her many times, Clara never married him. But together they shared the magic and music of the theremin.

MARCH 9, 1911–MAY 10, 1998

LITHUANIA

"I WAS FASCINATED BY . . .
THE IDEA OF PLAYING
IN THE AIR."
—CLARA ROCKMORE

CLARA SCHUMANN

PIANIST AND COMPOSER

By the time Clara was eight years old, she was already an extraordinary pianist.

After one of her concerts in a private home, she was approached by a 17-year-old boy. His name was Robert Schumann, and he was a pianist too. He told Clara that she was fantastic, and the two were soon good friends.

Clara traveled throughout Europe giving concerts, and she became one of the most famous composers and pianists of her time. Robert was also a great composer, and their shared love of music brought the two closer and closer, until they married when Clara was 21.

At the time, female musicians were expected to stop working after marriage. Some people believed that composing music would take away the energy needed to have and raise children. But for Clara, playing and composing music was not just a job, it was her passion, her skill, her reason for living. She had no intention of giving it up.

She and Robert would go on to have eight children, and Clara gave hundreds of concerts—more than any other contemporary pianist! She also composed more than 20 piano works, a concerto, some chamber music, and several shorter songs.

Clara and Robert loved each other dearly, and when he died, she stopped composing and devoted her life to playing his music for audiences around the world. Years later, as she herself lay dying, she asked her grandson to play the "Romance in F Sharp Major," a piece Robert had composed for her. She died before the last notes had faded away.

SEPTEMBER 13, 1819–MAY 20, 1896
GERMANY

ILLUSTRATION BY
CRISTINA AMODEO

"IF I HAVE KNOWN MUCH
TROUBLE IN MY YOUTH, I HAVE
ALSO KNOWN MUCH JOY."
—CLARA SCHUMANN

CLEMANTINE WAMARIYA

AUTHOR AND HUMAN RIGHTS ACTIVIST

"**O**nce upon a time" was Clemantine's favorite phrase. Every afternoon, she'd come home from kindergarten to play under the mango tree. And every night, she'd listen to the magical stories her nanny told her. She was a happy child in Rwanda.

One day, though, her beloved nanny disappeared. Shortly after, Clemantine stopped going to kindergarten. Then her parents forbade her to play outside. Then they all moved into the smallest room of their house, and they kept the lights off at night.

Finally, Clemantine's parents put her and her sister, Claire, in a car so they could be driven to their grandma's.

Six-year-old Clemantine and 15-year-old Claire arrived safely, but after two days, their grandma told them that they had to run. The same people who had made their nanny disappear were now looking for them.

The sisters walked for days, weeks, and months. Clemantine didn't know where she was or why her parents weren't there.

After spending six years on and off in African refugee camps, Claire and Clemantine eventually arrived in Chicago to start a new life. Clemantine went back to school, where she studied history and learned about the **Rwandan genocide**. She came to understand that in the world, there are many children who, like her and Claire, have been displaced and have lost their families due to wars or civil unrest.

She became a storyteller and a human rights activist. Through her writing and talks, she helps refugees cultivate courage, resilience, and hope, even in the middle of chaos.

BORN 1988

RWANDA

"SAFETY SHOULD BE
A BIRTHRIGHT."
—CLEMANTINE WAMARIYA

ILLUSTRATION BY
ALICE BARBERINI

CORRIE TEN BOOM

WATCHMAKER

Once upon a time, a girl named Corrie was born in a watch shop in Haarlem, Netherlands. Corrie's grandfather had been a watchmaker, as had her father, and when Corrie grew up, she decided to follow family tradition and became the first licensed female watchmaker in Holland.

But making watches wasn't the only family tradition Corrie followed. The ten Booms were devout Christians who believed in opening their house to anyone in need. So when Jewish people started being persecuted during the World War II, Corrie knew she needed to help.

She built a secret room behind a false wall in her bedroom, and she joined a network called the Dutch underground, which protected people being hunted by the Nazis. Corrie installed a buzzer to signal danger. Every time soldiers came to search the shop, she would ring the buzzer and the people hiding in her house would have about a minute to disappear into the secret room.

One day, a Dutch informant betrayed Corrie and sent the Nazi secret police, known as the Gestapo, to raid her home. They found evidence that she had been helping Jewish people and members of the Dutch underground, and they arrested her and her family. But they were unable to find the secret room, where six people were hiding.

Corrie, her sister, and her father were sent to prison before they died.

They saved more than 800 Jewish people, as well as many members of the Dutch underground. Corrie became a symbol of courage, unity, and unwavering dignity for people from all walks of life.

APRIL 15, 1892–APRIL 15, 1983

THE NETHERLANDS

ILLUSTRATION BY
CLAUDIA CARIERI

TEN BOOM HORLOGERIE

HAARLEM
1837

"LOVE IS LARGER
THAN THE WALLS
WHICH SHUT IT IN."
—CORRIE TEN BOOM

ELEANOR ROOSEVELT

POLITICIAN

Once there was a serious girl called Eleanor Roosevelt.

When she was a teenager, Eleanor was sent to school in London. There, she met an extraordinary teacher named Marie Souvestre. Ms. Souvestre wanted Eleanor to think for herself, to be free and independent. Eleanor studied with her for three years, before she was summoned home because her grandmother wanted her to get married.

Back in the United States, Eleanor met another Roosevelt. His name was Franklin Delano. They got married and soon after, he contracted polio. The disease left him paralyzed from the waist down, but Eleanor didn't let him give up on his dreams. With her determination and support, he went on to become president of the United States.

As first lady, Eleanor gave speeches, traveled throughout the country, and became a champion for human rights. She believed that human beings are born free and equal in dignity and rights, and she was determined to promote those rights in as many countries as possible.

After her husband died, Eleanor was named the US delegate to the United Nations. She became the chairperson of the Commission on Human Rights and led the creation of one of the most important documents of the 20th century: the Universal Declaration of Human Rights.

This powerful document inspired governments to pass laws protecting human life and encouraged citizens to take action when their fundamental rights were denied. Thanks to Eleanor—and to the tireless work of many representatives from all over the world—freedom, equality, dignity, respect, and safety became common goals for all people and all nations.

OCTOBER 11, 1884–NOVEMBER 7, 1962
UNITED STATES OF AMERICA

ILLUSTRATION BY
LIZZY STEWART

THE UNIVERSAL DECLARATION
OF HUMAN RIGHTS

"YOU MUST DO THE THING
YOU THINK YOU CANNOT DO."
—ELEANOR ROOSEVELT

ELLEN DEGENERES

One night, Ellen dreamed of a bird in a cage. In the dream, the bird realized that there was enough space between the bars to fly away.

Ellen knew exactly what the dream meant. She was a comedian, and she starred in a popular TV show where she played a woman who loved men. In reality, though, Ellen loved women. But she couldn't tell anybody.

At the time, her bosses thought that if the show's fans knew she was a lesbian, they would stop watching. But keeping silent didn't feel right to Ellen. She didn't want to hide anymore, and she wanted other gay people across the world to see that they were not alone. So in one of the episodes of her show, her character came out to her therapist, who was played by Oprah Winfrey. It was the first time in history that a lead character on a television program was openly gay. Next, Ellen told the public that she too was gay.

Her revelation sent shock waves through American media. Her show was eventually canceled, and Ellen found herself jobless and struggling with depression. For three years, she didn't receive any offers of work.

Then one day, the phone rang. *Would you like to play a fish with memory issues in a new Pixar movie?* the caller asked. Ellen was ecstatic. The fish—named Dory—became an iconic character.

Today, Ellen is a superstar. She received the Presidential Medal of Freedom for her courage and hosted her own talk show, *The Ellen DeGeneres Show*, which was watched by millions of people. "Find out who you are and figure out what you believe in," she likes to say, "even if it's different from what your neighbors believe in and different from what your parents believe in."

BORN JANUARY 26, 1958
UNITED STATES OF AMERICA

"PEOPLE ALWAYS
ASK ME, WERE YOU
FUNNY AS A CHILD?
WELL, NO, I WAS
AN ACCOUNTANT."
—ELLEN DEGENERES

FLORENCE CHADWICK

SWIMMER

The ocean was Florence's favorite place. Her parents would watch her from the beach as she swam and swam and swam. She was such a strong swimmer that everyone expected her to be chosen to compete in the Olympic Games.

But Florence didn't like swimming pools. She thought they were boring. She loved feeling the cold water of the sea, reading the currents, watching for sharks, and finding her rhythm with the waves. She loved to swim into the unknown. *In open water,* she thought, *you never know which fish you might encounter, or how the conditions might change.*

Even though she could swim farther than almost anyone else, Florence wasn't considered a professional athlete. Professional swimmers swam only in pools. So she took a job as a secretary in Saudi Arabia. Whenever she wasn't working, she was out swimming in the Persian Gulf. She saved every penny she could, because she had one goal in mind: *One day, I will swim across the English Channel.*

When she was ready, Florence returned to Europe. She used all her savings to buy her father a plane ticket from California to France. It was still night when she jumped in the water and started to swim. She had hired a boat so her father could follow as she crossed the Channel, encouraging her and giving her snacks along the way.

Florence became the first woman to swim across the English Channel in both directions, as well as the first woman to swim the Strait of Gibraltar, the Bosporus, and the Dardanelles. Sometimes she failed, but she never stopped looking for new channels to cross.

NOVEMBER 9, 1918–MARCH 15, 1995
UNITED STATES OF AMERICA

ILLUSTRATION BY
NOA SNIR

"I'M HAPPIEST IN THE WATER.
SOME PEOPLE GO FOR A
WALK. I GO FOR A SWIM."
—FLORENCE CHADWICK

GAE AULENTI

ARCIIITECT AND DESIGNER

Once there was a girl who couldn't stand seeing ruins. World War II had destroyed her school and all the other places she loved. *One day, I'll rebuild everything*, she promised herself. Her name was Gae.

When the war finally ended, Gae studied to be an architect. At the time, architecture was a field dominated by men, and she was one of only two women in a class of 20. But Gae wasn't easily intimidated. After graduating, she became one of the few female architects involved in rebuilding her home country of Italy after the war.

Gae saw architecture as a way to manipulate space with light. When she was asked to transform the old Gare d'Orsay railway station in Paris into a museum, she allowed natural light to flood into the huge main hall through a ceiling of glass. For an Olivetti showroom in Buenos Aires, Argentina, she used typewriters and mirrors to create a flight of steps seemingly multiplying into infinity.

Gae also worked as a theatrical set designer. "Theater taught me the value of action for architecture," she once said. "In architecture, a door is just a door. But onstage, a door can be a border, a crossing."

She constantly experimented with furniture and everyday objects. She designed a movable table using four bicycle wheels to hold up a floating glass top. For her iconic Pipistrello lamp, she created a lampshade shaped like the wings of a bat.

Gae worked her entire life designing buildings, museums, objects, and public spaces all over the world. She is regarded as one of the greatest architects of all time.

DECEMBER 4, 1927–OCTOBER 31, 2012

ITALY

ILLUSTRATION BY
GAIA STELLA

"DURING THE DAY,
A WINDOW IS A
BEAUTIFUL LAMP."
—GAE AULENTI

GEORGIA O'KEEFFE

PAINTER

Once upon a time, a woman saw a door. It was an ordinary door, weathered and old and set into an adobe wall. But the woman was no ordinary woman. Her name was Georgia O'Keeffe, and she was a great artist.

She spent the whole day making a painting of the door. Then she stepped back and looked at the canvas. There was something not quite right, something missing. So she started another painting. This one was better than the first, she decided, but it still wasn't quite right. She started again. And again. She made over 20 paintings of the same door!

Every time Georgia set out to paint something, she wanted to get at the heart of whatever it was—a flower, a hillside, an animal skull, or an ordinary old door. She wanted to paint not just what a flower *looked* like, but what it *was*—its very essence.

"When you take a flower and really look at it," she explained, "it's your world for the moment." Her paintings of flowers were huge—it was as though one flower could fill the entire sky. With simple shapes and blocks of color, Georgia created a whole new language of art.

She became the first female modernist painter. Everyone wanted to meet her, but Georgia liked being on her own. She lived in a place called Ghost Ranch in New Mexico. She loved it there, where the desert light was strong and clear, and the landscape was wild and free—just like her.

In 1997, the Georgia O'Keeffe Museum opened, making it the first museum in the United States dedicated to a major female artist.

NOVEMBER 15, 1887–MARCH 6, 1986
UNITED STATES OF AMERICA

ILLUSTRATION BY
ANA JUAN

"TO CREATE ONE'S OWN
WORLD TAKES COURAGE."
—GEORGIA O'KEEFFE

GERTY CORI

BIOCHEMIST

Once upon a time, there was a girl who was named after a warship. Gerty was 16 years old when she decided she wanted to study science. She was told she couldn't, however, because she didn't have enough background in Latin, mathematics, physics, and chemistry. But Gerty didn't give up. In two years, she managed to study the equivalent of eight years of Latin and five years of math, physics, and chemistry.

She was one of the first women to be admitted to the medical school at Charles University in Prague. There, Gerty became close friends with a fellow student called Carl Cori. He loved her charm, her sense of humor, and her passion for mountain climbing. They graduated, got married, immigrated to the United States, and stayed happily together for the rest of their lives.

In the United States, Gerty and Carl worked side by side in a laboratory and collaborated on scientific papers. Together they discovered how **glucose** is broken down by **enzymes** in the body to release energy. This process came to be known as the Cori cycle.

Their research has helped thousands of children with **diabetes**, and it also won them a Nobel Prize in Physiology or Medicine. Gerty was the first American woman to win a Nobel Prize in a scientific discipline, and the Coris were one of the very few married couples to win the prize jointly.

Theirs was a true partnership of equals. Gerty and Carl worked together on their scientific research until the end of their lives. When she was asked what was the secret to true happiness, Gerty replied: "The love for and dedication to one's work."

AUGUST 15, 1896–OCTOBER 26, 1957
CZECH REPUBLIC

ILLUSTRATION BY
CLAUDIA CARIERI

"I BELIEVE THAT IN ART
AND SCIENCE ARE THE
GLORIES OF THE HUMAN
MIND. I SEE NO CONFLICT
BETWEEN THEM."
—GERTY CORI

GIUSI NICOLINI

POLITICIAN

There was a young woman named Giusi who loved the little island of Lampedusa, where she was born. Criminal groups and ruthless corporations wanted to destroy Lampedusa's pristine beaches to build hotels and vacation homes, but Giusi wouldn't let them.

As the director of Lampedusa's natural reserve, she said, "It is my duty to protect this island with all my might." Her enemies burned down her father's shop. *You will not intimidate me*, she declared. Her car and her boyfriend's van were set on fire. *I will not back down!* she said.

Lampedusa is a tiny island in the Mediterranean Sea, between Europe and Africa. Many refugees who were fleeing Africa to escape war and build a better life in Europe landed there. The inhabitants of Lampedusa didn't know what to do. *Should we send these people back to protect our island?* they wondered. *Or should we welcome them?*

With these questions in mind, they went to vote for their next mayor. Giusi was one of five candidates. People knew she had given all she had to protect the island in the past, so they wanted to hear what she thought about the current situation. Giusi explained her point of view with four simple words: "Protect people, not borders."

Lampedusans elected her.

As mayor, Giusi reorganized the island's immigration center to be able to welcome as many people as possible. *We want to see many boats on our shores*, she insisted, *because that will mean that these people made it here and didn't drown.*

BORN MARCH 5, 1961
ITALY

"IT'S NATURAL FOR AN ISLAND TO BE WELCOMING!"
—GIUSI NICOLINI

ILLUSTRATION BY LAURA PÉREZ

GLORIA STEINEM

JOURNALIST AND POLITICIAL ACTIVIST

Once upon a time, there was a woman who traveled a lot. When she was a child, she traveled in her parents' trailer. When she grew up, she kept traveling by plane, train, bus—even on the back of an elephant! She traveled tens of thousands of miles, year after year, because she had an important message to spread and she wanted to deliver it in person to as many people as possible.

Her name was Gloria, and her message was simple yet revolutionary: she believed that women and men were equal. She believed that women should have the right to decide if they want children, that their salaries should be the same as men's, and that they should never have to suffer abuse from their husbands.

Gloria was a feminist.

At the time, many people thought a woman without a man wasn't really a complete person. Gloria thought that was ridiculous and remembered something she'd heard from another female journalist: "A woman needs a man like a fish needs a bicycle!"

She told women that they could choose whatever life they wanted, and that not everyone had to live the same way. They didn't have to have children if they didn't want to. She also believed that people form families in many different ways, and that any family can be happy—as long as everyone in it loves and respects one another.

To this day, Gloria inspires women all over the world to fight for their rights. *Sometimes, the truth can make you mad,* she admits, *but it will ultimately set you free.*

BORN MARCH 25, 1934
UNITED STATES OF AMERICA

ILLUSTRATION BY
MALIN ROSENQVIST

"POWER CAN
BE TAKEN BUT
NOT GIVEN. THE
PROCESS OF
THE TAKING IS
EMPOWERMENT
IN ITSELF."
—GLORIA STEINEM

HEDY LAMARR

ACTOR AND INVENTOR

Once upon a time, in Austria, a beautiful baby girl called Hedy was born. When Hedy grew up, she married a rich man and moved to a castle. At first, it seemed like a dream come true, but Hedy soon discovered that she and her husband didn't get along. "I was like a doll . . . . having no mind, no life of its own," she said. What's more, her husband sold weapons to Nazis and fascists, and she often had to sit in meetings about military technologies that would be used to advance the agendas of these evil regimes.

One day, Hedy decided she'd had enough, so she disguised herself as a maid and escaped to Paris. There, she met an important Hollywood producer named Louis B. Mayer. She followed him to Los Angeles, eventually becoming one of the world's biggest film stars.

In between movies, Hedy invented a new kind of traffic stoplight and a capsule that could make sparkling water, and she helped a tycoon build more efficient airplanes by suggesting modifications to their shape.

During the World War II, Hedy learned that the Nazis were able to protect their submarines from torpedoes by jamming the radio signals used to control them. *I can solve that problem*, she decided, and she got straight to work.

With the help of a musician friend, she invented a secret communication system that could automatically change the frequency of a torpedo's radio signal, making it impossible for enemies to jam.

Her work laid the foundation for the Wi-Fi and Bluetooth technologies we all use today.

NOVEMBER 9, 1914–JANUARY 19, 2000
AUSTRIA

ILLUSTRATION BY
MARTA SIGNORI

"ALL CREATIVE PEOPLE WANT
TO DO THE UNEXPECTED."
—HEDY LAMARR

HORTENSIA

ORATOR

Once there was a woman who knew how to win an argument. Her name was Hortensia, and she lived through a turbulent time in the history of ancient Rome.

The Roman emperor Julius Caesar had recently been killed, and he was replaced as ruler by Marc Antony, Augustus, and Marcus Aemilius Lepidus. Together, they were called the *triumvirs*.

The triumvirs wanted to declare war on the assassins of Julius Caesar, but they needed money to pay for the conflict. So they decided to tax the property of 1,400 rich Roman women to finance it. Hortensia was one of them. She didn't think it made sense that women had no say in a decision that affected them, so she decided to do something about it.

At first, she tried to persuade the triumvirs' wives to talk to their husbands, but she wasn't successful. Fulvia, Marc Antony's wife, was more interested in protecting her husband's decision than her own rights, and she threw Hortensia out of their house.

Outraged, Hortensia pushed her way into the tribunal and made her case with a memorable speech. *Why should we finance your war*, she demanded, *when we have no say in the government, no honors, and no part in public office? We would gladly pay taxes to help protect our country against a foreign invasion, but you cannot force us to sponsor your civil war.*

The triumvirs were furious. But Hortensia convinced so many people with her speech that the three rulers had to listen to her brilliant reasoning, and in the end, they changed their policy.

DATE OF BIRTH AND DEATH UNKNOWN
ITALY

· 68 ·

ILLUSTRATION BY
SARAH MAZZETTI

"WHY SHOULD
WE PAY TAXES
WHEN WE HAVE
NO PART IN
PUBLIC OFFICE?"
—HORTENSIA

ISADORA DUNCAN

DANCER

Once upon a time, there was a girl who didn't like school. Isadora hated sitting still at a desk when she longed to leap and spin and twirl—to express all the joy of being alive through her body. Deep inside, the girl knew she was born to dance.

By age six, Isadora had already become a dance teacher. At the time, everyone thought ballet was the most beautiful type of dance in the world, but Isadora did not. She didn't like the formal style of classical ballet. She found it "ugly and against nature."

Instead, Isadora wanted to dance like a wave on the ocean or a tree in the breeze—natural and free.

When she was 18, Isadora used her last few dollars to buy a ticket on a cattle boat from the United States to Europe. She traveled around all the great cities—Paris, Berlin, Vienna, and London. She performed onstage and set up groundbreaking dance schools. And she announced a rule for her schools: "I shall not teach the children to imitate my movements, but to make their own."

While dancing, Isadora wore loose white dresses and long trailing scarves. She wanted the cloth to echo and enhance the flowing movements of her limbs. Some people thought she was indecent. *Women should not be so wild and free*, they said. But Isadora didn't care! She declared herself to be a "dancer of the future . . . the highest intelligence in the freest body."

MAY 27, 1877–SEPTEMBER 14, 1927
UNITED STATES OF AMERICA

ILLUSTRATION BY
CRISTINA AMODEO

"I HAVE NEVER WAITED
TO DO AS I WISHED."
—ISADORA DUNCAN

J. K. ROWLING

AUTHOR

When she was six years old, Joanne wrote a short story about a rabbit and titled it "Rabbit." When she was 11, she wrote a novel about seven cursed diamonds.

She came from a poor family, and her parents hoped she would pursue a stable career in law or economics. But she decided to study literature.

One day, she found herself completely broke. As a single mother with no job and no money, Joanne experienced the pain of failure that her parents had always warned her about. Everything she owned was in a suitcase, including the first three chapters of a story about a boy with magic powers. That boy was called Harry Potter.

Her manuscript about Harry was rejected time after time, but finally one publisher took it on. They printed just a thousand copies and asked Joanne to change her name to J.K., as they feared young boys would not want to read a book written by a woman.

Her editor told her that she shouldn't expect to make money from her writing, but thankfully Joanne decided to keep going. The Harry Potter series went on to become the most incredible phenomenon in the history of publishing. The seven books have captured the imagination of hundreds of millions of children—and adults—all over the world, and they've redefined the meaning of children's literature.

Joanne always said failure was crucial to her success. "Had I really succeeded at anything else," she explained, "I might never have found the determination to succeed in the one arena I believed I truly belonged."

BORN JULY 31, 1965
UNITED KINGDOM

"IT IS IMPOSSIBLE TO LIVE WITHOUT FAILING AT SOMETHING, UNLESS YOU LIVE SO CAUTIOUSLY THAT YOU MIGHT AS WELL NOT HAVE LIVED AT ALL.
—J. K. ROWLING

ILLUSTRATION BY PAOLA ROLLO

JEANNE BARET

Once upon a time, a housekeeper called Jeanne disguised herself as a man and sailed around the world.

Jeanne looked after the house of a French naturalist named Commerson. One day, he was invited to sail to the New World on an expedition to find and identify new species of plants. Commerson was excited, but his health was poor and he needed someone to accompany him on this long, exhausting voyage.

At the time, women weren't allowed aboard French ships, so Commerson and Jeanne came up with a plan: at the very last minute, she would get on the ship disguised as a young man called Jean, and Commerson would hire this "stranger" as his assistant. The plan worked—and the ship's captain even gave his large cabin to them so they would have space for all the special equipment Commerson needed.

Jeanne took good care of Commerson, but he was so ill by the time they reached South America that she took over collecting and studying the plants herself. She was unstoppable. In Rio de Janeiro, Brazil, she found a brightly colored vine that Commerson named bougainvillea after the ship's captain, Bougainville.

When Jeanne's real identity was discovered, she and Commerson decided to leave the ship and stay in Mauritius, an island off the coast of Africa. They completed two more scientific expeditions—to Madagascar and the Bourbon Islands—but then Commerson died and Jeanne was stranded. When she finally made it back to France a year later, she had become the first woman in history to circumnavigate the globe.

JULY 27, 1740–AUGUST 5, 1807

FRANCE

JOAN BEAUCHAMP PROCTER

ZOOLOGIST

One day, a girl named Joan asked her mom and dad to get her a pet. *I don't want a puppy or a kitten*, she said. *I'd love a snake! And some lizards, please.* By the time she was 10, Joan was looking after lots of reptiles. One of them, a large Dalmatian wall lizard, was her favorite. They traveled everywhere together and even sat side by side at mealtimes. When she was older, Joan took her pet crocodile to school—much to the teacher's amazement!

These creatures fascinated Joan. She became a world expert in herpetology—the branch of zoology dealing with reptiles and amphibians—and got a job at the Natural History Museum. Then one day, the London Zoo asked her to design a new reptile house. She did an excellent job and became something of a celebrity. Crowds gathered to watch her handling pythons, crocodiles, and huge Komodo dragons. She was elected curator of reptiles.

A Komodo dragon named Sumbawa became Joan's special pet. Sumbawa followed her everywhere. Joan would stroke and pat her and feed her chicken, pigeon, and eggs. Sometimes, she "steered" the dragon along by holding her tail. Joan understood these animals so well that she knew when they were sick and exactly what to do to make them better.

Her own health problems, however, were harder to cure. She was constantly in pain and had been for much of her life. But this didn't stop her from following her passion—even when it meant going to work in a wheelchair, with Sumbawa lumbering along happily behind her.

AUGUST 5, 1897–SEPTEMBER 20, 1931

UNITED KINGDOM

ILLUSTRATION BY
MARIJKE BUURLAGE

JOHANNA NORDBLAD

ICE DIVER

Once upon a time, there was a free-diving champion named Johanna. She loved diving deep underwater on just a single breath, without the use of air tanks. As she swam down with nothing but the slow thump of her heartbeat in her ears, Johanna felt like she was flying.

Then one day, she had a terrible accident. Her leg was so badly broken that the doctors thought they might have to remove it. Although they were able to save her leg after intense surgery, the only way to help the pain was by plunging it in ice water. It was agonizing, but her leg slowly began to heal. And something else happened that no one had expected: Johanna started to enjoy the feeling of the icy coldness. "I felt it was the only place where I could get over the pain. Actually, it was very relaxing," she said.

When she was strong enough, Johanna decided to start swimming underneath ice. A short film called *Johanna* was made about one of her incredible dives. It shows a solitary figure dragging a sled to the middle of a frozen lake, leaving a trail of footprints behind her in the snow. She cuts a triangle into the ice with a saw and sits on the edge. Taking a deep breath, she slips into the black water. A different universe unfolds around her, silver and deep blue-black, silent and beautiful. She swims along like a mermaid, at peace with the world.

If it hadn't been for the accident, Johanna might never have discovered the joy of ice diving. *Sometimes*, she says, *a curse really is a blessing in disguise.*

BORN NOVEMBER 1975

FINLAND

ILLUSTRATION BY
GERALDINE SY

"THERE IS NO PLACE FOR FEAR.
NO PLACE FOR PANIC. NO PLACE
FOR MISTAKES. UNDER THE ICE,
YOU NEED TOTAL CONTROL."
—JOHANNA NORDBLAD

KATHERINE JOHNSON, DOROTHY VAUGHAN, AND MARY JACKSON

COMPUTER SCIENTISTS

Every day, Katherine, Dorothy, and Mary drove together to NASA, the agency responsible for the US space program. They were all brilliant scientists, and their job was to crack complex math problems to make sure that astronauts could travel safely to space.

When NASA bought its first IBM transistor-based computer, only a few people in the world knew how to use it for business—and no one knew how to use it for space travel! So Dorothy taught herself Fortran, the programming language the computer understood, and got the system working.

When astronaut John Glenn was about to take off for a trip orbiting Earth, he said he did not completely trust the computer and asked Katherine to check the trajectory calculations herself. "If she says the numbers are good, I'm ready to go," he said.

When the opportunity to work on the **Supersonic Pressure Tunnel** came about, Mary volunteered. She specialized in the behavior of air around planes, and she became the first Black female aeronautical engineer.

Katherine, Dorothy, and Mary overcame incredible odds, but their contributions to science and technology remained unknown for many years. Today, they are celebrated as three of the most inspiring figures in the history of space travel.

KATHERINE JOHNSON, AUGUST 26, 1918–FEBRUARY 24, 2020
DOROTHY VAUGHAN, SEPTEMBER 20, 1910–NOVEMBER 10, 2008
MARY JACKSON, APRIL 9, 1921–FEBRUARY 11, 2005
UNITED STATES OF AMERICA

ILLUSTRATION BY
CRISTINA PORTOLANO

"IN MATH, EITHER
YOU'RE RIGHT OR
YOU'RE WRONG."
—KATHERINE JOHNSON

KATIA KRAFFT

VOLCANOLOGIST

Katia loved volcanoes. She didn't just like to look at pictures of boiling rivers of lava—she wanted to see them for real.

In college, Katia met a young man called Maurice who was as passionate about volcanoes as she was. On their first date, they realized they shared the dream of filming a volcano as it was erupting—something no one had ever done before. They fell madly in love and planned their first trip to an active volcano.

From then on, they were hooked. Whenever they heard that a volcano was about to blow, they packed their bags and rushed to the scene. To get the best shots, they would scramble up to the edge of the crater. They wore protective silver suits and helmets so they could withstand the heat from the molten lava—which was more than a thousand degrees.

Katia and Maurice's dream was to ride a boat down a lava flow! They knew their work was extremely dangerous, but they didn't care. To them, there was no sight more beautiful than a volcano erupting right before their eyes.

One day, Katia and Maurice were on the slopes of Mount Unzen, an active volcano in Japan. They were a safe distance from the summit—or so they thought. But this time, their calculations were wrong. The explosion was far larger than anyone had predicted, and it sent a boiling cloud of gases, rocks, and ash rolling down the valley. Katia, Maurice, and the members of their team had no chance to escape, and all tragically died. Today, however, Katia is known as a pioneer for her incredible work in recording volcanoes.

APRIL 17, 1942–JUNE 3, 1991

FRANCE

"THERE IS THE PLEASURE OF APPROACHING THE BEAST AND NOT KNOWING IF HE IS GOING TO CATCH YOU."
—KATIA KRAFFT

ILLUSTRATION BY MARTINA PAUKOVA

KHOUDIA DIOP

MODEL

Once upon a time, there was a girl whose skin was as dark as night. Her name was Khoudia, and she lived in Senegal. At school, Khoudia was bullied because of the color of her skin. Other children would call her hurtful names, and every day Khoudia would look in the mirror to see if her skin had gotten any lighter.

Her sister showed her the pictures of the model Alek Wek. *You're beautiful!* she assured her. *See? You can be a model if you want!*

One day, Khoudia and her sister were walking down a street in Milan, Italy, when they passed a giant mirror. Khoudia saw how she stood out from all the other fair-skinned people around them. Every morning after that, she'd look in the mirror and tell herself, "Look at your skin. Look at your teeth and your smile. You are beautiful."

A couple years later, Khoudia accompanied an aunt who needed eye surgery to Paris. There, people would stop her in the streets to take pictures of her. She became a professional model and started an Instagram account, calling herself the Melanin Goddess.

Khoudia remembered how dark-skinned girls in Senegal would bleach their skin. She wanted to show girls that being different is beautiful.

Today, Khoudia campaigns to prevent bullying and is very proud that her 11-year-old brother, who is as dark as she is, told her, "I don't care anymore if other kids talk about my skin color."

BORN DECEMBER 31, 1996
SENEGAL

ILLUSTRATION BY
DEBORA GUIDI

"I'VE LEARNED TO IGNORE
THE NEGATIVE PEOPLE AND
JUST BE A LIVING EXAMPLE OF
CONFIDENCE AND SELF-LOVE."
—KHOUDIA DIOP

LAUREN POTTER

ACTOR

The day she was born, Lauren was diagnosed with **Down syndrome**. Because of her condition, she couldn't walk until the age of two, but shortly after taking her first steps, she started dancing and acting classes. She loved performing, and her mom encouraged her to follow her passion.

At school, however, her classmates were not as supportive. Bullies made fun of her—and even made her eat sand. "It was hard," Lauren remembered. "They hurt me."

As time went on, her passion for music and dance only grew stronger. She auditioned to be a cheerleader at her high school, but she didn't make the squad. A year later, though, a much bigger opportunity came her way: a chance to play a cheerleader on a TV show called *Glee*.

Out of the 13 girls who auditioned for the role, the one the show's producers picked was Lauren! The character she played, Becky Jackson, became so popular that kids in her former high school put posters of her on the walls. *I'm happy they can now see me as I always saw myself*, Lauren thought.

She enjoyed being an actor, but she also wanted to help other people with disabilities. Lauren wanted them to have the opportunity to follow their passions just as she had. She was appointed by Barack Obama to the President's Committee for People with Intellectual Disabilities, and she starred in commercials against bullying.

Today, she travels across the country giving speeches. She says, "It feels amazing to be a role model for people with and without disabilities."

BORN MAY 10, 1990
UNITED STATES OF AMERICA

ILLUSTRATION BY
ALICE BARBERINI

"IF YOU HAVE A DISABILITY,
KEEP WORKING HARD.
WHATEVER IT TAKES, DO IT!"
—LAUREN POTTER

LEYMAH GBOWEE

PEACE ACTIVIST

Once, in Liberia, a woman stopped a war.

Her name was Leymah, and she was a single mother of four. Her country was going through a violent civil war. Children were being recruited as soldiers, and hundreds of thousands of people were dying. Leymah worked hard to help those who had been traumatized by the fighting.

One day, she was invited to a conference organized by the West Africa Network for Peacebuilding. *Women like me had come from almost all 18 countries in West Africa*, Leymah recalled.

At the conference, she learned about conflict and conflict resolution. The women shared their experiences and talked about what war had taken from their lives. For Leymah, it was enlightening. *No one else*, she thought, *is doing this—focusing only on women and only on building peace.*

She became the leader of a program called the Women in Peacebuilding Network. To recruit other women, she went to mosques for Friday afternoon prayers, to the markets on Saturday mornings, and to churches every Sunday. All the women she spoke to were tired of a war they had never wanted in the first place—a war that was killing their children.

Leymah and the other women in her network pressured the factions at war to start peace talks. Then they gathered in front of the hotel where the negotiations were taking place to demand rapid progress. They even blocked the hotel exit to keep the negotiators from leaving until they had reached a deal.

When the Liberian civil war ended, Leymah was awarded a Nobel Peace Prize. "When women gather," she says, "great things will happen."

BORN FEBRUARY 1, 1972

LIBERIA

ILLUSTRATION BY
THANDIWE TSHABALALA

"WE MUST CONTINUE TO UNITE IN SISTERHOOD
TO TURN OUR TEARS INTO TRIUMPH . . ."
—LEYMAH GBOWEE

LILIAN BLAND

AVIATOR

The first time Lilian was in a plane, it was with her boyfriend. He took her up in his glider, but when she asked, *Can I fly it?* he said no, and Lilian got really mad.

Shortly after, Lilian's uncle Robert sent her a postcard of a monoplane flying over Paris. Lilian was in awe. She immediately wrote back, begging him to take her aboard as a passenger. But her uncle said no as well.

All right, I will have to do this myself, Lilian thought. But at the time, it wasn't easy to find a plane in Ireland. *No problem*, she said to herself. *I'll build one.*

Lilian read everything she could find by the Wright brothers and other famous aviators about how to build a plane. She succeeded in building a flyable biplane—an aircraft with two pairs of wings—then went on to build a full-scale glider, just like the one her boyfriend hadn't let her fly.

She called her glider the *Mayfly*—because, as she said, *It may fly, or it may not!*

Lilian fitted the *Mayfly* with an engine and found a nice level stretch of empty ground to use as a runway. She couldn't wait to see if her glider would get off the ground. The only problem was that the plane had no tank to hold the fuel. *Never mind*, she thought. *I'll use an empty bottle instead.* She did just that—and the plane soared along for about 10 seconds.

The *Mayfly*—designed, built, and flown by the amazing, inventive Lilian Bland—was the first fuel powered aircraft in Ireland.

SEPTEMBER 22, 1878–MAY 11, 1971
UNITED KINGDOM

ILLUSTRATION BY
NOA SNIR

"I HAVE FLOWN!"
—LILIAN BLAND

LORENA OCHOA

GOLFER

Once, a girl fell out of a tree and broke both her wrists. Her arms were in casts from her fingertips to her shoulders for three months. When the casts came off, her bones were completely mended. People thought the doctor gave her magical wrists!

Lorena grew up in Guadalajara, Mexico. Her house was near a country club that had a golf course. Sometimes, she would watch her dad play a round of golf on his day off.

At first, she only helped him steer his cart. But eventually, she started to play as well. It was immediately clear that, whether the doctor had something to do with it or not, Lorena had a magic touch.

At seven, she started competing in and winning golf tournaments. She also played tennis and excelled at that too! When she won the Junior World Championships in San Diego, though, she decided to focus on golf.

Lorena was tiny but strong. She became the top female golfer in the world. Her fans watched in awe as she hit drives longer than anyone else's. But her best game was with the short irons, which are golf clubs that have a short shaft for hitting short, high shots. The magic in her wrists made her unbelievably precise.

She became known as La Tigresa—the Tiger.

But Lorena wanted to do more than play golf. So she opened a foundation that operates an innovative school called La Barranca, where 250 underprivileged kids can get a great education and spend some fun time outdoors too—playing golf of course!

BORN NOVEMBER 15, 1981

MEXICO

ILLUSTRATION BY
CAMILLA PERKINS

"I HIT A LOT OF BAD SHOTS.
YOU NEED TO LAUGH ABOUT
THEM . . . AND KEEP MOVING."
—LORENA OCHOA

LOWRI MORGAN

ULTRAMARATHON RUNNER

Once upon a time, there was a girl named Lowri who loved to sing. She dreamed of becoming a professional singer. But life had other plans for her—plans that would take her far, far away from the hills of South Wales, where she was born. Lowri became an ultramarathon runner—someone who competes in races of great distances in extreme environments.

One day, as she ran through the Amazon jungle, exhausted and dripping with sweat, she wondered what life as a singer would have been like. *A lot easier, that's for sure*, she thought. She was running the Jungle Marathon—one of the toughest races on the planet. There were snakes in the trees and jaguars on the ground. She was attacked by angry hornets and had to swim across a river full of piranhas!

Then something magical happened: she heard her mother's voice say, *A glory is not by never falling but by getting up when you do so.* Lowri picked herself up and carried on until she reached the finish line in record time.

After running in one of the hottest places in the world, Lowri then ran in one of the coldest: the Arctic. She was so cold and tired during that race that her mind started playing tricks. She saw a park bench on the ice and thought, *How nice! I can sit down.* But it wasn't really there.

Lowri refused to give up. Like she had done in the Amazon, she kept going, over the snow and ice, past reindeers and polar bears, until she completed the entire 350-mile race.

She was the only person to complete the race that year!

BORN 1975
UNITED KINGDOM

ILLUSTRATION BY
SARAH WILKINS

"I'M NEVER GOING TO BE THE
FASTEST OR STRONGEST, BUT
I CAN BE THE BEST PREPARED."
—LOWRI MORGAN

LUO DENGPING

~~~

EXTREME ROCK CLIMBER

SCAN TO HEAR MORE

Once upon a time, there was a girl named Luo who loved climbing. She lived in Guizhou, a spectacular place in southern China with towering rock outcrops, lush dense jungles, and terraced fields covering the hills.

The men in Luo's village had a unique tradition. They climbed up and down the terrifyingly high cliffs with no climbing gear and no safety nets—nothing but their bare hands. They gathered medicinal herbs and collected swallow droppings to use as fertilizer. They were so agile and fast that people called them Spider-Men. Luo's father was one of them. As a little girl, Luo watched him climb nimbly from one ledge to the next, hundreds of feet in the air. *One day, I'll do that*, she thought to herself.

When she turned 15, Luo started practicing on small slopes. She was the only female rock climber in Guizhou, and at first no one wanted to train her. But eventually, she convinced her father to teach her all he knew. Soon, she was climbing as high and as fast as any of the Spider-Men. She was strong, brave, and extremely good at finding cracks in the sheer rock face to grab hold of.

Today, Luo is a professional climber. Tourists watch her death-defying feats in awe. Her hands are rough and calloused from hanging on to the rocks, and she loves her work. When she gets to the top, she waves a red flag. *It's a fantastic feeling*, she says, *like I'm on top of the world!* Everyone in her village is proud of Luo, their very own Spider-Woman.

~~~

BORN 1980

CHINA

ILLUSTRATION BY
LISK FENG

"THE OLD CUSTOM SAYS THAT ONLY
MEN ARE ALLOWED TO LEARN IT.
I WAS UNWILLING TO ACCEPT THAT
AND ASKED MY FATHER TO TEACH ME."
—LUO DENGPING

MADAM C. J. WALKER

SCAN TO
HEAR MORE

BUSINESSWOMAN

Once upon a time, on a cotton plantation in Louisiana, a girl named Sarah was born. Sarah's four older siblings had been born enslaved, as had their parents before them. But thanks to the Emancipation Proclamation, Sarah was the first in her family to be born free.

When Sarah was around 22, she moved to St. Louis, Missouri. There, she worked as a washerwoman for $1.50 a day. At night, she attended school.

During that time, Sarah started losing her hair, so she experimented with various products and treatments to help it grow back again. None of the available products was quite right for her, however. *What if I could create a hair treatment specifically for Black people?* she wondered.

Her husband, who worked in advertising, loved the idea. He suggested she change her name to Madam C. J. Walker to make her products more appealing, and so she did.

Sarah started traveling the country to promote her hair care line and give demonstrations of the Walker System: a hair care formula that used homemade pomade (a scented oil), heated combs, and a particular style of brushing to stimulate hair growth. Her demonstrations were so popular that, she started hiring other women to promote her products, and soon "Walker agents" became well known all over the country.

Sarah's success encouraged other women to create their own companies, and she supported many charities providing educational opportunities for Black people.

Madam C. J. Walker became the first female self-made millionaire in the United States.

DECEMBER 23, 1867–MAY 25, 1919
UNITED STATES OF AMERICA

ILLUSTRATION BY
CRISTINA SPANÒ

"I AM NOT SATISFIED IN MAKING MONEY
FOR MYSELF. I ENDEAVOR TO PROVIDE
EMPLOYMENT FOR HUNDREDS OF THE
WOMEN OF MY RACE."
—MADAM C. J. WALKER

MADAME SAQUI

ACROBAT

During the French Revolution, there was a short, stocky girl named Marguerite, who dreamed of being a tightrope walker. Her father had been an acrobat himself, but during the revolution, no one had money to give to circus performers, so he set up a stall selling home remedies and hoped his daughter would forget her dreams.

But Marguerite was determined.

She found an old family friend from her father's circus days and begged him to train her in secret. She was brilliant! She made her debut at the age of 11. People in the audience gasped when they saw her dance along a wire high over their heads. What incredible balance! Such grace! Such strength! Marguerite was an instant hit.

Her family formed a circus company with Marguerite as the star, and together they toured across France. When she was 18, she met another acrobat called Julian Saqui. They fell in love and were married, and she chose to become Madame Saqui.

Madame Saqui knew she was destined for greatness. At the height of her career, she performed at the world-famous Tivoli Gardens in Paris, walking up a steep rope with fireworks exploding all around her. Even Napoleon, the emperor of France, was captivated by her, and she devised a show to commemorate his victory in battle.

Her most daring feat was to walk on a rope stretched between the towers of Notre-Dame Cathedral, hundreds of feet in the air. She became a bright star shining in the sky of Paris, and her performances are still remembered as extraordinary displays of courage and talent.

FEBRUARY 26, 1786–1866

FRANCE

ILLUSTRATION BY
LAURA JUNGER

MADONNA

SINGER, SONGWRITER, AND BUSINESSWOMAN

Once, in a small town split in half by a river, a star was born. Her name was Madonna. She was smart and got top grades in school. But she always realized that she was a little bit different. More than anything, Madonna knew exactly what she wanted and would not let anyone change her dreams. Some people felt intimidated by her strength and clarity of mind, but Madonna didn't let them hold her back.

When she was 20 years old, she moved to New York City with just 35 dollars in her pocket. It was the first time she had taken a plane—the first time she had taken a cab! "It was the bravest thing I've ever done," she later said.

Madonna worked as a singer in clubs and as a waitress in coffee shops. She worked hard. She tried and failed and tried again, numerous times.

In those days, it was rare for female artists to be the masters of their own destiny: their male managers, producers, and agents would make most of their decisions for them. Not Madonna. *I am my own experiment*, she declared. *I am my own work of art.*

Through her music, Madonna inspired hundreds of millions of people to stay true to themselves and stand proud, even in the face of adversity. "People pick on me. That's just the way it is . . ." she explained. "I don't take it as personally as I used to, or it doesn't bother me as much as it used to."

Her huge talent, tremendous self-discipline, and fierce determination have made her one of the most influential pop artists in history.

BORN AUGUST 16, 1958
UNITED STATES OF AMERICA

"I HAVE THE SAME GOAL I'VE HAD
EVER SINCE I WAS A GIRL: I WANT
TO RULE THE WORLD."
—MADONNA

MARIE THARP

GEOLOGIST

Marie wanted to study Earth's crust, so she completed a master's degree in geology at the University of Michigan.

Today, we know that millions of years ago, almost all of Earth's land was united in a supercontinent called Pangaea and surrounded by a superocean called Panthalassa. In Marie's time, though, this was still just a theory based on the simple observation that the coastlines of South America and Africa looked like matching pieces of a gigantic jigsaw puzzle. In between the continents there were now huge oceans. To prove that such distant lands had once been united, the ocean floor had to be mapped.

People assumed that the bottom of the ocean was flat, and this idea wasn't challenged until geologists started to use **sonar** onboard ships. The sonar bounced sound waves off the bottom of the ocean, and it was Marie's job to make sense of the readings. She crunched numbers, took measurements by hand, and became the first person ever to piece together a map of the North Atlantic seafloor with its mountains and valleys. "The whole world was spread out before me," she recalled.

Marie discovered that at the bottom of the Atlantic Ocean, there was an incredibly deep valley that looked just like the Great Rift Valley in Africa. It formed part of a system that encircled the entire globe!

She showed that the ocean floor was spreading apart, which meant that the continents were drifting away from one another. This in turn proved that they had indeed been united millions of years ago, when the Earth was young.

JULY 30, 1920–AUGUST 23, 2006
UNITED STATES OF AMERICA

ILLUSTRATION BY
BARBARA DZIADOSZ

"I HAD. . . A FASCINATING JIGSAW
PUZZLE TO PIECE TOGETHER."
—MARIE THARP

MARINA ABRAMOVIĆ

PERFORMANCE ARTIST

Once upon a time, a woman in a long red dress sat silently at a wooden table. Her name was Marina, and she was a world-famous artist.

She was sitting in a plain white room inside the Museum of Modern Art in New York City. Marina had decided she would sit there eight hours a day for almost three months. On the other side of the table was an empty chair. Anyone who wanted to could sit across from her. If they kept silent and looked her in the eye, they could sit there as long as they liked.

Marina's idea was simple yet groundbreaking. A thousand people lined up for hours to sit with her and be in her presence—or even just to see her and another stranger staring at each other.

Many people were moved to tears by Marina's performance. It's not often we take the time to simply sit and look at each other, without saying anything. It's not often we feel truly "seen" by another person.

A record-breaking half a million people visited the show. For 40 years, Marina had been an artist. Not all of her performances were as successful as *The Artist Is Present*, but she never stopped experimenting—she never let fear get in her way. "If you experiment, you have to fail," she explained. "By definition, experimenting means going to territory where you've never been, where failure is very possible. How can you know you're going to succeed? Having the courage to face the unknown is so important."

BORN NOVEMBER 30, 1946

SERBIA

ILLUSTRATION BY
LIZZY STEWART

"THE HARDEST THING TO DO
IS SOMETHING THAT IS
CLOSE TO NOTHING."
—MARINA ABRAMOVIĆ

MARTA VIEIRA DA SILVA

~~~

SOCCER PLAYER

Marta loved to play soccer, and she was always the first to be picked by the boys when teams were made. Her mom couldn't afford to send her to school, so Marta used to sell fruit in the public market to help her family get by. In her spare time, she played soccer in the streets.

When Marta was 14, a famous soccer coach saw her playing with a group of boys. Her speed, superb control, and strong left foot amazed the coach. She knew that Marta would become a champion, and she helped her join the Vasco da Gama football club.

Despite her talent, Marta didn't have an easy career. In Brazil, soccer is still considered a man's game, and there isn't much funding for women's teams. When she was 17, Marta decided to accept an offer to move to Sweden. There, she won several league titles and a record five consecutive World Player of the Year Awards from FIFA, soccer's international governing body.

Her fancy footwork and blistering goals earned her the nickname Pelé de saias (Pelé with skirts), after the greatest soccer player of all time, but she didn't pay too much attention to that. She was captain of the Brazilian national team in her trademark number 10 yellow jersey, leading it to two silver medals at the Olympic Games in Greece and Beijing.

Marta was appointed a UN Women Goodwill Ambassador for her role in promoting equality in sport. "We need to score goals in the name of gender equality," she said.

~~~

BORN FEBRUARY 19, 1986

BRAZIL

ILLUSTRATION BY
ANNALISA VENTURA

"I FOUGHT BACK BY SHOWING
MY TALENT . . ."
—MARTA VIEIRA DA SILVA

MARY FIELDS

MAIL CARRIER

Mary was an incredibly strong woman.

When a friend who was a nun fell sick, she rushed to the convent to look after her. Mother Amadeus recovered, but Mary stayed on to help out. She took care of 400 chickens and drove a stagecoach to transport visitors to and from the convent.

One night, wolves attacked the stagecoach. Mary fought them off all night long, and in the morning, she made it back to the convent safe and sound.

Stagecoach Mary, as she was called, spent 10 years working there, but when a man complained that she was making two dollars more than he was each month, she got angry and grabbed her gun. There was a shoot-out. Six guns were emptied in the back of the nunnery, and the man was injured. The bishop fired Mary and gave the man a raise.

Mary opened a restaurant, but because she gave food to everyone, whether they could pay for it or not, she went out of business in just a few months. At 60 years old, she applied to be a mail carrier. She got the job because she was the fastest person to hitch up a team of six horses. She was the second woman and the first Black woman to work for the United States Postal Service.

Mary never missed a day on the job. No matter what, she was on her stagecoach delivering mail to the most remote homesteads in Montana. In her spare time, she babysat children, spending all the money she made to buy them presents.

CIRCA 1832–1914

UNITED STATES OF AMERICA

ILLUSTRATION BY
GABRIELLE TESFAYE

MARY KINGSLEY

EXPLORER

Once upon a time, there was a girl named Mary whose brother was sent to school. She wasn't. Her family wanted her to take care of the house. The only thing Mary was taught was German, because her father wanted her to translate some scientific books for him. She spent countless hours in his library. The books about voyages to faraway lands were her favorites.

When her parents died, Mary finally had time to do what she wanted with her life. She decided to travel to the most magical and unknown place she could think of: West Africa. Her friends and family all advised her against it. *It's dangerous*, they said. *A woman can't travel all that way alone. And why on Earth do you want to go to Africa?*

Mary didn't listen to them and went anyway. She traveled from village to village throughout West Africa. She canoed up the Ogowe River, and she was the first woman to climb Mount Cameroon. Being a white woman (and sometimes the first white person the local people had ever seen), she knew she was an oddity. Mary wanted to be a part of the community, not just a scientific observer, so she started trading cloth for rubber. She recorded information about the geography of West Africa, and she collected samples of **flora and fauna** from an area that was almost unknown to Europeans at the time.

She led a life of adventure, explored the complexity of African cultures, and challenged many of the racist stereotypes spread by other explorers.

OCTOBER 13, 1862–JUNE 3, 1900
UNITED KINGDOM

"THE GRIM, GRAND AFRICAN FORESTS ARE LIKE A GREAT LIBRARY. I AM NOW BUSILY LEARNING THE ALPHABET OF THEIR LANGUAGE . . ."
— MARY KINGSLEY

MARY SEACOLE

NURSE

Once there was a little girl named Mary who was great at curing her dolls. If one had a fever, Mary would lay a wet facecloth on her forehead. If another's tummy hurt, she'd give her pretend hot tea.

Mary's mother had learned the art of using herbs to make medicines, and she cured lots of illnesses in Kingston, Jamaica, the town where they lived. By the time she was 12, Mary was already helping her cure real people!

When she grew up, Mary started to travel, which was unusual for a woman at the time. She went to the Bahamas, Haiti, and Cuba to find out how the people there used herbs to treat the sick. In Panama, she risked her life to help local nurses and doctors cure patients during a cholera epidemic.

When the Crimean War broke out, Mary traveled to London to ask if the British Army needed help on the battlefront. The army said no because they were suspicious of women practicing medicine. So Mary went to Crimea on her own and opened the British Hotel, a place where wounded soldiers could recover their strength before making the long journey home.

Mary traveled right to the front lines with two mules to bring medicines and food to soldiers. For her, any wounded soldier was a wounded human being: she treated men from both sides without looking at uniforms, often while bullets flew and cannons thundered all around.

When she went back home, Mary wrote a best-selling book called *Wonderful Adventures of Mrs. Seacole in Many Lands.*

NOVEMBER 23, 1805–MAY 14, 1881
JAMAICA

ILLUSTRATION BY
ANNALISA VENTURA

"THE GRATEFUL WORDS
AND SMILE WHICH
REWARDED ME FOR
BINDING UP A WOUND
OR GIVING A COOLING
DRINK WAS A PLEASURE
WORTH RISKING LIFE FOR
AT ANY TIME."
—MARY SEACOLE

MARY SHELLEY

WRITER

Once upon a time, there was a girl named Mary whose mother died when she was just a baby. Her stepmother wasn't kind to her, and Mary missed having a mom tremendously. But she found comfort in the huge library they had at home. Every day, Mary would borrow a different book and go to her mother's grave to read it.

The books carried her away, far from the house where she felt lonely and unhappy. Soon enough, Mary started to write her own stories and poems.

One day, she met a young poet named Percy. They had their first date by Mary's mom's grave and fell deeply in love. They ran away to Paris to be together.

As they traveled across Europe, they became friends with many other artists and writers. One stormy night, Mary, Percy, and a few friends started telling one another scary stories. After a while, one of their friends proposed that they all go back to their rooms and write ghost stories and then see whose story was the most frightening.

That night, Mary came up with the idea of a mad scientist who builds a monster from bits of dead bodies and brings it to life using electricity. Everyone agreed: Mary's story of Dr. Victor Frankenstein was the scariest of them all.

Her novel, *Frankenstein; or, The Modern Prometheus*, became an incredible success, and even after 200 years, people still love to read about Dr. Frankenstein and the monster he created—all dreamed up by the amazingly imaginative Mary Shelley.

AUGUST 30, 1797–FEBRUARY 1, 1851

UNITED KINGDOM

ILLUSTRATION BY
ELISABETTA STOINICH

"BEWARE; FOR I AM FEARLESS,
AND THEREFORE POWERFUL."
—MARY SHELLEY

MARYAM MIRZAKHANI

MATHEMATICIAN

Maryam was never interested in math until the day her brother told her about a cool problem: "How do you add together all the numbers from 1 to 100?"

He explained that there were two ways to get the answer: a long and boring one, and a short and beautiful one that a mathematician called Carl Friedrich Gauss had discovered when he was still in elementary school.

Gauss took all the numbers and added them together in pairs—the first and the last, the second and the second to last, and so on. He noticed that 1 + 100 = 101, 2 + 99 = 101, 3 + 98 = 101, etc., so he was able to conclude that the total would be 50 lots of 101, which is 5050. Easy!

Maryam was hooked.

In high school, she competed in the International Mathematical Olympiad, winning the gold medal twice in a row. She became interested in the geometry of complex surfaces. *Everyone knows that the shortest path between two points on a flat surface is a straight line,* she thought, *but what about when the surface is curved, like a ball or a doughnut?* Maryam found joy in discovering simple, elegant solutions to these complicated problems. "The more I spent time on mathematics, the more excited I became," she said.

One day, her phone rang. *You've won the Fields Medal,* said a voice on the other end of the line. Maryam hung up, thinking it was a joke. But it wasn't! She was the first Iranian person—and the first woman in history—to win the world's most prestigious award for mathematics.

MAY 3, 1977–JULY 14, 2017

IRAN

ILLUSTRATION BY
GIORGIA MARRAS

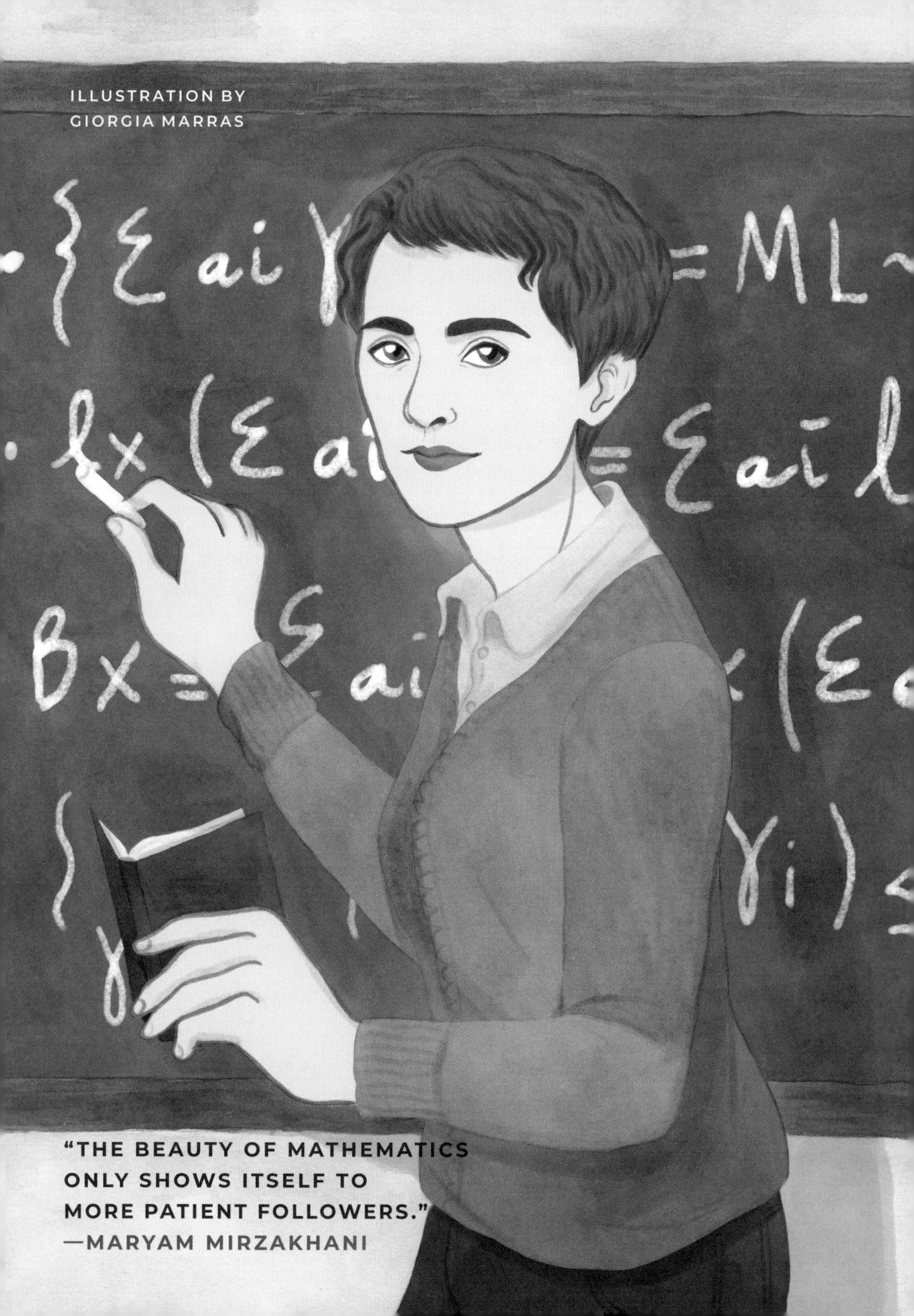

“THE BEAUTY OF MATHEMATICS
ONLY SHOWS ITSELF TO
MORE PATIENT FOLLOWERS.”
—MARYAM MIRZAKHANI

MATA HARI

SPY

Once upon a time, a young woman named Margaretha saw an advertisement in a newspaper. It said, "Wanted: bride." She answered the ad, married a military captain based in the Dutch East Indies, and moved to Indonesia. There, she studied the local traditions and joined a dance company.

But her marriage was unhappy, and when it ended, Margaretha moved to Paris. At that time, anything from "the exotic East" was very fashionable, so she pretended to be a Hindu temple dancer. She draped herself in veils and even gave herself a stage name: Mata Hari, meaning "eye of the day" in the Malay language.

She danced with the grace of a wild animal. She wore skimpy costumes, a bra studded with jewels, and skin-colored body stockings. She became an instant hit!

When Mata Hari was 40, she fell in love with a young Russian army captain who had lost an eye on a World War I battlefield. To support him, she needed a new job, so she became a spy for France.

She traveled across Europe by train and by boat. She dyed and changed her hairstyle many times and became a master of disguise. She found out about German submarines along the coast of Morocco and sent the information back to France in letters written with invisible ink.

But the French wrongly suspected that she was also spying for the Germans, and they arrested her as a double agent. She was sentenced to death. As she stood before the firing squad, she blew the soldiers a kiss. Mata Hari died as she had lived: fearless and free.

AUGUST 7, 1876–OCTOBER 15, 1917
THE NETHERLANDS

ILLUSTRATION BY
MONICA GARWOOD

"I WAS NOT CONTENT AT
HOME . . . I WANTED TO
LIVE LIKE A COLORFUL
BUTTERFLY IN THE SUN."
—MATA HARI

MATILDA OF CANOSSA

FEUDAL RULER

Long ago, in an ancient time of kings, popes, and castles, there was a woman so powerful that everyone wanted to become her friend.

Matilda ruled over a huge realm that spanned black forests and green lakes, white mountains and golden shores. She lived in Italy in a time called the Middle Ages, when the two biggest powers were the Roman Catholic Church and the Holy Roman Empire. The head of the Holy Roman Empire was Henry IV, Matilda's cousin. The head of the Catholic Church was Pope Gregory VII, Matilda's friend.

One day, Henry realized that Gregory was becoming too powerful. So he declared that the people of the Holy Roman Empire no longer had to be loyal to the pope. Gregory was furious and gathered a huge army to fight back.

Henry asked Matilda for help. She had a powerful army of her own, and she could have backed her cousin in his campaign. But Matilda refused.

I will only help you obtain the pope's forgiveness, she said.

She arranged a meeting between the two men at her magnificent castle in Canossa, in northern Italy. It was winter, and the forest surrounding her castle was covered in snow.

Henry spent three days and three nights kneeling barefoot in the snow, to show repentance. When he was finally allowed to enter the castle, the pope forgave him. But their truce didn't last long.

The battle between the Holy Roman Empire and the Catholic Church had just begun, and Matilda had to lead many military expeditions against the emperor's army to protect the pope. After 20 years of battles, she was crowned imperial vicar and vice-queen of Italy.

MARCH 1046–JULY 24, 1115

ITALY

MERRITT MOORE

QUANTUM PHYSICIST AND BALLERINA

Once upon a time, there was a girl who loved science and ballet. She was equally talented at both, but everyone said: *You'll have to choose. Science or art? Physics or ballet?*

Merritt tried to give up ballet many times. She even burned her pointe shoes! But she always started dancing again. Eventually, she joined the Zurich Ballet Company and became a professional ballerina. At the same time, she was researching physics at Harvard University. One minute she would be in her tutu and pointe shoes, and the next she'd be in a lab coat.

"There have been times that I have felt overwhelmed," she said, "when I have been in the lab for 20 hours a day, literally sleeping there." But she would take a break from work, sneak out to a stairwell, and practice ballet. When she did, she found that she returned to the lab with a fresh perspective. And she discovered that physics helped her understand dance too. "I think it's so important for a scientist to explore art, because you have to think about concepts with imagination and creativity."

The two parts of her life came together beautifully in a dance piece called *Zero Point*, which explored a concept from **quantum physics** called **zero-point energy**.

Merritt finished her PhD at Oxford University, and she keeps on dancing. Her favorite quote is from one of the greatest scientists in history, Albert Einstein: "Life is like riding a bicycle. To keep your balance, you must keep moving." And that's just what Merritt intends to do!

BORN FEBRUARY 24, 1988
UNITED STATES OF AMERICA

"I WANT TO SHATTER ALL THE STEREOTYPES.
THE DREAM IS TO CONTINUE COMBINING
PHYSICS AND DANCE."
—MERRITT MOORE

ILLUSTRATION BY
MARINA MUUN

MOLLY KELLY, DAISY KADIBIL, AND GRACIE FIELDS

FREEDOM FIGHTERS

One day, a white man in a car chased three Aboriginal girls and a woman through the Australian desert. The woman screamed, kicked, and tried to protect Molly, Daisy, and Gracie, but the man caught hold of the girls and drove away, disappearing in a cloud of dark orange sand.

At the time, white settlers in Australia abducted children who had both white and Aboriginal parents so they could detain them in camps and train them to work as servants for white families. The settlers wanted to strip the Aboriginal culture from the children and force them to conform instead. The man took the three girls to one of these camps.

Molly was 14 when she decided to flee with her sister, Daisy, and their cousin, Gracie. *Look,* she said to the two younger girls, pointing at a dark cloud on the horizon. *It's about to rain. Now's our chance to run. The rain will wash away our tracks!*

As they walked, Molly, Daisy, and Gracie hunted for food, waded across rivers, slept under bushes, and took turns carrying each other. They knew there was a fence built to keep rabbits from getting into the farmland that ran across Australia from north to south. So they followed it north to find their village. They walked for nine weeks. Finally, they made it!

Years later, Molly's daughter wrote a book, *Follow the Rabbit-Proof Fence*, which inspired a film about Molly, Daisy, and Gracie's story.

MOLLY KELLY, 1917–JANUARY 13, 2004
DAISY KADIBIL, 1923–MARCH 30, 2018
GRACIE FIELDS, 1920–JULY 1983

AUSTRALIA

ILLUSTRATION BY
SARA OLMOS

"I WANTED TO GO HOME—TO MOTHER."
—MOLLY KELLY

NADIA COMĂNECI

GYMNAST

When she was six years old, Nadia wanted to do only one thing: cartwheels. At the time, cartwheels were a very big deal in her country of Romania, but Nadia didn't know that yet.

One day, she was playing in the schoolyard when she was spotted by a famous gymnastics coach named Béla Károlyi. He thought that with the right training, Nadia could become a great gymnast and bring glory to the Communist regime in Romania.

Training was hard. If the kids made a mistake, Béla would beat them with his huge hands. They had to train for six hours a day, seven days a week. He wanted his gymnasts to be perfect.

And Nadia became perfect—literally. At the age of 14, she scored a 10 at the Olympic Games in Montreal. No gymnast had ever received a perfect score before. People were amazed at her faultless performances on the beam, the vault, and the uneven bars. Nadia became a legend.

In fact, she became so famous that the Romanian leader grew worried she would overshadow him. He wouldn't let her leave the country for any reason other than to compete.

So Nadia decided to escape. One morning, she walked for six hours through muddy woodlands and crossed the border into Hungary on foot. From there, she moved to the United States, where she was welcomed as a refugee.

In the US, Nadia started a family and built a business. She loved gymnastics and worked to promote it the way she liked the most: as a free woman.

BORN NOVEMBER 12, 1961
ROMANIA

ILLUSTRATION BY
ELINE VAN DAM

"YOU MUST
FIGURE OUT
YOUR OWN
DESTINATION
AND THE BEST
ROUTE TO GET
THERE BECAUSE
NO ONE ELSE
KNOWS THE WAY."
—NADIA COMĂNECI

NADIA MURAD

HUMAN RIGHTS ACTIVIST

In the village of Kocho, there was a girl named Nadia who dreamed of becoming a history teacher or a makeup artist. Nadia belonged to the Yazidi religion, an ancient faith indigenous to northern Iraq.

One terrible day when Nadia was around 20, a terrorist group called ISIS invaded Kocho, killed her brothers, and kidnapped her and many other Yazidi women.

Nadia was held hostage by men who hurt her badly. She was desperate, but she constantly looked for opportunities to escape. One day, she noticed that her captors had forgotten to lock the door. Without a moment's hesitation, she slipped out and ran!

A neighboring family helped her leave the region and reach a refugee camp, where she would be safe. *I might not be a history teacher or a makeup artist*, she thought, *but I'll do all I can to help other women who are still prisoners of ISIS.*

Nadia was resettled in Germany, where she started working with a nonprofit organization.

It was hard for her to talk about what she'd been through. But Nadia realized that if she kept silent, no one would know what was happening to girls like her. She found the courage to speak out.

She told her story to journalists and spoke before the United Nations. Thanks to her testimony, global leaders learned about the terrible violence being perpetrated by ISIS fighters.

Nadia won the Nobel Peace Prize in 2018 for advocating on behalf of women everywhere.

BORN 1993
IRAQ

ILLUSTRATION BY
PING ZHU

"I WILL GO BACK TO MY LIFE WHEN
WOMEN IN CAPTIVITY GO BACK
TO THEIR LIVES, WHEN MY COMMUNITY
HAS A PLACE, WHEN I SEE PEOPLE
ACCOUNTABLE FOR THEIR CRIMES."
—NADIA MURAD

NADINE GORDIMER

~~~

AUTHOR AND POLITICAL ACTIVIST

O nce upon a time in South Africa, there was a girl who cared deeply about justice and equality. Her name was Nadine. Back then, South Africa was still under a brutal system called apartheid, which segregated and discriminated against Black people. Nadine was white and could see what a difference this single fact made to her life. She could go to any school, but her Black friends couldn't. She could go to movie theaters, but her Black friends couldn't. She could enter any shops she liked, but her Black friends couldn't.

When the police opened fire on a crowd of protesters, killing 69 people, Nadine decided to join the anti-apartheid movement. She wanted to tell the world the truth about what was happening in South Africa.

One day, she met a brilliant man called Nelson Mandela—a lawyer who would later become the country's first Black president. Nelson was determined to end apartheid through peaceful political means, and he and Nadine immediately became friends. When Nelson was arrested and tried for his political activism, Nadine helped him edit a famous speech he gave in his own defense, called "I Am Prepared to Die."

Nadine wrote several books addressing apartheid that the South African government banned for years. But she continued to write relentlessly. The whole world had discovered her voice and wanted to listen to her epic message of freedom and justice. She received a Nobel Prize for Literature and lived long enough to see the apartheid era come to an end.

~~~

NOVEMBER 20, 1923–JULY 13, 2014

SOUTH AFRICA

"THE TRUTH ISN'T
ALWAYS BEAUTY,
BUT THE HUNGER
FOR IT IS."
—NADINE GORDIMER

NEFERTITI

QUEEN

Long ago in ancient Egypt, there ruled a mysterious queen called Nefertiti. Her name meant "a beautiful woman has come," but it offered no clue as to where she had come from. Nefertiti was as **enigmatic** as she was powerful.

She had six daughters and reigned alongside her husband, Akhenaten. The two wore the same crown and fought side by side in battles. Nefertiti promoted a radically new art style, and she changed Egypt from a polytheistic society, or one that believed in many gods, into a culture that worshipped only one: Aten, the sun god.

Then one day, Nefertiti disappeared.

Even now, no one knows what happened to her. If she had died, she would have received a royal burial like other kings and queens, but her tomb has never been found. Some believe that she outlived her husband, because images of her stood at each corner of his tomb. Some believe that when her husband died, she began to dress as a man and changed her name to Pharaoh Smenkhkare to become Egypt's sole ruler.

A few years ago, archaeologists were working in the tomb of another great king, Tutankhamun. One of them noticed some strange cracks in a wall. Could there be another burial chamber hidden behind it? Using a special underground radar, the archaeologists discovered that there was, in fact, a room there!

Was it the tomb of ancient Egypt's long-lost queen? Nobody knows— yet. Until they can open the chamber without damaging the fragile walls, Nefertiti's fate will remain wrapped in mystery.

CIRCA 1370 BCE–CIRCA 1330 BCE

EGYPT

ILLUSTRATION BY
ELENI KALORKOTI

OPRAH WINFREY

TV HOST, ACTOR, AND BUSINESSWOMAN

Once there was a little girl who interviewed crows. She also interviewed her corncob dolls. And she was so good at reciting from the Bible that people nicknamed her the Preacher.

Her name was Oprah, and she loved to talk, but her family didn't listen. Her mother brushed her away, saying, *Be quiet! I don't have time for you.* Her grandmother never let her cry. *People will think you're weak*, she'd say.

But keeping everything bottled up inside was unbearable.

So Oprah kept looking for opportunities to speak out. She kept looking for people who would listen to what she had to say. First, she joined the public speaking team in high school, then she took a job at a local radio station, and eventually she joined a Baltimore TV news show as a co-anchor.

Her family and friends were excited. But deep inside, Oprah wasn't sure that reporting the news was what she loved the most. She was fired from the show and given a low-rated early morning talk show. Oprah thought her career was over. Instead, while interviewing an ice-cream seller, she discovered her greatest talent: connecting with compassion. People started to love the show because she really listened to her guests. If they cried, she felt their sadness. If they were angry, she understood their pain. And if they were happy, she laughed with them.

Oprah became the queen of talk shows. She moved on to national television. She launched her own TV network and became a multi-billionaire and one of the most generous philanthropists in history.

BORN JANUARY 29, 1954
UNITED STATES OF AMERICA

"YOU GET IN LIFE WHAT YOU HAVE
THE COURAGE TO ASK FOR."
—OPRAH WINFREY

ILLUSTRATION BY
PALESA MONARENG

PAULINE LÉON

REVOLUTIONARY

Pauline was born in a chocolate shop in Paris. Her parents, like most people in France at that time, were simple, hardworking folk. They were part of what was known as the Third Estate—people who were neither rich landowners nor priests in the Catholic Church.

The people of the Third Estate worked hard every day, but for most, there was never enough food on the table. The rich didn't pay as much in taxes—a situation that people like Pauline thought was unfair. She wanted freedom and equality for everyone—and she wanted it now.

At the age of 21, Pauline helped to start a revolution. At the time, women were not supposed to get involved in politics, but Pauline didn't care. She wanted to fight for her country. She believed that it was a citizen's duty to protect their nation, regardless of their class or gender.

One morning, about a thousand people decided to storm a Parisian fortress called the Bastille. Pauline was among them, armed with a pike. It was the beginning of the mother of all revolutions, the French Revolution—an event that would shape the future of Europe for centuries to come.

Pauline encouraged other women to take part in the revolution, and she founded a group called *femmes sans culottes*, or "women without breeches." Breeches were fancy silk pants worn by the nobility. Revolutionaries wore sturdy trousers instead.

Eventually, the French Revolution overthrew the monarchy, established a republic, and altered the course of history. And it's all thanks to citizens such as Pauline Léon, the revolutionary born in a chocolate shop.

SEPTEMBER 28, 1768–OCTOBER 5, 1838

FRANCE

ILLUSTRATION BY
SARAH MAZZETTI

"THE RHETORIC OF
THE REVOLUTION MUST
BE APPLIED TO BOTH
SEXES EQUALLY . . ."
—PAULINE LÉON

PEGGY GUGGENHEIM

ART COLLECTOR

Once upon a time, there was a girl who inherited a fortune. Her name was Peggy, and her dad had died tragically when the *Titanic* sank. She was just 14 years old.

Peggy loved to travel, but even more than that, she loved art and artists. To meet as many artists as she could, she worked as a clerk in an avant-garde bookstore in Manhattan, and later she moved to Paris, where she became friends with some of the world's most talented writers and painters.

Peggy was on a mission to build a collection of the finest works of modern art in the world. She chose carefully, buying one painting a day with a very clear idea of who should be included in her collection.

During World War II, Peggy was terrified that her priceless paintings would be destroyed by the bombs falling on Paris. She asked curators at the Louvre Museum for help, but they told her she didn't have anything worth protecting. *Braque, Picasso, Klee, Dalí, Magritte—not worth protecting?* Peggy was outraged. She ended up storing her paintings in a friend's barn outside Paris.

After the war, Peggy moved to Venice, Italy. She floated around the city in her private gondola with her beloved dogs on her lap, always sporting a pair of jazzy sunglasses.

She was a driving force in the male-dominated art world of the 20th century. The Peggy Guggenheim Collection—one of the most important museums in Italy—is located in her former Venetian home, right on the banks of the Grand Canal.

AUGUST 26, 1898–DECEMBER 23, 1979
UNITED STATES OF AMERICA

ILLUSTRATION BY
KATE PRIOR

"I LOOK BACK ON MY LIFE
WITH GREAT JOY . . .
I ALWAYS DID WHAT I
WANTED AND NEVER CARED
WHAT ANYONE THOUGHT."
—PEGGY GUGGENHEIM

POORNA MALAVATH

MOUNTAINEER

Once upon a time, a girl called Poorna went on a rock climbing expedition with her classmates. When they arrived at the Bhongir rock, in southern India, she looked up at the huge cliff that she was supposed to climb. Her legs shook and there were tears in her eyes. *I'll never make it*, she thought.

But Poorna's teacher, a local police officer, encouraged her. *You can do it*, he said. So she tried. When she reached the top, she shouted for joy. *I'm not afraid of anything now*, she said. *I can conquer Mount Everest!* And she wasn't just saying it—Poorna actually wanted to climb the highest mountain in the world.

Before setting off for that next adventure, she had to train hard. She built up her stamina playing *kabaddi*—a sport similar to a high-energy version of tag. She traveled to the high plateaus of northern India in the freezing winter, and she climbed to the top of Mount Renock, one of the most challenging peaks in the Himalayas.

When she was ready, she joined an expedition to scale Mount Everest. She wasn't at all afraid when she first saw the mighty mountain. *It's not that tall*, she said to her coach. *We can do that in a day.*

Well, it took 52 days to get to the top, but when she reached the summit, Poorna, age 13, became the youngest girl ever to make it.

Poorna went on to climb to the top of Mount Kilimanjaro, in Tanzania, but her highest aspiration is to become a police officer—just like the teacher who helped her conquer her fear.

BORN JUNE 10, 2000

INDIA

"I WANTED TO PROVE THAT GIRLS CAN DO ANYTHING."
—POORNA MALAVATH

ILLUSTRATION BY
PRIYA KURIYAN

QIU JIN

REVOLUTIONARY

Once upon a time, a girl named Qiu Jin followed her father's orders and married a wealthy merchant she didn't love. Unsurprisingly, theirs was not a happy marriage.

"[His] behavior is worse than an animal's. . . . He treats me as less than nothing," Qiu Jin wrote. She dreamed of becoming a famous poet, but her husband made fun of her and told her she'd never reach her goals.

At that time, China was evolving from an empire ruled by a dynasty into a republic run by the people. Every day, revolutionary groups formed and underground newspapers spread new ideas about the future of the country. Qiu Jin wanted to be part of this transformation, so she left her abusive husband and moved to Japan.

There, she educated herself about women's rights, and she learned that the ancient practice of **foot-binding** was hurting millions of Chinese girls.

When she returned home, Qiu Jin founded the *Chinese Women's Journal*. She also began encouraging women to overthrow the Qing dynasty. "With all my heart," she wrote, "I beseech and beg my two hundred million countrywomen to assume their responsibility as citizens. Arise! Arise! Chinese women, arise!"

Qiu Jin opened a school that was supposed to train sports teachers but actually trained revolutionaries. She was warned that government officials were on their way to arrest her, yet she refused to flee. *I'm willing to die for the cause*, she said.

She was executed, but she became a national hero and a symbol of women's independence in China and all over the world.

NOVEMBER 8, 1875–JULY 15, 1907

CHINA

ILLUSTRATION BY
GIORGIA MARRAS

"DON'T TELL ME WOMEN ARE
NOT THE STUFF OF HEROES."
—QIU JIN

RACHEL CARSON

ENVIRONMENTALIST

Once there was a girl who loved to write stories about animals. Her name was Rachel, and she would grow up to become one of the world's most passionate guardians of the environment.

After graduating college with a degree in zoology, Rachel went back home to care for her aging mother. She found a job writing a series of radio shows about fish. No one else could make marine biology sound so exciting, and Rachel's program, called *Romance Under the Waters*, was a big hit. It showed that she was not only an amazing scientist but also a fine writer.

Despite having to earn a living and care for her mother, Rachel found time to write two beautiful books, called *The Sea Around Us* and *The Edge of the Sea*. And when her sister died, she even adopted her two nieces, raising them as her own.

Years later, Rachel and her mother moved to a little town in the countryside. There, she started to notice the impact of pesticides on wildlife. At that time, farmers routinely sprayed chemicals on their crops to protect them from insects. What Rachel discovered was that these chemicals were poisoning other plants, animals, birds, and even humans. She wrote a book about it called *Silent Spring*.

The people who sold pesticides tried to stop her, but Rachel kept on talking about what she'd learned. *Silent Spring* was voted one of the most important science books ever written. It has inspired millions of people to join the environmental movement and campaign for the well-being of all species on Earth, not just our own.

MAY 27, 1907–APRIL 14, 1964
UNITED STATES OF AMERICA

ILLUSTRATION BY
SARAH WILKINS

"IN NATURE NOTHING
EXISTS ALONE."
—RACHEL CARSON

RIGOBERTA MENCHÚ TUM

POLITICAL ACTIVIST

Once there was a girl who was told she didn't matter. She lived high in the mountains of Guatemala. But she and her family had to work down in the valleys picking coffee beans. The plantation owners worked them hard and beat them if they did not pick fast enough. The workers were treated like enslaved people. They were paid hardly anything. *Your life is not worth a bag of beans*, her bosses told her.

My name is Rigoberta, she replied, *and my life is worth just as much as yours.*

Rigoberta was proud of her people and her culture. The Mayans of Guatemala could trace their history back to ancient times. They had a rich and wonderful civilization. But they had been forced into poverty. They were beaten and even killed by soldiers if they dared to protest.

Rigoberta started fighting for better conditions and equal rights for her people. She organized strikes and demonstrations. Although she could not read or write, she spoke with such conviction that more and more people joined her cause. Many were taken away and killed, including Rigoberta's own parents and her brother. The government tried to silence her. Local landowners tried to break her, but no one could crush her fearless spirit. She insisted on telling her story—not because it was hers but because it was the story of oppressed Indigenous peoples everywhere.

Rigoberta played a large part in ending the civil war in Guatemala. For this and for her life's work campaigning for the rights of the poor, she was awarded the Nobel Peace Prize.

BORN JANUARY 9, 1959
GUATEMALA

"I AM LIKE A DROP OF WATER ON A
ROCK. AFTER DRIP, DRIP, DRIPPING
IN THE SAME PLACE, I BEGIN TO
LEAVE A MARK, AND I LEAVE MY
MARK IN MANY PEOPLE'S HEARTS."
—RIGOBERTA MENCHÚ TUM

ROSALIND FRANKLIN

CHEMIST AND X-RAY CRYSTALLOGRAPHER

Once upon a time, there was a girl who discovered the secret of life. Her name was Rosalind, and she was an extraordinary chemist. She was also an X-ray **crystallographer** who worked as a researcher in the biophysics lab at King's College London.

Rosalind studied DNA, a molecule carrying information that tells our bodies how to develop and function. Today, we know that DNA is shaped like a double helix—basically a twisted ladder—but in Rosalind's time, the scientific community had no idea what DNA looked like.

Rosalind spent hundreds of hours using X-rays to photograph DNA fibers and trying to unveil the secret of life. She even improved the machines she used so she could get the best possible picture.

Each photo took about a hundred hours to develop. One day, her team got an incredible shot that provided groundbreaking information about the structure of DNA. They called it *Photograph 51*.

One of the scientists working with Rosalind, Maurice Wilkins, didn't like her, so without telling her, he sent the photo to two competing scientists who were also studying DNA. When those two scientists, James Watson and Francis Crick, saw the picture, their jaws dropped. They used *Photograph 51* as the basis of their 3D model of DNA, which eventually won them a Nobel Prize in Physiology or Medicine.

Rosalind left King's College London to work in other areas. She made crucial discoveries about how viruses spread infection. For this—and for her vital contribution to the discovery of DNA—she is now acknowledged as one of the most important scientists of the 20th century.

JULY 25, 1920–APRIL 16, 1958

UNITED KINGDOM

"SCIENCE AND EVERYDAY LIFE CANNOT AND SHOULD NOT BE SEPARATED."
—ROSALIND FRANKLIN

ILLUSTRATION BY LIEKELAND

RUBY BRIDGES

CIVIL RIGHTS ACTIVIST

Once upon a time in New Orleans, there lived an incredibly brave girl named Ruby. She had to walk miles to get to her school, even though there was one closer to her home. But that school was all-white, and Ruby was Black. *You can't stop my child from going to a school because of the color of her skin*, said Ruby's mom. *It's wrong. And it's against the law.*

Even though members of the school board didn't want to admit it, they knew Ruby's mom was right. They made Ruby take a tough exam to get in—hoping that she would fail. But Ruby aced the test!

She was excited to go to her new school, but when she and her mom arrived on her first day, they found a crowd of angry people shouting racist slogans at the gate. "I didn't actually know that all of that was there because of me," remembered Ruby. She was just six years old. And when she entered the building, parents rushed in to pull their children from the school, until a total of 500 students walked out.

Each day, Ruby went to school with four United States Marshals to protect her. The sight of this small girl flanked by her big bodyguards inspired the artist Norman Rockwell to produce a famous painting called *The Problem We All Live With*.

Ruby grew up to be a brilliant civil rights activist and icon. She even went to the White House to meet President Barack Obama, and together they looked at Rockwell's painting, which hung outside the Oval Office. "We should never look at a person and judge them by the color of their skin," Ruby said. "That's the lesson I learned in first grade."

BORN SEPTEMBER 8, 1954
UNITED STATES OF AMERICA

"I REFUSE TO BELIEVE THERE IS
MORE EVIL THAN GOOD."
—RUBY BRIDGES

ILLUSTRATION BY
GIULIA TOMAI

SAMANTHA CRISTOFORETTI

ASTRONAUT

Once there was an engineer who brewed espresso in outer space. Her name was Samantha, and she was also an astronaut.

Samantha had studied mechanical engineering and aeronautics in college. After she graduated, she joined a flight school and finished at the top of her class. Samantha became a fighter pilot in the Italian Air Force, but she wanted to fly even higher.

So she applied to the European Space Agency to join its space program. Only six pilots out of more than 8,000 applicants were selected. Samantha was one of them.

For two years, she trained. At an underwater military training camp in Houston, Texas, Samantha had to learn how to assemble equipment at the bottom of a pool four times deeper than a normal one, how to swim while wearing a space suit, and how to fight under water. She even had to learn how to speak Russian!

Once she had mastered all that, she was ready to go.

At the International Space Station, Captain Cristoforetti performed experiments for 200 days to study how the human body reacts to long stretches of time spent in zero gravity. *In the future*, she predicted, *the human race will live on multiple planets, so it's important to know what happens to our bodies in outer space.*

During the mission, Samantha also experimented with different kinds of food. *Who would want to live on Mars*, she asked, *if they could only eat stuff squeezed out of a tube?* She was the third European woman to travel to space—and the first person to brew espresso there!

BORN APRIL 26, 1977
ITALY

· 154 ·

ILLUSTRATION BY GIULIA TOMAI

"WHEN IT SEEMS TO YOU THAT THERE IS NO WAY OUT, STOP, BREATHE, AND CHANGE YOUR PERSPECTIVE."
—SAMANTHA CRISTOFORETTI

SAPPHO

POET

Along time ago, on a small island in the Aegean Sea called Lesbos, there lived a poet. Her name was Sappho.

Sappho had dark hair and a sweet smile. She ran a special boarding school where girls were educated in art and religion. She also wrote poems that were read and sung during public ceremonies, often as a farewell to the students who were ready to leave the school.

Sappho wrote about the intense emotional bond between girls and young women. In ancient Greece at that time, married women weren't able to have the close friendships they had enjoyed at school. Instead, they were mostly confined to their husbands' homes. Sappho's poems celebrated the loving relationships that existed between girls, to remind older women of the friendships they had enjoyed in their younger days. The greatest writers and thinkers of the time praised her work, and she inspired many others. She even created a new form of poetry, called the **Sapphic stanza**.

She wrote her lines of verse on papyrus scrolls, some of which were carefully stored in the Great Library of Alexandria in Egypt. But over the centuries, most of the fragile scrolls were lost. Although Sappho wrote more than 10,000 lines during her life, only a few fragments of her poems have survived to the present day.

Sappho's poetry is so romantic that for thousands of years she has symbolized women's love around the world. And that is why women who love women are called lesbians, after the beautiful Greek island where Sappho lived.

CIRCA 610 BCE–CIRCA 570 BCE

GREECE

ILLUSTRATION BY
ELENI KALORKOTI

"I DECLARE THAT LATER ON,
EVEN IN AN AGE UNLIKE
OUR OWN, SOMEONE WILL
REMEMBER WHO WE ARE."
—SAPPHO

SARA SEAGER

Once upon a time, there lived a girl whose mind seemed to work much faster than everyone else's. She could make connections between things in the blink of an eye. She didn't watch TV because it seemed slow and boring. She preferred to be up in her bedroom looking through her telescope.

While other people looked at the moon or the stars, Sara looked at the spaces in between. She knew that in the dark spaces, there were billions more stars, and that most of those had planets circling around them, just like Earth orbits the sun. Were they far enough from their own suns not to burn up? Were they near enough not to be permanently frozen? Were they in that sweet spot—that one chance in a million—where life could form?

Sara grew up to be a real-life alien hunter. At her job at the Massachusetts Institute of Technology, she looked for signs of life on exoplanets—planets beyond our own solar system that orbit stars in distant galaxies. In the hallway outside her office, she had a poster of one of them: a rocky desert with two suns burning in the sky, just like Luke Skywalker's home planet, Tatooine, in the *Star Wars* movies.

Sara eventually had two boys who are proud of their mom—a certified genius and one of the top astrophysicists in the world. She says she is not very practical and admits that she couldn't change a light bulb at home. Although she sometimes can't find her boys' socks, she might just find a whole new Earth!

BORN JULY 21, 1971
CANADA

"BEING A SCIENTIST IS LIKE BEING AN EXPLORER."
—SARA SEAGER

ILLUSTRATION BY JOANA ESTRELA

SARINYA SRISAKUL

FIREFIGHTER

One day, a young woman went to her father with some exciting news. *Dad*, she said, *I've signed up to become a firefighter!* Her father was stunned. *It's dangerous*, he said. *It's not a very good job for a woman. And anyway, we're from Thailand—there aren't any Asian people in New York's fire department.* But Sarinya was determined.

She went through a tough three-month boot camp, where she learned how to fight kitchen and car fires, how to maneuver aerial ladders, and how to handle lots of other challenges. She was the only woman trainee, and one of the very few who wasn't white. It was extremely hard, but she made it.

Firefighters need to be fit to deal with all sorts of emergencies, so to keep in shape, Sarinya began to bike from home to work and back again. Every day she faced new and unexpected situations: stuck elevators, suspicious packages, floods, car accidents, gas leaks, and more. "I never knew what to expect when I walked in the fire station door," Sarinya explained. "Being a firefighter is really fun and exciting, and you get to help people."

Whenever there was a woman who needed help, Sarinya was always first on the scene. "Sometimes seeing a face that looks like yours gives a huge relief to someone's emotional state," she says. The fact that she spoke several languages was also a big advantage in New York City, where there are so many people from different cultures and not everyone speaks English.

There are now twice as many women in the New York City Fire Department than there were when she started. "I am also the first and only Asian woman firefighter in the FDNY," says Sarinya. "I am psyched for number two, and more, to come along one day!"

BORN CIRCA 1980
UNITED STATES OF AMERICA

"THE MAIN THING ABOUT BEING 'HEROIC' IS HELPING OTHERS."
—SARINYA SRISAKUL

ILLUSTRATION BY LISK FENG

SELDA BAĞCAN

SINGER AND SONGWRITER

Once there was a girl in Turkey who spent every night playing and singing with her brothers, pretending to be the Beatles. When she grew up, Selda moved to the city of Ankara to study physics. Her brothers had also moved there, and they ran a popular music club called Beethoven.

Every night, Selda would put down her books, pick up her electric guitar, and head to Beethoven. The club was packed whenever Selda played. She put a rock twist on Turkish **folk music**. Nobody had ever heard anything like it before!

Selda's music was political, and her lyrics directly challenged the government. "Why is it so hard to make new roads?" she would sing. When a military regime took power in Turkey, Selda was banned from appearing on TV and arrested three times. The government even took away her passport so she couldn't leave the country.

But nobody could stop Selda's music.

Millions of people all over the world danced to her songs. When she was finally free to travel again, she headed for London, England, where thousands of fans were waiting for her.

Selda started touring and even set up her own record label. When she found out that an American rapper had sampled her music without her permission and without paying her, she sued his record company. She didn't win, but she wasn't mad at the artist. She said she was proud that he'd used her song to rap about the Black American human rights activist Malcolm X. *Yes, he cheated me*, she thought. *But for a good cause.*

BORN 1948
TURKEY

SELDA

ILLUSTRATION BY
GIULIA TOMAI

"SONGS ARE MORE
DANGEROUS THAN
WEAPONS, YOU KNOW."
—SELDA BAĞCAN

SERAFINA BATTAGLIA

ANTI-MAFIA WITNESS

Serafina owned a coffee shop. Her husband was a criminal. He belonged to a violent organization called the Mafia. He and his friends would meet at her coffee shop to plot all sorts of crimes.

Serafina heard the men plotting, but she never spoke up or tried to stop them. In her twisted world, people who went to the police were despised, while those who robbed and killed were admired.

One fateful day, the men in her husband's gang turned against him. They killed him and Serafina's son. Many other women had seen their loved ones killed, but none of them had spoken out. For Serafina, though, this was too much. She realized that her silence had allowed terrible things to happen.

Wrapped in a mourning shawl, she went to court to face the men accused of killing her son. There, the most powerful Mafia bosses in Italy stood behind bars like animals in a cage. Serafina held the bars and looked the men in the eye. "You drank my son's blood," she said, "and here, before God and man, I spit in your face." And she did. Then she turned to the judge and said, "Mafia bosses have no honor."

That was the start of a 10-year collaboration between Serafina and the police. Thanks to her, officers arrested hundreds of criminals. Some of them later bribed the judges and walked free, but even so, Serafina had set an example. After her, many more women started to speak out.

"If all the women talked about what they know of their men," she said, "the Mafia would no longer exist."

1919–SEPTEMBER 9, 2004
ITALY

ILLUSTRATION BY
GIORGIA MARRAS

per
Cesare
Terranova

"JUSTICE IS MY WEAPON."
—SERAFINA BATTAGLIA

SHAMSIA HASSANI

GRAFFITI ARTIST

SCAN TO HEAR MORE

Once upon a time, there was a girl who was an incredibly fast painter. In just a few minutes, she would create a mural and be gone. Her name was Shamsia, and she lived in Kabul, Afghanistan.

There was a good reason for Shamsia to be so quick: if she got caught making art in the streets, she would be harassed by people who believed an Afghan woman should be at home, not painting on walls. Afghanistan could be a dangerous place for women—especially those who wanted to change the rules.

Shamsia used her art to advance women's rights in her country. *Graffiti is a friendly way to fight,* she thought. *Most people don't go to art galleries or museums. But if I create my art in the streets, they will see it.*

Shamsia couldn't paint on big buildings, however, because each mural would take too much time to complete, increasing the risk of getting caught. Instead, she chose staircases, walls of narrow streets, back alleys—hidden passages that people still used on a daily basis.

She mainly painted women—big, tall women. In one of Shamsia's murals, a girl is playing a red electric guitar. In another one, on a cracked wall near a staircase, a tall woman wearing a light blue **burka** is looking up toward the sky. She wanted people to notice them and begin to see women in a new way.

"Art cannot change anything directly," she says, "Art can only change people's minds, and then people's minds can change the society. That is what I hope for."

BORN 1988

AFGHANISTAN

ILLUSTRATION BY
CRISTINA PORTOLANO

"I WANT TO SHOW
THAT WOMEN HAVE
RETURNED TO
AFGHAN SOCIETY
WITH A NEW,
STRONGER SHAPE."
—SHAMSIA HASSANI

SIMONE VEIL

POLITICIAN

Simone could not understand war. *Why would one country want to attack another?* she wondered. She was a Jewish girl living through World War II—one of the most violent conflicts the world had ever seen—and her whole family had been sent by the Nazis to a concentration camp.

By the time the war came to an end, Simone had lost her mom, her dad, and her brother.

She had witnessed so much injustice that she felt a great urge to do something about it. She studied law and became a judge in France.

Simone got married to a man who worked in aeronautics. One day, the French president visited their home to ask her husband if he would like to join the government. By the end of the president's visit, it was Simone who was offered the job. She became the health minister in the president's cabinet.

When France and other countries decided to unite their citizens in the European Union, Simone ran to become a member of the European Parliament. She won—and even became its first president!

As president, Simone focused on reconciliation, even when that meant working with Germany, whose Nazi regime had once caused so much pain to her people. But she knew war was not—and had never been—an answer. She believed that peace and justice were worth fighting for. Simone thought that was what the European dream was about, and she devoted her life to it.

"The idea of war was for me something terrible," Simone Veil once told a journalist. "The only possible option was to make peace."

JULY 13, 1927–JUNE 30, 2017

FRANCE

"EUROPE'S
DESTINY AND
THE FUTURE OF
THE FREE WORLD
ARE ENTIRELY
IN OUR HANDS."
—SIMONE VEIL

SKY BROWN

SKATEBOARDER

Once upon a time in Japan, there was a little girl called Sky. Sky's dad was a skateboarder, and she loved watching him zoom up slopes and perform amazing stunts. Although she could barely walk, Sky used to balance on his skateboard and try to copy him.

At first, Sky's dad was afraid she'd fall and hurt herself, but then he realized that she was a natural at skateboarding. He bought her a board of her very own.

When Sky went to the skate park to practice, the older boys would sometimes cut in front of her. What could this little girl know about skateboarding? Well, she knew quite a bit.

Being underestimated pushed Sky to train harder, to jump higher, and to learn more tricks. Soon, she was the youngest skater ever at the Vans US Open Pro Series, a professional skateboarding tour.

Nobody gets good at skating without suffering their share of bloody knees, scraped elbows, and the occasional broken bone, and Sky has tumbled off her board many times. Once, she fell in a steep bowl during a competition. She couldn't climb out on her own, but three of her fellow skaters helped her clamber to the top. They gave her a high five when she made it out.

It's okay to fall, she thought, *when you can count on people to pick you up! I want to be just like them: a good skater and a good person.*

Sky continues to push the limits and challenge much older competitors in the male-dominated skateboarding world.

BORN JULY 7, 2008

JAPAN

SOFIA IONESCU-OGREZEANU

NEUROSURGEON

O nce there was a girl with wonderful hands: strong and steady, with long, elegant fingers. *With hands like those, you could be a pianist or a painter,* said her schoolteachers. Art and music were all very well, but Sofia had something else in mind. A young friend of hers had died following brain surgery. Sofia wanted to become a neurosurgeon to help save the lives of people like her friend.

At that time, there were hardly any female doctors in Romania, and female neurosurgeons were extremely rare anywhere in the world. Sofia's teachers didn't think she was smart enough to even get into medical school. But she studied hard by the light of a streetlamp shining through her bedroom window, and with her mother's constant support, she passed all her courses and exams and became a doctor.

During World War II, Sofia volunteered to take care of wounded soldiers in the hospital near her home. She operated on them—mostly performing amputations when their arms or legs had been so badly damaged that they could not be saved. But she still wanted most of all to be a neurosurgeon, operating on the brain.

One day, she got her chance. A boy was rushed into the hospital with terrible injuries to his head. As bombs fell around them, Sofia took up a scalpel and looked at her hands—they were strong and steady as always. That day, she saved the young boy's life.

After the war, Sofia trained as a neurosurgeon, and through her long and distinguished career, she saved many, many more lives.

APRIL 25, 1920 – MARCH 21, 2008
ROMANIA

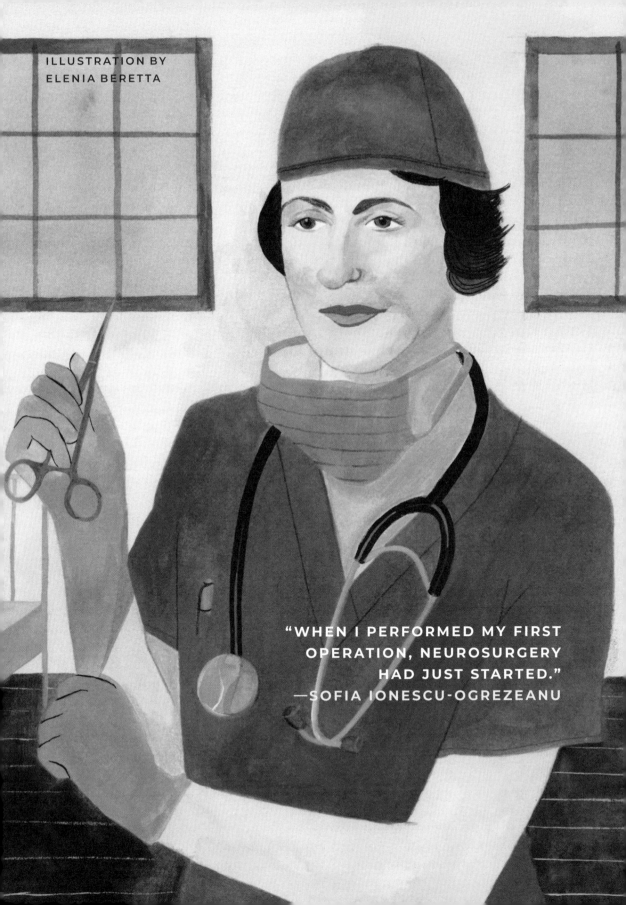

ILLUSTRATION BY
ELENIA BERETTA

"WHEN I PERFORMED MY FIRST
OPERATION, NEUROSURGERY
HAD JUST STARTED."
—SOFIA IONESCU-OGREZEANU

SOJOURNER TRUTH

SCAN TO
HEAR MORE

ABOLITIONIST AND
WOMEN'S RIGHTS ACTIVIST

sabella had a powerful voice. But she couldn't use it because she was born into slavery.

When she grew up, Isabella fell in love with a man named Robert and wanted to marry him, but the family who kept him enslaved forbade him from being with her. She was forced to be with another man. With him, she had five children. But Isabella never knew if she would see her children from one day to the next—they could be taken away and sold at any time. It was terrifying.

Then New York state announced that all enslaved people would soon be legally free. The man who held her captive, Dumont, promised he would set Isabella and her children free one year earlier than that date. But when the day came, he broke his word. Outraged, Isabella escaped.

She stayed with a nearby family, who paid Dumont for Isabella's safety. Finally, Isabella was free. Now she could use her voice.

One of her sons, Peter, had been sold to an enslaver in Alabama, but Isabella knew it was illegal to sell enslaved people across state lines. She took the white man to court and won! Peter returned with her to New York.

Isabella changed her name to Sojourner Truth. *Sojourner* means "one who travels," and she set out across the country giving speeches about the true meaning of slavery and the importance of equal rights for all people. "That man over there says that women need to be helped into carriages and lifted over ditches and to have the best place everywhere," she said in one speech. "Nobody ever helps me into carriages or over mud-puddles! And ain't I a woman?"

CIRCA 1797–NOVEMBER 26, 1883

UNITED STATES OF AMERICA

ILLUSTRATION BY
CRISTINA AMODEO

"LOOK AT MY ARM! . . .
AIN'T I A WOMAN?"
—SOJOURNER TRUTH

SONIA SOTOMAYOR

SUPREME COURT JUSTICE

Once there was a girl who wanted to be a detective. Her name was Sonia.

When she was six, Sonia was diagnosed with **diabetes**. *You can't be a detective*, she was told. *You need to find something else!* But Sonia didn't give up. Her favorite TV show was a legal drama starring a brilliant lawyer named Perry Mason. He wasn't as exciting as her favorite detective, Nancy Drew, but he was great at solving crimes.

Fair enough, she thought. *I'll be a lawyer like Perry Mason.*

Sonia came from a poor family that had moved to New York from Puerto Rico. When she was nine, her father died, leaving her mother to provide for the entire family. She worked six days a week, and she kept telling Sonia that she had to get an excellent education.

Sonia didn't disappoint her. She studied hard and became one of the few Hispanic female students accepted by Princeton University at that time. "I felt like an alien," she later recalled. But she still managed to graduate with top grades, and she continued her studies at the prestigious Yale Law School.

She became a judge and worked at every level of the judicial system. When Barack Obama was elected president, he nominated her to the **Supreme Court** of the United States, and Sonia became the first Latina to serve in that position.

Sonia played a major role in some of the country's most important legal cases, including the historic decision to make same-sex marriage legal in all states.

BORN JUNE 25, 1954
UNITED STATES OF AMERICA

ILLUSTRATION BY
KATHRIN HONESTA

"THE LATINA IN ME IS AN EMBER
THAT BLAZES FOREVER."
—SONIA SOTOMAYOR

SOPHIA LOREN

ACTOR

Sophia's nickname was Toothpick.

She grew up in Naples, Italy, during World War II, sharing a small apartment with her mom, her sister, her grandparents, and her aunt and uncle. Nobody ever had enough to eat.

Sophia's mom had often dreamed of becoming an actor, so when she heard that extras were needed on a film shoot in Rome, she packed her bags and headed off, taking Sophia with her. Sophia was still a teenager, but she realized that she liked being on set, so she decided to stay in Rome and try to become an actor herself.

By this time, the skinny little toothpick had blossomed into a beautiful young woman. Sophia worked as a model for magazines and in fashion shows while she tried to break into the movies.

Directors were attracted first by her beauty. But they quickly found out that Sophia was also an incredible actor. Soon enough, she became the face of Italian cinema. Comedies, dramas, thrillers—she starred in them all.

With her mischievous sense of humor, her passion, and her strong personality, Sophia embodied the whole country's determination to bounce back after the long, hard years of war and work toward a brighter future.

Hollywood also noticed Sophia's talent, and before long, producers were falling over one another to sign her to their next big film. She put that special sparkle into the golden age of American cinema.

"If you have fear, you have to conquer it," Sophia once said. "Anything that you want in life. Anything, not just acting. If you're stubborn enough, one day you will get it."

BORN SEPTEMBER 20, 1934
ITALY

ILLUSTRATION BY
MARTA SIGNORI

"AT THE DRESSING TABLE,
EVERY WOMAN HAS A CHANCE
TO BE AN ARTIST ..."
—SOPHIA LOREN

SOPHIE SCHOLL

POLITICAL ACTIVIST

Once upon a time, a girl named Sophie would stand outside her town's prison walls playing her flute, hoping that one particular prisoner would hear. The tune she played was "*Die Gedanken sind frei*" (Your Thoughts Are Free), and the prisoner listening in his cell was her father. He had been thrown in jail because he was opposed to the Nazis and their leader, Adolf Hitler.

When she was younger, Sophie had supported Hitler. She and her brother Hans had even marched in parades for him. But then they started reading about the terrible things the Nazis were doing. They learned about the mass murder of Jewish people and other groups Hitler deemed undesirable, and they realized their father had been right from the start: Adolf Hitler was not a good man.

Sophie and Hans formed a group called the White Rose and produced flyers and pamphlets encouraging Germans to resist the Nazis.

At that time, every school, church, college, and street was full of spies, and anyone who dared criticize Hitler was reported to the police and arrested. That didn't stop Sophie. She knew in her heart that opposing the Nazi Party was the right thing to do, and she wasn't afraid of the consequences.

How can we expect justice to prevail if we don't give ourselves up for a just cause? she thought.

Sadly, Sophie and the other members of the White Rose were arrested, tried, and executed by the Nazis, but their example inspired people all over the world to fight for freedom.

MAY 9, 1921–FEBRUARY 22, 1943
GERMANY

ILLUSTRATION BY
CRISTINA PORTOLANO

"WHAT DOES MY DEATH
MATTER IF, THROUGH US,
THOUSANDS OF PEOPLE ARE
STIRRED TO ACTION?"
—SOPHIE SCHOLL

STEFFI GRAF

TENNIS PLAYER

Once there was a little girl who loved tennis. Steffi would watch her father coaching all the other players and follow him around, pestering him to let her play too.

Papa, I want a racket, she'd beg. *I want to play tennis like you.*

You're too small, her father would reply. *Wait until you have grown up a little more.*

Steffi bugged him so much that finally he gave in. He picked up a tennis racket and chopped the handle in half.

There, he said. *Now you can play.*

Steffi was thrilled. She made her own little tennis court in the basement, tying a piece of string between two chairs for the net. She spent hours downstairs, blissfully banging the ball with her racket. She was very happy. Her mother was not so happy, though—a lot of lamps got broken!

When she was just six years old, Steffi won her first tennis tournament, and from then on, there was no stopping her. She grew up to be one of the most brilliant tennis stars in the world. She won 22 Grand Slam singles titles, captured an Olympic gold medal, and was voted German Sportsperson of the Year a record-breaking five times!

Now she loves spending time with her son, Jaden, who plays baseball, and her daughter, Jaz, who prefers roller-skating and hip-hop dance to tennis. Steffi doesn't mind. She believes everyone should be free to do what they love and what makes them happy.

BORN JUNE 14, 1969
GERMANY

"A NEW DAY MEANS A NEW CHANCE TO
BE THE PERSON YOU WANT TO BE."
—STEFFI GRAF

ILLUSTRATION BY
GIULIA FLAMINI

TEMPLE GRANDIN

PROFESSOR OF ANIMAL SCIENCES

SCAN TO HEAR MORE

Once upon a time, there was a girl who invented a hug machine. Her name was Temple, and she didn't speak until she was three and a half years old. Luckily, her parents realized she needed a little extra help and hired a speech therapist for her.

Temple's mom could see that her daughter was different, but she didn't realize until later that she was autistic. Autistic people's brains are wired slightly differently, and their experience of the world is different from other people's as a result.

Like many autistic children, Temple had super-sensitive skin. She found clothes really itchy, so she always wore soft pants and shirts. She also didn't like to be hugged, but she loved the feeling of being pressed, so she invented a machine that could hug her just the way she wanted.

At that time, people didn't understand autism. They didn't want to be labeled as autistic, even though the term can mean many different things. Autistic people are on a spectrum ranging from having genius-level skills to having severe developmental disabilities or no language at all. But Temple was not afraid to speak about her autism and explain the different way her brain worked. "I don't think in language," she liked to say. "I think in pictures."

Temple instinctively understood how animals make sense of the world. She became a world-famous professor of animal sciences and argued strongly for the humane treatment of livestock in a brilliant book called *Animals Make Us Human*.

BORN AUGUST 29, 1947
UNITED STATES OF AMERICA

"THE MOST IMPORTANT THING
PEOPLE DID FOR ME WAS TO
EXPOSE ME TO NEW THINGS."
—TEMPLE GRANDIN

TROOP 6000

Giselle Burgess was a single mother with five children.

She worked hard to pay the rent on a low-cost apartment. But when her landlord sold the building, she couldn't afford another place, and she and her kids found themselves without housing.

The city of New York had rented 10 floors to shelter families without homes at a motel in a neighborhood in Queens, and that's where Giselle and her children went.

At the time, Giselle was working at the Girl Scouts of Greater New York, so she thought, *Why not start a troop in the shelter?* And she did.

At the first meeting, there were just eight girls, and three of them were Giselle's own daughters. She needed to spread the news. Through word of mouth and flyers, Troop 6000 grew to 28 members, some as young as five years old. Eventually, it welcomed more than 600 members!

Giselle hopes the girls in Troop 6000 learn that tough times "are just seasons in their lives. And that they will surpass it."

Troop 6000 is the first one for girls without homes in New York City, but many more will follow—unfortunately, homelessness is still a serious problem across the United States. "We are like a pack," said Giselle's daughter Karina. "If one of us is down, the rest of us will be there to pick them back up."

Like other Girl Scouts and Girl Guides, Karina and her friends love adventure. They cultivate courage and honesty, responsibility and strength. They know that no matter where you're from or where you live, that's what being a Girl Scout is all about!

STARTED FEBRUARY 2017

UNITED STATES OF AMERICA

"THERE IS SO MUCH MORE OUT THERE THAT THEY ARE CAPABLE OF ACCOMPLISHING."
—GISELLE BURGESS

ILLUSTRATION BY
ALICE BARBERINI

VALENTINA TERESHKOVA

COSMONAUT

Once upon a time, there was an 80-year-old woman who wanted to volunteer for a one-way trip to Mars. Her name was Valentina, and back when she was 24, she was the first woman to travel to outer space.

Valentina loved to fly. She would parachute every weekend, during the day or at night, onto land and into water. When Russia started selecting women to train as cosmonauts, Valentina did her best to get into the program. After months of hard training, she was chosen to fly aboard the spacecraft *Vostok 6*.

Soon after takeoff, though, Valentina realized that something was wrong. The settings for reentry were incorrect, and at the end of the mission, the craft would shoot off into outer space instead of back to Earth. As much as she loved flying, Valentina wasn't ready to leave Earth for good just yet! So she got in touch with the engineers back at mission control, and everyone worked frantically to correct the settings before it was too late.

Her bosses were horrified and didn't want to admit they'd made a mistake. They made Valentina promise she'd never tell anyone. Thirty years passed before she could reveal the truth about her mission.

Now that she's an old woman, Valentina would love to blast off into space on one final voyage. She says the view of the Earth from space shows "a planet at once so beautiful and so fragile" and encourages us all to do our best to protect it.

BORN MARCH 6, 1937

RUSSIA

"HEY, SKY, TAKE OFF YOUR HAT.
I'M ON MY WAY!"
—VALENTINA TERESHKOVA

CCCP

VALERIE THOMAS

ASTRONOMER AND INVENTOR

O ne day, a young girl picked up a book called *The Boys' First Book of Radio and Electronics*. Valerie thought to herself, *I'm not a boy. But who cares? This is really fascinating!*

When her dad took apart their television to fix it, Valerie wanted to help. *This is too complicated for girls*, her father said, but she wanted to find out how things worked.

After college, she got a top job at NASA working on something way more complicated than a television: the world's first satellite. *Landsat 1* was launched into space, and it sent back images of Earth that helped predict weather patterns and crop cycles.

Then one day, Valerie visited a science museum and saw something that would change her life. It was a light bulb, sitting on its own, not connected to anything, and still shining brightly! How did they do that?

The answer was a clever optical illusion created by a hidden second light bulb and **concave mirrors** that made it *look* as if the first bulb was on. That gave Valerie a great idea. She began to research concave mirrors and light, and she came up with a brilliant invention called the **illusion transmitter**. This amazing piece of technology is still used in NASA's space exploration programs, and scientists like Valerie are developing ways to use it to look inside the human body. One day, it may also project 3D videos from your television right into your living room!

BORN FEBRUARY 1943
UNITED STATES OF AMERICA

ILLUSTRATION BY
FANESHA FABRE

"I LIKE TO SHARE
KNOWLEDGE WITH
YOUNG PEOPLE.
AND I WOULD LIKE
TO SEE THEM TAKE
THE KNOWLEDGE
TO THE NEXT LEVEL."
—VALERIE THOMAS

VIOLETA PARRA

COMPOSER AND MUSICIAN

Once upon a time, there was a girl who sang songs with her sister while cleaning gravestones at the cemetery. Her name was Violeta.

Violeta didn't have beautiful dresses to wear. Her family was poor, so her mother made her dresses from scraps of material. Violeta didn't mind. In fact, she thought her clothes were so beautiful that even when she was grown up and had money of her own, she decided to keep dressing that way.

One day, she and her sister passed a farm and heard some workers singing a beautiful tune. *I love that song so much!* Violeta exclaimed. As soon as she got home, she found her father's guitar and began to play. Her fingers danced across the strings, making the most enchanting music.

When she got older, Violeta started to travel across Chile. With a recorder and a notebook in hand, she went to the most remote corners of the country, gathering songs and memories from all the people she met. Many of the songs she learned had been passed from generation to generation, but no one had ever written them down or recorded them before Violeta came along.

Her music was inspired by the traditional folk culture she had absorbed during her journey. Violeta became a national hero. Her songs spoke of legends, history, love, and life.

Violeta was also a sculptor, a poet, and a painter. And she embroidered pictures that were so magnificent they were exhibited at the Louvre Museum in Paris after her death.

Today, Violeta's songs are sung all over the world.

OCTOBER 4, 1917–FEBRUARY 5, 1967
CHILE

"THANKS TO LIFE, WHICH HAS GIVEN ME SO MUCH."
—VIOLETA PARRA

ILLUSTRATION BY PAOLA ROLLO

VIRGINIA HALL

SPY

O nce upon a time, there was a woman with a wooden leg. Her name was Virginia, and she called her leg Cuthbert.

Though she walked with a limp, Virginia was amazingly determined. When World War II broke out, she joined the British Special Operations Executive and set off across the English Channel to help the French Resistance fight the Nazis. Three years later, she learned of the United States' Office of Strategic Services and worked as a spy for them too.

Virginia was a master of disguise. One time, she pretended to be an elderly milkmaid. She dyed her hair gray, put on a long skirt, and shuffled along so no one could see she had a limp. She managed to send out secret radio messages telling the Allies about German troop movements. It was incredibly dangerous, and Virginia knew that if she were discovered she would be tortured and killed. But she carried on anyway.

The Limping Lady, as she was known, was considered the most dangerous of all Allied spies. The Nazi secret police put up wanted posters all over France, but Virginia always stayed one step ahead of them.

Once, she almost died crossing the Pyrenees Mountains on foot in the middle of winter. She radioed a message to London: "Having trouble with Cuthbert." They didn't realize she was talking about her leg. "If Cuthbert is giving you difficulty," they replied, "have him eliminated!"

By the war's end, the Limping Lady's team had destroyed four bridges, derailed several freight trains, blown up a railway line, cut down telephone wires, and captured hundreds of enemy soldiers. Virginia was declared America's greatest female spy and received a medal for her bravery.

APRIL 6, 1906–JULY 8, 1982
UNITED STATES OF AMERICA

ILLUSTRATION BY
DALILA ROVAZZANI

"AFTER ALL, MY NECK
IS MY OWN. IF I AM
WILLING TO GET A CRICK
IN IT, I THINK THAT'S
MY PREROGATIVE."
—VIRGINIA HALL

VIVIAN MAIER

PHOTOGRAPHER

Once there was a nanny who was a secret photographer. She would walk the streets of Chicago with the children she was looking after and photograph strangers going about their daily lives. Her name was Vivian. She never showed her pictures to anyone.

Vivian lived for 40 years with the families she worked for. She didn't like to talk and asked for locks for her room, which she forbade anyone to enter. She was so secretive that when she took her film rolls to be developed, she never gave her real name. Over the course of her life, she took more than 100,000 pictures, but nobody ever knew she was a photographer.

Vivian kept all her negatives and prints in a rented storage space. Two years before she died, she failed to pay the rent, and everything inside was put up for sale. At the auction, all of her work was bought by three photo collectors. They had no idea they had found a treasure trove.

Despite having no formal training, Vivian had captured the street life of postwar America with the rawness and intensity of a master. Her photos showed people eating doughnuts, shopping for groceries, going to museums, being arrested, kissing, selling newspapers, and cleaning shoes. Sometimes she also took pictures of herself—as seen in the reflection of shop windows or even as a shadow on a wall.

She became a worldwide sensation.

Vivian often used a Rolleiflex camera, held at chest level so she could maintain eye contact with the person she was photographing. Many of her most memorable shots are of people staring straight at her.

FEBRUARY 1, 1926–APRIL 21, 2009
UNITED STATES OF AMERICA

"I'M SORT OF A SPY."
—VIVIAN MAIER

ILLUSTRATION BY
SARA OLMOS

WISŁAWA SZYMBORSKA

POET

Once, many years ago, a little girl handed a piece of paper to her father. On it was a poem she had written. Her father put on his glasses and studied the wobbly handwriting very seriously. Then he nodded, reached into his pocket, and pulled out a penny. *It is a good poem, Wisława*, he said, giving the coin to his daughter with a smile.

Wisława's house was full of books. She read everything she could and wrote poetry throughout her childhood. Although her family wasn't rich, it was a happy house, full of chatter and laughter and books and cats.

Everything changed when World War II broke out. Led by Hitler, the German army invaded Wisława's homeland of Poland when she was 16. It was a terrible time. Many people were deported, and intellectuals were often executed. In Nazi-occupied Poland, there was no place for poets. Wislawa's work, her freedom, and even her life were at risk. She took a job as a railway officer, but she secretly kept on writing, and she survived.

Years later, she wrote a poem about Hitler. In it, she imagined him as a cute baby boy, "a little fellow in his itty-bitty robe." When he was a kid, after all, no one could possibly imagine who he would become as a grown-up. People everywhere loved her poetry because it was surprising. Wislawa wrote simply and beautifully about all sorts of things: "chairs and sorrows, scissors, tenderness, transistors, violins, [and] teacups . . ." She found fun and laughter in unexpected places.

When she won the Nobel Prize in Literature, she joked that it was all because her friend had a "magic sofa." If you sat in it, you would get the prize!

JULY 2, 1923–FEBRUARY 1, 2012
POLAND

"IN EVERY
POSSIBLE ANSWER,
THERE SHOULD BE
ANOTHER QUESTION."
—WISŁAWA
SZYMBORSKA

YEONMI PARK

HUMAN RIGHTS ACTIVIST

Once upon a time, in North Korea, people were not free to sing, wear what they wanted, read a newspaper, or make a phone call abroad.

Yeonmi was born there. Like many North Koreans, she was so scared of the country's supreme leader that she thought he could read her mind and would imprison her if he didn't like her thoughts.

When Yeonmi was 14, her family decided to escape.

It was a dangerous journey. She and her mother crossed a frozen river and three mountains to get to the Chinese border. There, they were treated very badly. When refugees have no option but to enter a country illegally, they have no laws to protect them and can fall victim to all sorts of criminals.

Yeonmi and her mother lived in hiding, terrified that the Chinese authorities would find them and send them back to North Korea. It was so scary that they fled again to Mongolia.

They walked across the Gobi Desert using a compass. When it stopped working, they followed the stars. At the Mongolian border, the guards told them they couldn't cross. Having lost all hope, Yeonmi and her mother threatened to kill themselves. The guards let them pass.

A few years later, Yeonmi was living safely in New York City. She told her story in a powerful speech at the One Young World Summit in Ireland. Her words moved the world, and she became a full-time activist for human rights. Every day, she works to liberate her birth country from its terrible dictatorship and to protect North Korean refugees.

BORN OCTOBER 4, 1993
NORTH KOREA

ILLUSTRATION BY
JOANA ESTRELA

CHINA

NORTH
KOREA

YELLOW
SEA

SOUTH
KOREA

1984

GEORGE
ORWELL

"I FELT
ONLY THE
STARS WERE
WITH US."
—YEONMI PARK

WRITE YOUR STORY

O nce upon a time, _____

_____

_____

_____

_____

_____

_____

_____

_____

_____

_____

_____

_____

_____

_____

_____

_____

_____

_____

_____

_____

_____

_____

_____

_____

DRAW YOUR PORTRAIT

GLOSSARY

BOYCOTT to choose not to buy something or not to participate in an event as a form of protest

BURKA a loose garment that some Muslim women women wear to cover their face and body

CALICO CLOTH a fabric made of heavy cotton

CONCAVE MIRROR a mirror with the reflecting surface curved inward

CRYSTALLOGRAPHER a scientist who studies how atoms are arranged in crystalline solids such as table salt, diamonds, or snowflakes

DIABETES a disease that affects how the body processes glucose

DOWN SYNDROME a condition caused by an extra chromosome. People with Down syndrome may have health problems, learning impairments, and physical limitations

ENIGMATIC something that is mysterious or difficult to understand

ENZYMES substances that speed up biochemical reactions in plants or animals

FLORA AND FAUNA all the plant life (flora) and animal life (fauna) present in a particular region

FOLK MUSIC traditional music originating with the ordinary people of a country or area and usually transmitted orally from generation to generation

FOOT-BINDING an ancient Chinese tradition that required little girls to have their feet broken and tightly bound, in order to change the shape of their feet and keep them impossibly small. Girls with bound feet could barely walk on their own, but their small feet were considered a sign of beauty

GLUCOSE
the main type of
sugar in the blood
and the main source
of energy for the
body's cells

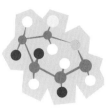

ILLUSION TRANSMITTER
a device that uses
concave mirrors
to create the
illusion of a
3D object

QUANTUM CHEMISTRY
the study of subatomic particles,
which are the particles that make
up atoms. These include protons,
neutrons, and electrons

QUANTUM PHYSICS the study
of energy and matter that explores
how atoms and subatomic particles
interact with each other

RWANDAN GENOCIDE the
mass killing of a people called the Tutsi
by members of another group called
the Hutu in the East African country of
Rwanda in 1994

SALSA a type of Latin
American dance
music or a popular
form of dance
performed to
this music

SANTERÍA a religion developed
by people of West African descent and
originally practiced in Cuba

SAPPHIC STANZA a group of
verses of four lines, each with a specific
pattern of accents and number
of syllables

SONAR a system that is used to
detect objects under water or
measure the water's depth

SUPERSONIC PRESSURE TUNNEL
an enormous wind tunnel where NASA
scientists tested space vehicles before
launching them into orbit

SUPREME COURT the highest court
in the United States. It hears cases on
criminal and constitutional matters

ZERO-POINT ENERGY
the lowest possible energy that a
quantum
mechanical
system may have

REBELS' HALL OF FAME

Let's hear it for the Rebel kids who were early believers in *Good Night Stories for Rebel Girls 2* on Kickstarter! They come from all over the world, and they are going to change the world.

ABBIGAIL SKETCHLEY

ABBY AND PAIGE LAROCHELLE

ABIG SUSSMAN

ABIGAIL COHEN

ABIGAIL AND MADELINE SHERLOCK

ADA TAFLINGER-AHMAD

ADA WHITMAN

ADDISON AND ANDREA KANNAS

ADDISON MOYER

ADELINE HOLMSTROM

ADELKA VYCHODILOVA

ADILYNN CROCKER

AINSLEY BRIGHT

ALAINA BOWMAN

ALANA MARTINEZ HERNANDEZ

ALBA MOORE

ALDEN ECKMAN

ALEX SKALETSKY

ALEX WATKINS

ALEXA CONNELLY

ALEXANDRA FRANCES RENNIE

ALEXANDRA LISTER

ALICE BRYANT

ALICE VINCENT

ALINA GRICE

ALINA SUESS

ALISON GARCIA

ALISZA DEVIR

ALLISON COOPER

ALMA MY AND MARIE ELISE AGERLUND KAABER

ALMA OPHELIA AND HARLOW MAGDALENA ZELLERS

AMELIA AND KRISTINA CLARK

AMELIA LOOKHART

AMELIA JANE AND LOLA ELIZABETH STINSON

AMELIE BLECHNER

AMÉLIE WILLIAMS

ANA MARTIN

ANARCELIA CHAVEZ

ANGELISE KIARA RODRIGUEZ

ANIKA AND CLAUDIA STADTMUELLER

ANISHA NAYYAR

ANITA AND ANGELINA BAGGIO BARRETO

ANNA GRAFFAGNINO

ANNABEL ROSE MURPHY

ANNE DARWIN BROOKS

ANNIKA KAPLAN BASDEVANT

ANONYMOUS REBEL MOM

ANOUK AND FELIX FREUDENBERG

ANOUSHKA AND OSKAR ROBB

ANUSHRI KAHN

ARWEN AND HANNAH GREENOUGH

ARYANNA HOYEM

ASHLEY AND SHAVEA SCHLOSS

ATHENA FLEARY

AUDREY GIUSTOZZI

AVA AND KEIRA KLISS

AVA EMILY AND NOA STARLIGHT MESLER

AVA TSIGOUNIS

AVELYN CLARE CUTLER

AVERIE ANNE EVINS

AVERY AND MILA DOROGI

AVERY KEPLINGER

AYAKO ROSE SAFRENO

AYLA AND ASHLEA GRIGG

AZUL ZAPATA-TORRENEGRA

BABOOMBA TERRY

BELLA AND GIA DI MARTINO

BELLA AND GABI RIDENHOUR

BIANCA AND FEDERICO BARATTA

BILLIE KARLSSON

BRESYLN, ARROT, AND BRAXON PLESH
  STOCK-BRATINA

BRIANA FEUERSTEIN

BROOKLYN CRISOSTOMO

CAITLIN AND IMOGEN O'BRIEN

CAMILA ARNOLD

CAMILLE HANLEY

CARA QUINN LARKIN

CAROLINE ROCCASALVA

CAROLINE ROMPEL

CAROLINE SMYTH

CASSIA GLADYS CADAN-PEMAN

CATHERINE AND BECCA VAN LENT

CHANDLER GRACE OCTETREE

CHARLEE VINCELETTE

CHARLIE GRACE EVANS

CHARLIE TRUSKOSKI

CHARLOTTE AND EISLEY CLINE

CHARLOTTE KENNEDY

CHARLOTTE MOSER-JONES

CHARLOTTE POOLOS

CHIHARU BRIDGEWATER

CHLOE ANGYAL

CHLOE AND GRACE HALE

CHLOE HOBBS

CLAIRE BUSENBARK

CLAIRE DAVIS

CLAIRE POGGIE

CLAIRE RUFFY

CLAIRE AND SLOANE STOLEE

CLARA BOTELHO HOFFMANN

CLARA TOULMIN

CLEMENTINE TAFLINGER

COCO CANTRELL

COLETTE AND ASTRID UNGARETTI

CONSTANÇA VIEIRA

CORA AND IVY BRAND

DAKOTA ALLARD

DANIELA MENDEZ CASTRO

DAPHNE MARIE BARRAILLER

DASCHA MAKORI

DEBRA LOUISE AND MILLIE RUSSELL MCLEOD

DEEDEE AND NAIMA REISS-REINITZ

DELANEY KUHN

DELANEY MCSHANE

DELANEY O'CONNER

DIYA AND ISHA THOBHANI

DYLAN COOPER

EADIE MCMAHON

ELAINA MAE SCOTT

ELENA HOROBIN-HULL

ELENA WOLFE

ELIANA AND ARABELLA ARCHUNDE

ELISE LEHRKAMP

ELIZABETH "BETSY" NAGLE

ELIZABETH WEBSTER-MCFADDEN

ELLA MAGUIRE

ELLA AND AUDREY THOMPSON

ELLIA AND VICTORIA WHITACRE

ELLIE DIEBLING

ELLIE HUGHES

ELLISON AMERICA MARUSIC-REID

ELSA PORRATA

EMERI PEERY

EMERY MATTHEW

EMIE WATSON

EMILIA LEVINSEN

EMILY ALESSANDRA AND ANDREA JULIANNA DIFEDERICO

EMILY FENSTER

EMILY SMITH

EMMA AND LILIANNE BRUNNER

EMMA AND CHARLOTTE DAVISON

EMMA DEEG

EMMA GOMEZ

EMMA AND LUCY GROSS

EMMA HERON

EMMA ROSE MORRIS

EMMALINE JOANNE SINCLAIR

ENARA BECK

EVE NUNNIKHOVEN

EVELYN AND LYDIA HARE

EVIE GRACE CUNNINGHAM

EVIE AND JESSICA HIGGINSON

FIONA CARIELLO

FLORENCE GRACE AND AUDREY ROSE ARCHER

FRANCESCA PORRAS

FREDRICA THODE

FREJA AND JULIANA HOFVENSCHIOELD

FREYA BERGHAN-WHYMAN

GABBY AND ALEX SPLENDORIO

GABRIELA CUNHA

GABRIELLA AND GALEN VERBEELEN

GEMMA AND DARA WOMACK

GIULIA AND GIORGIA PERSICO

GRACE MARIE ASHMORE

GRACE AND SOFIA MCCOLLUM

GRACIE FOWLER

GRETA AND LUCY HUBER

GRETCHEN PELLE

HADLEY WELLS

HALLIE JO VAUGHN

HANA AND SAMANTHA HALE

HANA HEGAZY

HANNA HART

HANNAH HUNDERMARK

HANSON CCC

HARRIET STUART

HAZEL MAE CARDENAS

HELEN CLARK

HELENA AND NANCY MARTINEZ

HELENA VAN DER MERWE

HENRY TIGER AND BILLY JAMES BEVIS

TEAM HOWARD

ILAINA AND ELIAS NEWBERRY

ILORA AND VIVIKA PAL

IMOGEN OAKENFOLD

INGRID PALACIOS

IONA MARQUIST

ISABELLA ROSE FARRELL-JACKSON

ISABELLA SINENI

ISLA IYER

JACK WILLIAM AND BILLIE ROSE OLIVER

JADE REISTERER

JAHNAVI KAKARALA

JANE AND NORA ANNA BEGLEY

JASMINE GOODSON

JAZMIN ELENES-LEON

JENIFER AND ELIZABETH PATTERSON

JENNA BERARIU

JENNIFER MCCANN

JILLIAN JOY WELLS

JODI HOLLAND

JOHANA "JO-JO" HAARMAN-FOWLER

JOSEPHINE AND LUCIA MOXEY

JOSEPHINE WEBSTER-FOX

JOSIE HOPKINS

JOSIE AND NORA HUTTON

JOY AND GRACE BRADBURY-SMITH

JULIA AND PAULINA KIRSTEN

JUNIPER RUTH MARKS

JUPITER ROSE JAY

KAHUTAIKI AND AWATEA CALMAN

KAIA MARIE PADILLA

KATE TYLER

KATERYNA ZIKOU

KATHLEEN AND DAISY KELLY

KATIE MCDOWELL

KATIE MCNAB

KATIE AND LIZZIE STANDEN

KAYA GASTELUM

KAYLAH PAYNE

KELLY ROTH

KIERA JOHNSON

DR. KRISTEN LEE

KRYSTIN AND ELISSA SCHLEH

KYLA PATEL

KYLEE CAUSER

KYLIE AND KAITLYN SCOTT

KYRA MAI

LANA VERONITA DAHL

LARA IDA AND DERYA KINAY

LAUREN KROFT

LEELA AIYAGARI

LENNON AND ARIA BACKO

LEO LALONDE

LEONIE POMPEI

LILA YINGLING

LILIANA GAIA POPESCU

LILITH AND ROSE WATTERS

LILLY HAWES

LILY SCHMITT

LOLA VEGA

LUCILE ORR

LUIZA AND EMILIJA VIKTORIA GIRNIUS

LUNA PUCKETT

MACY JANE HEWS

MACY AND KATE SCHULTE

MADELEINE DALE

MADELINE GIBBS

MADELINE ANNE TERESA HAZEL-
GOLDHAMER AND SARA NEIL LEA HAZEL

MADELINE PITTS

MADELINE AND ELAINE WOO

MADELYN O'BRIEN

MADISON ROSE HORGAN

MADISYN, MALLORY, AND RAPHAEL PLUNKETT

MAE AND EVE BUTLER

MAE BETTY AND MARGOT ROATH

MAGGIE CRISP OXFORD

MAHREYA AND CHRYSEIS GREEN

MAISIE MAZOKI

MAPLE SAN

MARGARET QUINN

MARGAUX BEDIEE

MARIELLA SCHWIETER

MARLOE MARIE NELSON

MATHILDE AND LINDA GIO COIS

MATILDA WINEBRENNER

MAYA AND NOA GUIZZI

MAYA AND SONIA TOLIA

MIA AND JADE GAVONI

MIA MICHUDA

MIA VENTURATO

MILA KONAR

MILLIE AND SLOANE KAULENTIS

MIRABELLE CHOE

MISCHA BAHAT

MOLLY DEANE

MOXIE INES GOTTLIEB

MOXIE MARQUIS

NADIA GARBE

NATALIA MACIAS PEREZ

NATALIA AND GABRIELA SHANER LOPEZ

NATALIE HEPBURN

NAYARA VIEIRA

NIAMH CAVOSKI MURPHY

NINA JOANNA ARYA

NINA HEWRYK

NORA BAILEY-RADFORD

NORA BELCHER

NORA IGLESIAS POZA

NORAH WALSH

NORENE COSTA

NORI ELIZABETH COOPER

OLIVE SARAH AND EDIE QUINN COLLINGWOOD

OLIVE SHEEHAN

OLIVIA AND MILA CAPPELLO

OLIVIA ANNA CAVALLO STEELE

OLIVIA AND AMELIA O'CONNELL

OLIVIA REED

OLIVIA YIATRAS

PEARL FUHRMAN

PENELOPE SCHNEIDER RIEHLE

PENELOPE JOY ARGUILLA TULL

PENELOPE WHITE

PEYTON AND CAMBRIA HINCY

PHOEBE BISHOP

PIPPA LUNA BARTON

PIXI JUDE RUDY

QUINN SCHULTE

REBECCA WHITE

RILEY KNEZ

RILEY AND GABRIELA ROSARIO

ROBIN AND ANNALISE NORDSTROM

ROSA AND AUSTIN KEREZSI

ROSE GOUGH

ROSE LANDRUM

ROSE LEIGHTON

ROSE TYLER

ROWAN WEBER

ROXY LEVEY

RUBY JANE MCGOWAN

RUTH BROWN

RUTHIE GEISDORFER

RYAN ACKERMAN

RYAN AND SHANE COMSTOCK FERRIS

SAOIRSE AND FELICIA BEDRIN

SARA SAEZ

SHAI MANDELL

SIENNA AND ALEXA MARTINEZ CORZINE

SIRI DIRIX

SLOANE ZELLER

SOFÍA RUÍZ-MURPHY

SOFIE PETRU

SONIA AND BEN TWEITO

SONORA SOFIA GOEL

SOPHIA AND MAYA CRISTOFORETTI

SOPHIA MARTIN

SOPHIA VUU

SOPHIE WEBB

SORAYA ALIABADI

STEIN FT

STELLA ANDERSON

STELLA MESSINA

SYDNEY BROOK

SYDNEY KERPELMAN

SYDNEY MESSER

SYLVIE FRY

SYNIA CASPER

TARA AND TALIA DAIL

TARA LEIJEN

TATE HINERFELD

TATE PITCHER

TATUM STEVELEY

TEAGAN HALEY

TEAGEN AND ANNEN GOUDELOCK

TEDDY ROSE WYLDER HEADEY

VALENTINA NUILA

VANESSA EMSLEY

VANJA SCHUBERT

VICTOR CASAS

VICTORIA AND EMMA HEDGES

VICTORIA PAYTON WOLF

VIOLET SUDBURY

VIVIAN HARRIS

VIVIAN LEE WARTHER

VIVIANA GUTIERREZ

WALLIS STUNTZ

WEDNESDAY FIONA WHITE

WILEMS GIRLS

WYNN GAUDET

ZELDA NATIV

ZOE AND SELLA ALPERIN

ZOE MAE JACKSON

ZOE AND CAILEY MCKITTRICK

ZOIE JONAKIN

ZOYA ESFAHANI

ILLUSTRATORS

Fifty-one extraordinary female artists from all over the world created the portraits of the trailblazing Rebels in this book. Here they are.

ALICE BARBERINI ITALY, 47, 87, 187

ALICE BENIERO ITALY, 27, 113

ANA JUAN SPAIN, 33, 35, 59

ANNALISA VENTURA ITALY, 109, 115

BARBARA DZIADOSZ GERMANY, 21, 105

BEATRICE CEROCCHI ITALY, 185

CAMILLA PERKINS UK, 93

CLAUDIA CARIERI ITALY, 49, 53, 61

CRISTINA AMODEO ITALY, 45, 71, 133, 175

CRISTINA PORTOLANO ITALY, 19, 81, 167, 181

CRISTINA SPANÒ ITALY, 43, 99

DALILA ROVAZZANI ITALY, 195

DEBORA GUIDI ITALY, 85, 149

ELENIA BERETTA ITALY, 11, 173

ELENI KALORKOTI UK, 41, 135, 157

ELINE VAN DAM NETHERLANDS, 23, 103, 129

ELISABETTA STOINICH ITALY, 117, 123

EMMANUELLE WALKER CANADA, 25

FANESHA FABRE USA, 191

GABRIELLE TESFAYE USA, 111

GAIA STELLA ITALY, 57

GERALDINE SY PHILIPPINES, 79

GIORGIA MARRAS ITALY, 15, 119, 145, 165

GIULIA FLAMINI ITALY, 183

GIULIA TOMAI ITALY, 3, 153, 155, 163

JOANA ESTRELA PORTUGAL, 159, 201

KATE PRIOR USA, 141, 171

KATHRIN HONESTA INDONESIA, 177

LAURA JUNGER FRANCE, 101

LAURA PÉREZ SPAIN, 63

LIEKELAND NETHERLANDS, 151, 169

LISK FENG CHINA, 97, 161

LIZZY STEWART UK, 51, 107

MALIN ROSENQVIST SWEDEN, 65, 189

MARIJKE BUURLAGE NETHERLANDS, 77

MARINA MUUN AUSTRIA, 125

MARTA SIGNORI ITALY, 17, 67, 179

MARTINA PAUKOVA SLOVAKIA, 7, 83

MARYLOU FAURE UK, 31, 75

MONICA GARWOOD USA, 29, 121

NOA SNIR ISRAEL, 55, 91

PALESA MONARENG UK, 39, 137

PAOLA ROLLO ITALY, 73, 193

PING ZHU USA, 37, 131

PRIYA KURIYAN INDIA, 143

SALLY NIXON USA, 5

SARA OLMOS SPAIN, 127, 197

SARAH MAZZETTI ITALY, 13, 69, 139

SARAH WILKINS NEW ZEALAND, 95, 147

THANDIWE TSHABALALA SOUTH AFRICA, 89

ZOSIA DZIERŻAWSKA POLAND, 9, 199

ACKNOWLEDGMENTS

Our biggest, most heartfelt, loudest thank-you goes to our Rebel community on Kickstarter. All of you—once again—responded with such generosity and enthusiasm to *Good Night Stories for Rebel Girls 2*. Not only did you back the campaign, but you helped us find these incredible stories, you cheered for us along the way, and above all, you kept believing in us.

A special thank-you also goes to all the Rebel boys and men who are reading these stories and are brave enough to fight this battle alongside the women in their life.

Thank you, dads who are raising free, independent, strong daughters.

To our own dads, Angelo and Uccio, thank you for always supporting us. Even when we challenged you, even when you didn't understand our choices, you were *always* on our side. Thank you for instilling in us a burning desire for discovery and adventure and a deep love for the places we come from.

Thank you, thank you, thank you, Rebel team. It is an honor to work with you every day.

LISTEN TO MORE EMPOWERING STORIES ON THE REBEL GIRLS APP!

Download the app to listen to beloved Rebel Girls stories, as well as brand-new tales of extraordinary women. Filled with the adventures and accomplishments of women from around the world and throughout history, the Rebel Girls app is designed to entertain, inspire, and build confidence in listeners everywhere.

ABOUT THE AUTHORS

ELENA FAVILLI is a *New York Times* best-selling author, journalist, and breaker of glass ceilings. She is the cofounder of Rebel Girls and serves on the board, leading all impact initiatives. Elena has written for the *Guardian*, *Vogue*, *ELLE*, *COLORS* magazine, *McSweeney's*, *RAI*, *Il Post*, and *La Repubblica*, in addition to authoring four books within the Rebel Girls series.

FRANCESCA CAVALLO is an activist, an entrepreneur, and the *New York Times* best-selling coauthor of *Good Night Stories for Rebel Girls*. Recipient of the 2018 Publishers Weekly StarWatch Award for her work at Rebel Girls, Francesca launched some of the most successful crowdfunding campaigns in the history of publishing. In 2019, she founded Undercats, Inc., a company with the mission of radically increasing diversity in children's media.

REBEL GIRLS is a global, multi-platform empowerment brand dedicated to helping raise the most inspired and confident global generation of girls through content, experiences, products, and community. Originating from an international best-selling children's book, Rebel Girls amplifies stories of real-life women throughout history, geography, and field of excellence. With a growing community of nearly 20 million self-identified Rebel Girls spanning more than 100 countries, the brand engages with Generation Alpha through its book series, award-winning podcast, events, and merchandise. With the 2021 launch of the Rebel Girls app, the company has created a flagship destination for girls to explore a wondrous world filled with inspiring true stories of extraordinary women.

JOIN THE REBEL GIRLS COMMUNITY
    Facebook: facebook.com/rebelgirls
    Instagram: @rebelgirls
    Twitter: @rebelgirlsbook
    Web: rebelgirls.com
    App: rebelgirls.com/app

If you liked this book, please take a moment to review it wherever you prefer!

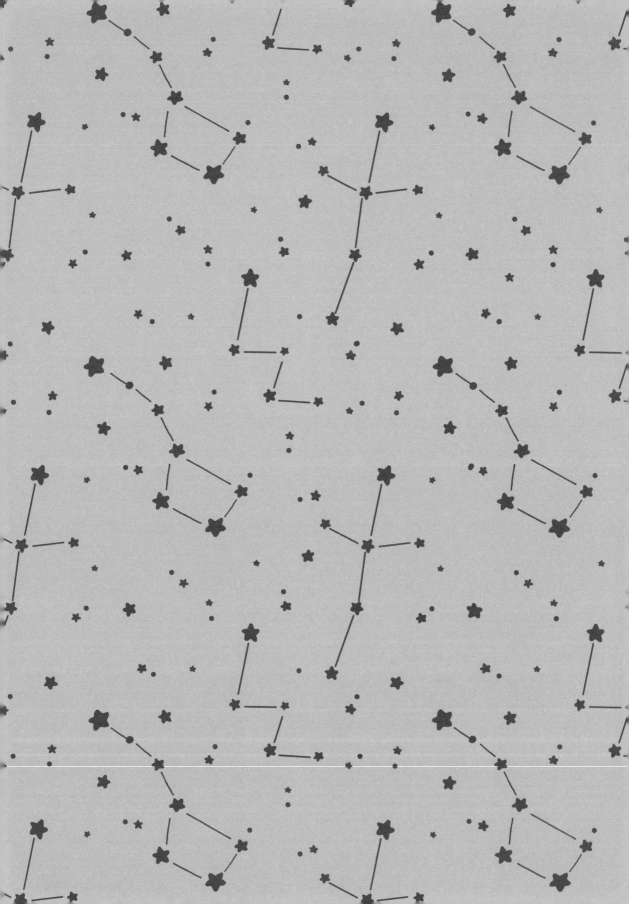

THIS BOOK
BELONGS TO

—————————————————

—————————————————

Good Night Stories for Rebel Girls

GOOD NIGHT STORIES FOR REBEL GIRLS

100 TALES OF EXTRAORDINARY WOMEN

ELENA FAVILLI AND FRANCESCA CAVALLO

REBEL GIRLS

Good Night Stories for Rebel Girls and all other Rebel Girls titles are available for bulk purchase for sale promotions, premiums, fundraising, and educational needs.
For details, write to sales@rebelgirls.com.

This is a work of creative nonfiction. It is a collection of heartwarming and thought-provoking bedtime stories inspired by the life and adventures of 100 heroic women. It is not an encyclopedic account of the events and accomplishments of their lives.

www.rebelgirls.com

Printed in China, 2021
20 19 18 17 16 15 14 13

Editorial direction and art direction by Francesca Cavallo and Elena Favilli
Cover design by Pemberley Pond
Graphic design by Cori Johnson

Good Night Stories for Rebel Girls is FSC® certified.

ISBN: 978-0-997-89581-0

To the rebel girls of the world:

Dream bigger

Aim higher

Fight harder

And, when in doubt, remember

You are right.

OTHER BOOKS FROM REBEL GIRLS

• CONTENTS •

There are many reasons why this book will always be special to us. Some are obvious: the record-breaking amount of money we raised through crowdfunding (more than one million dollars! *Good Night Stories for Rebel Girls* is the most funded original book in the history of crowdfunding), the astonishing number of backers from more than 70 countries, and the privilege of working with dozens of unbelievably talented female artists from all over the world.

Some reasons, though, are less obvious: the messages of soon-to-be moms and dads who told us that this is the first book they have bought for their daughters. The friend of a friend who said that this campaign gave her the confidence to start working on a project close to her heart that she had kept on hold for a long time because "what if I fail?" The email from a mom ecstatic to have a book that could help her share her perspective on the world with her three sons, not only as a mother, but as a woman. Above all, the deep trust that our backers have put in us.

This amount of trust is not something women get to experience very often. We do not take it for granted. How could we? Most of the extraordinary women featured in this book never experienced this kind of trust. No matter the importance of their discoveries, the audacity of their adventures, the width of their genius—they were constantly belittled, forgotten, and in some cases, almost erased from history.

It is important that girls understand the obstacles that lay in front of them. It is just as important that they know these obstacles are not insurmountable—that not only can they find a way to overcome them, but that they can remove those obstacles for those who come after them, just like these great women did.

Each of the 100 stories in this book proves the world-changing power of a trusting heart.

May these brave pioneers inspire you. May their portraits impress upon our daughters the solid belief that beauty manifests itself in all shapes and colors and at all ages. May each reader know the greatest success is to live a life full of passion, curiosity, and generosity. May we all remember every day that we have the right to be happy and to explore wildly.

Now that you're holding this book, all we can feel is hope and enthusiasm for the world we're building together. A world where gender will not define how big you can dream, how far you can go. A world where each of us will be able to say with confidence: "I am free."

Thank you for being part of this journey.

Elena Favilli
Francesca Cavallo

BONUS! AUDIO STORIES!

SCAN TO HEAR MORE!

Download the Rebel Girls app to hear longer stories about some of the extraordinary women in this book. You will also unlock creative activities and discover stories of other trailblazing women. Whenever you come across a bookmark icon, just scan the code, and you'll be whisked away on an audio adventure.

Good Night Stories for Rebel Girls

ADA LOVELACE

MATHEMATICIAN

Once upon a time, there was a girl named Ada who loved machines. She also loved the idea of flying.

She studied birds to work out the perfect balance between wing size and body weight. She tested out materials and tried out several designs. She never managed to soar like a bird, but she created a beautiful book full of drawings called *Flyology* where she recorded all of her findings.

One night, Ada went to a ball. There, she met a grumpy old mathematician named Charles Babbage. Ada was a brilliant mathematician herself, and the two soon became good friends. Charles invited Ada to see a machine he had invented. He called it the *Difference Engine*. It could automatically add and subtract numbers. No one had ever done that before.

Ada was hooked.

"What if we built a machine that could make more complicated calculations?" she said. Excited, Ada and Charles started working. Their machine was huge, and it required an enormous steam engine.

Ada wanted to go further: "What if this machine could play music and show letters as well as numbers?"

She was describing a computer, way before modern computers were invented!

Ada wrote the first computer program in history.

DECEMBER 10, 1815–NOVEMBER 27, 1852

UNITED KINGDOM

"THAT BRAIN OF MINE IS SOMETHING MORE THAN MERELY MORTAL; AS TIME WILL SHOW."
—ADA LOVELACE

· ALEK WEK ·

SUPERMODEL

Once upon a time, there was a girl named Alek who would stop by a mango tree to get a snack on her way home from school.

In Alek's village, there was no running water or electricity. She had to walk to a well for drinking water, but she and her family lived a simple, happy life.

Then a terrible war broke out, and Alek's life changed forever. As the warning sirens wailed over their village, Alek and her family had to run away from the fighting. It was the rainy season. The river had flooded, the bridges across it were underwater, and Alek could not swim. She was terrified of drowning, but her mom helped her to cross safely to the other side. During their journey, Alek's mom foraged for food and sold packets of salt until she saved enough to buy passports for her family. They managed to escape from the war and make their way to London.

One day, she was in a park when a talent scout from a famous modeling agency approached her. He wanted to recruit Alek as a model. Alek's mother did not want to hear about it. But the agent persisted, and she finally agreed. Alek looked so different from any other model that she instantly became a sensation. Alek wants every girl on the planet to know she's beautiful.

"I felt that girls growing up needed to see somebody different . . . It's OK to be quirky, it's fine to be shy. You don't have to go with the crowd."

BORN APRIL 16, 1977
SOUTH SUDAN

"WHEN BEAUTY SHINES
FROM WITHIN, THERE
CAN BE NO DENYING IT."
—ALEK WEK

ALFONSINA STRADA

CYCLIST

O nce there was a girl who could ride a bike so fast that you could barely see her. "Don't go so fast, Alfonsina!" her parents would scream. Too late—she had already whizzed past.

At age 20, Alfonsina set a women's record that stood for 26 years!

When she got married, her family hoped she would finally give up the crazy idea of becoming a cyclist. Instead, on her wedding day, her husband gave her a new racing bike. They moved to Milan, and Alfonsina started to train professionally. She was so fast and so strong that a couple of years later, she entered the Giro di Lombardia, one of the toughest races in the world. No other woman had ever attempted it before. Of the 54 cyclists who started out, only 29 made it across the finish line. Alfonsina was one of them.

A few years later, Alfonsina enrolled in the Giro d'Italia, which was traditionally only for men. It was a strenuous 21-day race along some of the steepest mountain roads in Europe. "She'll never make it," people said. But nobody could stop her. After three weeks of racing, Alfonsina finished in 36th place. She was greeted as a hero. The next year, she was barred from competing. "Giro d'Italia is a men's race," the officials declared.

She raced all the same and continued to compete against men and women in Italy, Spain, France, and Luxembourg.

She would be happy to know that things have changed a lot since then.

MARCH 16, 1891–SEPTEMBER 13, 1959
ITALY

ILLUSTRATION BY
CRISTINA PORTOLANO

"NOBODY CAN
STOP MY BIKE."
—ALFONSINA STRADA

ALICIA ALONSO

BALLERINA

Once upon a time, there was a blind girl who became a great ballerina. Her name was Alicia.

Alicia grew up sighted. She was already a wonderful ballerina with a great career ahead of her when she fell ill. Her eyesight got worse and worse. She was forced to stay in bed for months without moving, but Alicia had to dance—so she danced in the only way she could. "I danced in my mind," she said. "Blinded, motionless, flat on my back, I taught myself to dance *Giselle*."

One day, the American Ballet Theatre's prima ballerina injured herself. They called Alicia to step in. She was already partially blind, but how could she say no? The ballet was *Giselle*!

As soon as she started to dance, the audience fell in love. Alicia danced with grace and confidence even though she could barely see. She trained her partners to be exactly where she needed them at just the right time.

Her style was so unique that she was asked to dance all over the world. But her dream was to bring classical ballet to Cuba, her home country. Back from her travels, she started to teach classical ballet to Cuban dancers. She founded the Ballet Alicia Alonso company, which later became the Ballet Nacional de Cuba.

Alicia was eventually named Cuba's prima ballerina assoluta, the highest honor in ballet reserved for the most notable of dancers.

DECEMBER 21, 1920–OCTOBER 17, 2019
CUBA

"A DANCER SHOULD LEARN
FROM ALL THE ARTS."
—ALICIA ALONSO

AMEENAH GURIB-FAKIM

PRESIDENT AND SCIENTIST

On an island nation in the Indian Ocean called Mauritius, there lived a girl who wanted to know everything about plants. Her name was Ameenah.

Ameenah studied biodiversity. She analyzed hundreds of aromatic and medicinal herbs and flowers. She studied their properties and traveled to rural villages to learn from traditional healers how they used plants in their rituals. For Ameenah, plants were like friends.

Her favorite tree was the baobab because it is so useful. It stores water in its trunk, its leaves can cure infections, and its fruit (called monkey bread) contains more protein than human milk.

Ameenah knew that a lot could be learned from plants—plants like benjoin, for example. "The leaves of benjoin are different shapes and sizes," she said. "Animals won't eat plants they don't recognize. So they tend to leave this plant alone . . . Quite smart, don't you think?"

Ameenah thought of plants as living, biological labs, full of vital information for humans and every other species. "Every time a forest is cut down, every time a marsh is filled in, it is a potential lab that goes with it and which we will never, ever recover."

Ameenah Gurib-Fakim was President of Mauritius from 2015 to 2018, and she fought hard for all the inhabitants of her country: people, animals, and of course, plants.

BORN OCTOBER 17, 1959
MAURITIUS

ILLUSTRATION BY
GERALDINE SY

"I THINK NOT JUST AS
A BIOLOGIST, BUT AS A
WOMAN BIOLOGIST."
—AMEENAH GURIB-FAKIM

SCAN TO HEAR MORE

AMELIA EARHART

AVIATOR

Once upon a time, a girl called Amelia saved enough money to buy a yellow airplane. She called it "The Canary."

A few years later, she became the first woman to fly solo across the Atlantic Ocean. It was a dangerous flight. Her tiny plane was tossed around by strong winds and icy storms. She kept herself going with a can of tomato juice, sucked through a straw. After almost 15 hours, she touched down in a field in Northern Ireland, much to the surprise of the cows. When a few farmers came out to see what had landed, Amelia blurted out "I'm from America!"

Amelia loved to fly and she loved to do things no one had ever done before. Her biggest challenge was to be the first woman to fly around the world.

She took only a small bag, as all the space in the plane had to be used for fuel. Her long flight was going well. She was supposed to land on the tiny Howland Island, but never got there.

In her last transmission, Amelia said she was flying through clouds and was running low on fuel. Her plane disappeared somewhere over the Pacific Ocean and was never found.

Before leaving, she wrote, "I am quite aware of the hazards. I want to do it because I want to do it. Women must try to do the same things that men have tried. If they fail, their failure must be a challenge to others."

JULY 24, 1897–CIRCA JULY 2, 1937

UNITED STATES OF AMERICA

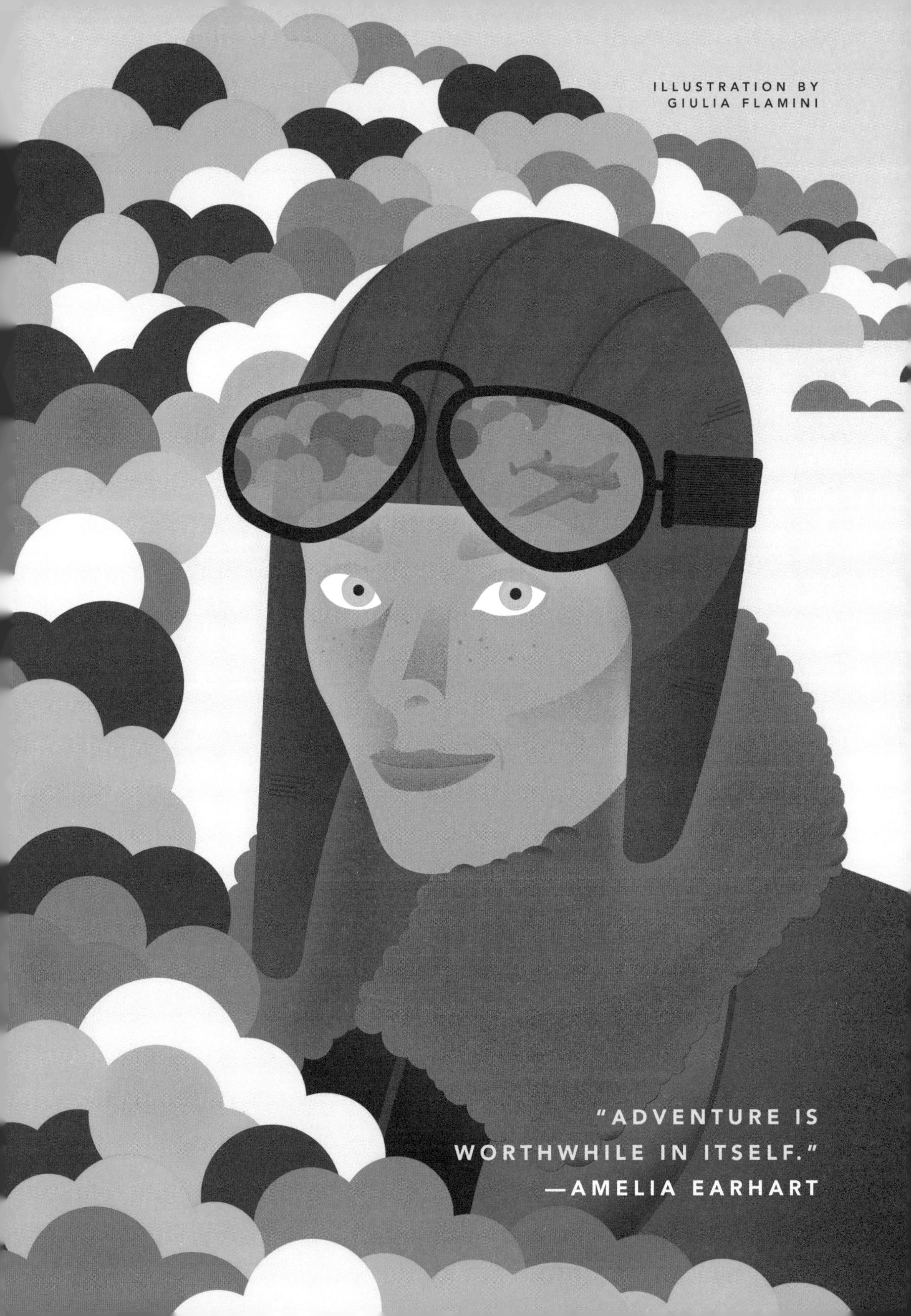

ILLUSTRATION BY
GIULIA FLAMINI
"ADVENTURE IS
WORTHWHILE IN ITSELF."
—AMELIA EARHART

AMNA AL HADDAD

WEIGHTLIFTER

Once upon a time, there was a journalist named Amna. Amna was not happy. She was overweight and unfit. One day, she said to herself, "You can do much more than this. You can be better than this. Just go and do something. Go for a walk." And that's what she did.

She enjoyed her walks so much she wanted to go farther. She ran long distances. She sprinted. She started to work out at the gym. When she discovered weight lifting, she knew it was the sport for her.

Amna's life changed when the International Weightlifting Federation decided to allow Muslim women to compete in a unitard (an outfit that covers the whole body). She started competing in Europe and the United States and became an icon for Muslim girls across the world.

"I like being strong," says Amna. "Being a girl does not mean you can't be as strong as a boy, or even stronger!"

She liked weight lifting so much that she started training for the Olympic Games in Rio de Janeiro, Brazil. She qualified for the games, but was unfortunately injured before she could compete.

Amna believes everyone should find a sport they like and practice it. "Whatever your age, religion, or ethnicity, sport is good for everyone," she says. And what advice does she have? "No matter what the challenges are, never walk away from your dream. The more you persist, the closer you are going to get to your goals. When things get tough, just get tougher."

BORN OCTOBER 21, 1989
UNITED ARAB EMIRATES

"NOBODY CAN TELL ME WHAT
I CAN AND CANNOT DO."
—AMNA AL HADDAD

ANN MAKOSINSKI

INVENTOR

Once upon a time, a girl named Ann visited a friend's home that didn't have electricity. It was too dark for them to study!

Ann was great at building things, and she was especially passionate about transistors, devices that regulate the flow of electric current.

"What if I could invent a flashlight that is powered by your body?" Ann asked her friend. "After all, our bodies give off lots of energy in the form of heat." The girls got very excited.

"Just think how many people could have electricity if this worked!"

Ann was just 15 years old, but she already had a lot of experience taking things apart and putting them back together.

So she started to work on this mysterious new flashlight. She called it the "Hollow Flashlight" because she built it using a hollow aluminum tube that cooled the heat collected from the holder's hand.

When she presented it to the Google Science Fair, she won first prize! It's the first flashlight that doesn't need batteries, wind, or sun—just body heat.

Today Ann is considered one of the most promising inventors of our time. Her dream is to make the battery-free Hollow Flashlights available to anyone in the world who can't afford electricity.

"I like the idea of using technology to make the world a better place and to keep our environment clean," she always says.

BORN OCTOBER 3, 1997
CANADA

ILLUSTRATION BY
CLAUDIA CARIERI

"IF YOU ARE ALIVE, YOU
PRODUCE SOME LIGHT."
—ANN MAKOSINSKI

ANNA POLITKOVSKAYA

JOURNALIST

Once upon a time, in Russia, many books were forbidden. Some of these were by writers that a little girl named Anna loved. Anna's parents used to smuggle in her favorite books so she could read to her heart's content.

Anna grew up and became a journalist.

When a part of Russia called Chechnya wanted to break away and become an independent nation, the Russian government sent in troops to stop them. A brutal war broke out. Anna decided that she had to write. She wanted to tell the world what was really happening in Chechnya. The Russian government did not like that at all.

"Why are you putting your life at risk?" her family asked her over and over. "Risk is part of my profession," she answered. "I know that something may happen to me. I just want my articles to make the world better."

Many bad things happened, but Anna was brave.

Once, she had to run all night long in the Chechen hills to escape from the Russian Security Services. People on both sides wanted to stop her from telling the truth—someone even put poison in her tea to try and get rid of her. But despite these dangers, she bravely carried on telling the truth about everything she saw.

Anna continued to risk her life until she died, writing the truth in order to make the world a better place.

AUGUST 30, 1958–OCTOBER 7, 2006
RUSSIA

ILLUSTRATION BY
LEA HEINRICH

"WHAT MATTERS IS THE
INFORMATION, NOT WHAT
YOU THINK ABOUT IT."
ANNA POLITKOVSKAYA

SCAN TO
HEAR MORE

ARTEMISIA GENTILESCHI

PAINTER

Once there was a girl who was an amazing painter. Her name was Artemisia and she was beautiful and strong.

Her father, Orazio, was also a painter. He trained her in his studio from the time she was little. By the time she was 17 years old, Artemisia had already painted several masterpieces. Yet people were skeptical about her. "How can she paint like this?" they whispered to one another.

At that time, most women were not even allowed to get close to famous artists' studios.

One day, her father asked his friend, the famous painter Agostino Tassi, to teach Artemisia perspective, how to create a three-dimensional space on a flat surface.

Agostino wanted his star pupil to also be his lover. "I promise I will marry you," he told her. Artemisia kept saying no.

Things became so bad that Artemisia finally told her father what was going on. Artemisia's father believed her, and even though Agostino was a powerful man and a dangerous enemy, Orazio took him to court.

During the trial, Agostino denied doing anything wrong. Artemisia faced terrible pressure but stuck to the truth and didn't give in. In the end, Agostino was found guilty. Today, Artemisia is considered one of the greatest painters of all time.

JULY 8, 1593–CIRCA 1653

ITALY

ILLUSTRATION BY
MONICA GARWOOD

"AS LONG AS I LIVE, I WILL HAVE
CONTROL OVER MY BEING."
—ARTEMISIA GENTILESCHI

ASHLEY FIOLEK

MOTOCROSS RACER

A little girl called Ashley was playing in the kitchen when some pans fell off the table with a massive crash. Ashley didn't even turn around. Her mom and dad decided to get her hearing tested. When the results came back, they found out that their daughter was deaf.

They learned sign language and sent Ashley to camp with other deaf kids so she could learn from them and build up her self-confidence.

Ashley's father and her grandfather loved motorcycles, so they gave her a peewee motorbike when she was three. The three of them would head to the woods, each of them on their own motorcycle. Ashley loved these outings, and she started dreaming about becoming a motocross racer.

Most people told her it was impossible. "Hearing is really important in motocross," they said. "The sound of the engine tells you when to shift gears. You have to be able to hear where the other riders are."

But Ashley could feel from the engine's vibration when to change gears. She looked for shadows in the corner of her eye and knew when someone was getting close. In five years, she won four national titles. She fell many times. Ashley broke her left arm, her right wrist, her right ankle, her collarbone (three times!), and her two front teeth, but she always recovered and got back on her bike.

Ashley has a pickup truck parked in her driveway. On the back, a bumper sticker reads "Honk all you want, I'm deaf!"

BORN OCTOBER 22, 1990
UNITED STATES OF AMERICA

"I DON'T THINK ABOUT VIBRATIONS; I DON'T THINK ABOUT ANYTHING AT ALL. I'M PART OF THE BIKE NOW."
—ASHLEY FIOLEK

ILLUSTRATION BY
KATE PRIOR

ASTRID LINDGREN

WRITER

Once there was a girl who lived on a farm with her big family. She spent entire days roaming free in the fields with her brother and sisters. She also helped take care of the farm animals—not just the small ones like chickens and ducks, even the big ones like cows and horses!

Her name was Astrid, and she had quite a rebellious spirit.

She was strong, brave, never scared of being alone, and she could do all sorts of things: clean, cook, fix a bike, walk along rooftops, fight off bullies, make up fantastic stories . . . Sound familiar? Well, if you've ever read about another little girl who was strong, brave, and fearless called Pippi Longstocking, you won't be surprised to learn that Astrid was the author of that brilliant book.

When *Pippi Longstocking* was published, lots of adults disapproved. "Pippi is too rebellious," they said. "Our children will think being disobedient is okay." Children, on the other hand, absolutely loved it. Pippi didn't just say *no* without any reason. She showed young readers the importance of being independent while always caring for others.

Today *Pippi Longstocking* is one of the best-loved books in children's literature. Astrid went on to write and publish many more books, always depicting strong children in charge of their own adventures.

So, whenever you're in trouble for something you did, grab a copy of *Pippi Longstocking*. She will always be there to help you!

NOVEMBER 14, 1907–JANUARY 28, 2002
SWEDEN

"S'NOT SOMETHING YOU PLAN,
MISCHIEF, IT JUST HAPPENS."
—ASTRID LINDGREN

AUNG SAN SUU KYI

POLITICIAN

Once there was a young woman named Suu Kyi. She came from a rich Burmese family who traveled the world.

Suu Kyi, her husband, and their two children were living in England when the phone rang. "My mom has fallen ill," she said to her children. "I have to return to Myanmar."

She planned to stay for only a few weeks, but from the moment she landed, she found herself protesting a military dictator. He had taken over the country and imprisoned anyone who opposed him.

Suu Kyi spoke out and quickly gained support. The dictator realized that she was a powerful threat and gave her a tough choice: "You can leave and never come back or be a prisoner in your own home."

Suu Kyi thought about it. "I'll stay," she said. She spent 15 years locked in her house spreading messages of peace. She inspired millions of people across the world, all without leaving her home.

After being released, she was elected to parliament and later became the state counsellor of her country. Sadly, her administration was accused of horrible crimes. The military silenced journalists and activists, then persecuted and killed Rohingya* people, just like the dictator before Suu Kyi. As the leader of her country, the world began to see her differently. Some people still admire her conviction, but many think her actions as head of state outweigh any past achievements as a peace activist.

*The Rohingya are a minority ethnic group in Myanmar who are predominantly Muslim.

BORN JUNE 19, 1945
BURMA

ILLUSTRATION BY
LIZZY STEWART

"SINCE WE LIVE IN
THIS WORLD, WE HAVE
TO DO OUR BEST FOR
THIS WORLD."
—AUNG SAN SUU KYI

BALKISSA CHAIBOU

ACTIVIST

Once there was a girl who wanted to become a doctor. Her name was Balkissa, and she was really good at school. One day, she discovered that her uncle had promised her in marriage to one of her cousins. Balkissa was horrified. "You can't force me to get married!" she insisted. "I want to be a doctor."

Unfortunately, the country where Balkissa lived allowed parents to arrange weddings for their daughters when they are still children.

"Just let me stay in school five more years," Balkissa begged.

Her parents agreed to postpone the marriage, but after five years, Balkissa's love of learning had only grown stronger. The night before her wedding, she escaped from her house and ran to the nearest police station to ask for help. She decided to challenge her uncle in court.

She was terrified that her whole family would turn against her, but her mother quietly encouraged her to keep fighting. The judge agreed with Balkissa, and when her uncle threatened her, he was forced to leave the country. "When I put on my school uniform, I felt my life was renewed," she says.

Balkissa went to medical school to become a doctor. She visits schools and speaks to tribal chiefs about the issue. She campaigns for other young girls to follow her example and say 'no' to forced marriage. "Study with all your might," she tells them. "Those studies are your only hope."

BORN 1995
NIGER

ILLUSTRATION BY
PRIYA KURIYAN

"I WILL SHOW THEM WHAT
I CAN DO WITH MY LIFE."
—BALKISSA CHAIBOU

BRENDA CHAPMAN

DIRECTOR AND STORY ARTIST

Once there was a girl who had curly red hair and loved to draw. Her name was Brenda.

When she was 15 years old, Brenda called up Walt Disney Studios. "I'm really good at drawing," she said. "Will you give me a job?" They told her to get back in touch when she was older and had some training.

That's exactly what she did. She studied character animation at CalArts, and a few years later found herself exactly where she'd always dreamed: working on animated films for Disney in Los Angeles. She soon discovered that she was one of the very few women animators there. Brenda suspected that was why the princesses in the movies always seemed so powerless. She promised herself that she would create a new type of princess: strong, independent, and . . .

". . . *Brave*," she thought. "What a great name for a film!"

Princess Merida in *Brave* is anything but helpless. She's a fantastic archer, who gallops around on her horse, fighting off bears and having amazing adventures. Brenda based the character on her own little girl, Emma—a strong, free-spirited girl, just like her mom! "She is my Merida . . . and I adore her." Brenda won an Oscar and a Golden Globe for her film.

She also worked on many other award-winning films, like *Beauty and the Beast* and *The Lion King*. Brenda became the first woman to direct an animated feature for a major Hollywood studio with *The Prince of Egypt*.

BORN NOVEMBER 1, 1962
UNITED STATES OF AMERICA

"I DREW SINCE I WAS A
LITTLE KID—AND I WANTED
TO DRAW IN MY CAREER."
BRENDA CHAPMAN

THE BRONTË SISTERS

WRITERS

In a cold, bleak house in northern England, there once lived three sisters. Charlotte, Emily, and Anne were often alone. They wrote stories and poems to entertain themselves.

One day, Charlotte decided to send her poems to a famous poet to ask what he thought of them. He dismissed them and responded, "Literature cannot be the business of a woman's life, and it ought not to be."

Charlotte kept on writing.

One night, she found a notebook lying open on Emily's desk. "Why have you not shown us your poems before?" Charlotte asked. "They are beautiful." Emily was furious at her sister for reading her private papers without permission. But once Emily calmed down, Charlotte asked, "Why don't we write a book of poetry together?" Emily and Anne agreed.

When they finally published the book, it sold only two copies. But they didn't give up. They kept working in secret, discussing their writing at the dinner table. This time, they each worked on a different novel. When the novels came out, they were hugely successful. People at the time couldn't believe that they had been written by three country girls, so the sisters had to travel to London to prove that they were indeed the authors.

Their books have been translated into many different languages and read by millions of people across the world.

CHARLOTTE, APRIL 21, 1816–MARCH 31, 1855
EMILY, JULY 30, 1818–DECEMBER 19, 1848
ANNE, JANUARY 17, 1820–MAY 28, 1849
UNITED KINGDOM

"I AM NOT AN ANGEL, AND I
WILL NOT BE ONE TILL I DIE:
I WILL BE MYSELF."
—CHARLOTTE BRONTË

CATHERINE THE GREAT

EMPRESS

Once there was a queen who disliked her husband.

Her name was Catherine and her husband, Peter, was the emperor of Russia. The Russian people found him mean and arrogant.

Catherine knew she would do a better job of ruling the country. All she had to do was to figure out a way of replacing her husband.

Six months after becoming emperor, Peter went on vacation, leaving Catherine behind. This was her chance. Catherine gave a rousing speech to the royal soldiers to get them on her side. They switched their loyalty from Peter to Catherine, and a priest declared her the new ruler of Russia. She then ordered a suitably magnificent crown to be made for herself.

Catherine's magnificent crown took two months to create! It was made of gold and silver encrusted with 4,936 diamonds, 75 pearls, and a huge ruby on top.

One of the first things she did as empress was to order her husband to be arrested and put in jail.

During her reign, Catherine expanded the Russian empire, winning many wars and uprisings.

Lots of people were envious. They said nasty things about her behind her back when she was alive, and when she died, they said she must have fallen off the toilet! In fact, she died in her bed and was buried in a golden tomb in Peter and Paul Cathedral in Saint Petersburg.

MAY 2, 1729–NOVEMBER 17, 1796

RUSSIA

ILLUSTRATION BY
MARIJKE BUURLAGE

"I AM ONE OF THE
PEOPLE WHO LOVE
THE WHY OF THINGS."
—CATHERINE THE GREAT

CHOLITA CLIMBERS

MOUNTAINEERS

Once upon a time, at the foot of a beautiful mountain in Bolivia, there lived a woman called Lidia Huayllas.

All her life, Lidia and her friends had cooked for mountaineers before they set off from base camps to climb the mountain. She used to watch them put on their helmets, strap on their backpacks, tighten their boots, and fill their water bottles. She saw the excited looks in their eyes.

Lidia and the other women did not know what it was like on top of the mountain. Their husbands did, and their sons did. It was their job to act as mountain guides and porters, taking groups of climbers safely up to the peaks and back down again, while the women stayed at camp in the valley.

One day, Lidia said, "Let's go up and see for ourselves."

As the women pulled on their boots and crampons under their long, colorful skirts (polleras), the men laughed. "You can't wear polleras," they said. "You have to wear proper climbing gear."

"Nonsense," Lidia said, strapping on her hardhat. "We can wear what we like. We are the *cholita* climbers!"

Through snowstorms and high winds, the women climbed peak after peak. "We are strong. We want to climb eight mountains," they said.

As you read this, they are probably tramping through the snow, the wind swirling their multi-colored skirts, filled with the excitement of seeing the world from yet another peak.

FOUNDED 2015

BOLIVIA

"BEING ON THE TOP IS WONDERFUL.
IT'S ANOTHER WORLD."
—LIDIA HUAYLLAS

CLAUDIA RUGGERINI

PARTISAN

Once there was a girl who had to change her name. "Hey, Marisa!" her friends would call out. Nobody could know that her real name was Claudia. It was too dangerous.

Claudia lived at a time when Italy was ruled by a tyrannical man called Benito Mussolini. During Mussolini's dictatorship, you couldn't read certain books, you couldn't watch certain movies, you couldn't express your opinion, and you couldn't vote. Claudia believed in freedom and decided to fight this man with all her strength, so she joined a group of partisans (*partigiani* in Italian) to help bring down the dictator.

Claudia's group was made up of university students. They would meet in secret after class to bring out their own newspaper. But how could they spread their message with Mussolini's police everywhere?

Claudia was incredibly brave. She cycled around delivering newspapers and messages from one secret location to another for almost two years. One day, the regime finally collapsed. The national radio announced that Italy was free from fascism, and people flooded onto the streets to celebrate.

Claudia—Marisa—had one last task. With a small group of partisans, she entered the offices of one of Italy's daily newspapers, *Corriere della Sera*, and officially liberated it from censorship after 20 years. Finally, they were free to print the truth—and Claudia's friends could call her by her real name at last.

FEBRUARY 1922–JULY 4, 2016

ITALY

ILLUSTRATION BY
CRISTINA PORTOLANO

"STRONGER THAN FEAR IS THE
DESIRE TO FIGHT FOR FREEDOM."
—CLAUDIA RUGGERINI

CLEOPATRA

PHARAOH

Once upon a time, in ancient Egypt, a pharaoh died and left his kingdom to his 10-year-old son, Ptolemy XIII, and his 18-year-old daughter, Cleopatra.

The two had such different ideas about how to run the country that soon Cleopatra was kicked out of the palace, and a civil war broke out.

Julius Caesar, the emperor of Rome, traveled to Egypt to help Cleopatra and Ptolemy find an agreement. "If only I could meet Caesar before my brother does," Cleopatra thought, "I could convince him that I'm the better pharaoh." But she had been banished from the palace. The guards would block her at the entrance.

Cleopatra asked her servants to roll her up inside a carpet and smuggle her into Caesar's rooms. Impressed by her daring, Caesar restored Cleopatra to the throne. They became a couple and had a son. Cleopatra moved to Rome but returned to Egypt after Caesar was killed.

The new Roman leader, Mark Antony, had heard a lot about this strong Egyptian queen and wanted to meet her. This time, she arrived on a golden barge, surrounded by precious jewels and silk.

It was love at first sight. Cleopatra and Mark Antony were inseparable. They had three children and loved each other to the end of their lives.

When Cleopatra died, the empire ended with her. She was the last pharaoh to rule Ancient Egypt.

69 B.C.–AUGUST 12, 30 B.C.

EGYPT

ILLUSTRATION BY
KIKI LJUNG

"I WILL NOT BE
TRIUMPHED
OVER."
—CLEOPATRA

· COCO CHANEL ·

FASHION DESIGNER

Once upon a time, in central France, there was a girl who lived in a convent, surrounded by nuns dressed in black and white. Her name was Gabrielle Chanel.

In the convent, girls were taught how to sew, but they didn't have many colors to choose from. They used the same material as the nuns did, so all their dolls were dressed in black and white, too!

When she grew up, Gabrielle worked as a seamstress by day and a singer by night. The soldiers she sang for at the bar called her *Coco*, and the nickname stuck with her for the rest of her life.

Coco dreamed of having her own shop in Paris. One day, a wealthy friend of hers lent her enough money to make her dream come true.

Coco's clothes looked fabulous, even if the cloth was plain. "Where did you buy that?" the chic French ladies would ask her. "I made it myself," she'd say. "Come to my shop and I can make one for you, too." Business grew quickly, and Coco soon repaid all the money to her friend.

Her most successful design was her classic "little black dress." She transformed the color that had always been associated with funerals into something perfect for a glamorous evening out. The shape of many of the clothes we wear now was heavily influenced by Coco Chanel.

Unfortunately, her alignment with the Nazi party during WWII left a stain on her legacy, but her pioneering designs are still celebrated today.

AUGUST 19, 1883–JANUARY 10, 1971
FRANCE

"SOME PEOPLE THINK THAT LUXURY IS THE OPPOSITE OF POVERTY. NOT SO. IT IS THE OPPOSITE OF VULGARITY."
—COCO CHANEL

SCAN TO HEAR MORE

CORA CORALINA

POET AND BAKER

Once upon a time, in a house on a bridge, there was a little girl called Cora who knew she was a poet.

Her family did not think so. They did not want her to read books, and they did not want to send her to high school. They thought her job was to find a good husband and raise a family.

When she grew up, Cora fell in love with a man, and they got married. She moved with him to the big city, and they had six children. She worked at all sorts of jobs to make sure her children could go to school.

Cora had a busy life, but she never forgot she was a poet. She wrote every single day.

When she was 60 years old, she moved back to the house on the bridge. She decided it was time to start her career as a poet. Cora still needed money, so she baked cakes to sell on her doorstep along with her poems.

Cora's poems started to be appreciated by other poets and writers. She won prizes and medals, and when she was 76 years old, she published her very first book.

Journalists came from all over the country to interview her while she was baking. And when they left, she sat back down at her desk and started to write again, surrounded by the delicious smells of pies, cookies, and cakes.

AUGUST 20, 1889–APRIL 10, 1985

BRAZIL

ILLUSTRATION BY
ELENIA BERETTA

"I'M THAT WOMAN WHO
CLIMBED THE MOUNTAIN OF
LIFE, REMOVING STONES AND
PLANTING FLOWERS."
—CORA CORALINA

• COY MATHIS •

ELEMENTARY SCHOOL STUDENT

Once upon a time, a child named Coy was born. At the time, doctors said Coy was male.

But Coy wanted to be addressed as "she." She preferred dresses and bright, shiny shoes to the clothes that were made for boys. So, Coy's parents let her wear whatever she wanted.

One night, Coy asked her mom, "When are we going to the doctor to have me fixed into a girl-girl?"

The doctor explained that usually boys feel okay with being boys, and girls are fine with being girls. But there are some boys who know they are female, and some girls who know they are male. They're called transgender, and Coy is a transgender girl. She was born in a boy's body, but deep inside, she knew she was a girl.

From then on, Coy's mom and dad asked everyone to treat Coy as a girl. But when she started first grade, the family ran into an unexpected problem. "Coy has to use either the boys' bathroom or the bathroom for children with disabilities," the teachers said.

But Coy was not a boy, and she didn't have a disability. "The school is being mean to me!" Coy wailed.

Coy's parents talked to a judge. The judge thought about it and decided: "Coy should be allowed to use whichever bathroom she wants." Coy's parents threw her a big party with a big cake to celebrate.

BORN CIRCA 2007
UNITED STATES OF AMERICA

ILLUSTRATION BY
MARTA LORENZON

"I WANT TO GO TO SCHOOL.
WE PLAY GAMES AT RECESS."
—COY MATHIS

ELIZABETH I

QUEEN

Once upon a time, there was a king who wanted to leave his kingdom to a son.

When his wife gave birth to a daughter, King Henry VIII was so mad that he left her, sent the child away, and married another woman. He believed that only a man would be able to rule the country after he died and was delighted when his new wife gave birth to a boy: Edward.

Meanwhile, Henry's daughter, Elizabeth, grew up a bright and brilliant girl, with striking red hair and a fiery temper.

Edward was only nine when his father died and he became king. A few years later, he also became ill and died, and his sister Mary became queen. Mary thought that Elizabeth was plotting against her, so she locked up Elizabeth in the Tower of London.

One day, the Tower guards burst into her cell. "The Queen is dead," they shouted. Then they fell to their knees in front of her. Elizabeth instantly went from being a prisoner in the Tower to the country's new queen.

Elizabeth's court was home to musicians, poets, painters, and playwrights. The most famous was William Shakespeare, whose plays Elizabeth adored. She wore sumptuous gowns decorated with pearls and lace. She never married. She valued her own independence as highly as that of her country.

Her people loved her dearly and, when she died, Londoners took to the streets to mourn the greatest queen they had ever known.

SEPTEMBER 7, 1533–MARCH 24, 1603

UNITED KINGDOM

ILLUSTRATION BY
ANA GALVAŃ

"A CLEAR AND INNOCENT
CONSCIENCE FEARS
NOTHING."
—ELIZABETH I

· EUFROSINA CRUZ ·

ACTIVIST AND POLITICIAN

When Eufrosina's father told her that women could only make tortillas and children, she burst into tears and promised to show him that it wasn't true. "You can leave this house, but don't expect a single cent from me," he told her.

Eufrosina started out by selling chewing gum and fruit on the street to pay for her studies. She got a degree in accounting and came back home with a job as a teacher. She taught young Indigenous girls like herself, so they could also find the strength and the resources to build their own lives.

One day, she decided to run for mayor of her town. She won many votes, but despite that, the townsmen canceled the election. "A woman as mayor? Don't be ridiculous," they said. Furious, Eufrosina worked even harder. She founded an organization called QUIEGO, to help Indigenous women fight for their rights. Their symbol was a white lily. "Wherever I go, I take this flower to remind people that Indigenous women are exactly like that: natural, beautiful, and resilient," Eufrosina said.

A few years later, Eufrosina became the first Indigenous woman to be elected president of the state congress. When the first lady of Mexico came to visit, Eufrosina walked arm-in-arm with her, in front of the local population.

She showed her father—and the whole world—that there is nothing that the strong, Indigenous women of Mexico cannot do.

BORN JANUARY 1, 1979
MEXICO

"WHEN YOU CHANGE A WOMAN, YOU CHANGE A FAMILY, THEN A TOWN AND STEP BY STEP WE CAN CHANGE THE ENTIRE COUNTRY."
—EUFROSINA, CRUZ

ILLUSTRATION BY PAOLA ROLLO

EVITA PERÓN

POLITICIAN

Once upon a time, in South America, there lived a beautiful girl named Eva. As a child, Eva dreamed of escaping her life of poverty by becoming a famous actress and film star.

When she was just 15 years old, Eva moved to the big city of Buenos Aires. With her talent, good looks, and determination, she soon became a celebrated actress onstage and on the radio. But Eva wanted more. She wanted to help people less fortunate than herself.

One night, at a party, she met Colonel Juan Perón, a powerful politician. They fell in love and got married shortly after.

When Juan Perón was elected president of Argentina one year later, Eva quickly became known by her affectionate nickname, Evita. The people loved her passion and her commitment to helping the poor. She fought hard for women's rights and helped women win their right to vote.

She became such a legendary figure that she was asked to run as vice president to help govern alongside her husband. Although she was loved by the poor, many powerful people feared her charisma and power. "They just can't deal with a young, successful woman," she used to say.

After discovering she had a serious illness, Evita decided not to run, although she did help her husband win a second term as president. When she died, only a few months later, the announcement came on national radio: "We have lost the spiritual chief of our nation."

MAY 7, 1919–JULY 26, 1952
ARGENTINA

ILLUSTRATION BY
CRISTINA AMODEO

"YOU MUST WANT! YOU
HAVE THE RIGHT TO ASK!
YOU MUST DESIRE."
—EVITA PERON

FADUMO DAYIB

POLITICIAN

Once there was a girl whose childhood was spent trying to escape from war. Fadumo and her family had to stay one step ahead of the fighting, and she could not go to school. She did not learn to read and write until she was 14 years old.

One day her mother told her, "You must leave the country. Take your brother and sister and go!" Fadumo knew her mother was right. War-torn Somalia was one of the most dangerous places in the world for children.

When they finally arrived in Finland, Fadumo and her brother could do all the things that children can do when they live in a peaceful, democratic country. They had a home and beds. They had food every day. They could play and go to school. They were never beaten, and they could see a doctor for free if they were ill. But Fadumo never forgot about Somalia.

She wanted to learn everything she could so she could go back to her own country and help her people regain freedom and peace. After earning three master's degrees, she left her family in Finland and started to work with the United Nations to set up hospitals across Somalia.

"I have to be there," she told her husband.

In 2016, Fadumo became Somalia's first female presidential candidate. No Somali woman had ever run for president before because it was extremely dangerous. But she had no doubts: "My mother always told me, 'You hold all life's possibilities in the palm of your hands.' And that's true."

BORN 1972
SOMALIA

"WE WILL NO LONGER NEGOTIATE
FOR OUR EXISTENCE."
—FADUMO DAYIB

FLORENCE NIGHTINGALE

NURSE

Once upon a time, a baby was born to an English couple traveling in Italy. They decided to name their daughter after the beautiful city where she was born, so they called her Florence.

Florence loved traveling, she loved math and science, and she loved collecting information. Whenever she went to a new place, she would note down how many people lived there, how many hospitals there were, and how big the city was.

She loved numbers.

Florence studied nursing and became so good at it that the government sent her to manage a hospital for injured soldiers in Turkey.

As soon as she arrived, Florence started collecting and examining all the data she could find. She discovered that most of the soldiers died not because of their wounds but because of infections and diseases contracted in the hospital.

"The very first requirement in a hospital is that it should do the sick no harm," she said.

She made sure that everyone working there washed their hands frequently and kept everything clean. At night, she carried a lamp as she made her rounds, talking to her patients and giving them hope.

Thanks to her, many more soldiers made it home safely, and she became known as "The Lady with the Lamp."

MAY 12, 1820–AUGUST 13, 1910
UNITED KINGDOM

ILLUSTRATION BY
DALILA ROVAZZANI

"I ATTRIBUTE MY SUCCESS
TO THIS—I NEVER GAVE
OR TOOK ANY EXCUSE."
—FLORENCE NIGHTINGALE

• FRIDA KAHLO •

PAINTER

Once upon a time, in a bright blue house near Mexico City, there lived a small girl called Frida. She would grow up to be one of the most famous painters of the twentieth century, but she almost didn't grow up at all.

When she was six, she nearly died from polio. The disease left her with a permanent limp, but that didn't stop her from playing, swimming, and wrestling just like all the other kids.

Then, when she was 18, she was involved in a terrible bus accident. She almost died again—and again she spent months in bed. Her mother made her a special easel so that she could paint while lying down, for more than anything else, Frida loved to paint.

As soon as she was able to walk again, she went to see Mexico's most famous artist, Diego Rivera. "Are my paintings any good?" she asked him. Her paintings were amazing: bold, bright, and beautiful. He fell in love with them—and he fell in love with Frida.

Diego and Frida got married. He was a big man in a large floppy hat. She looked tiny beside him. People called them "the elephant and the dove."

During her life, Frida painted hundreds of beautiful portraits of herself, often surrounded by the animals and birds that she kept. The bright blue house where she lived has been kept just as she left it, full of color and joy and flowers.

JULY 6, 1907–JULY 13, 1954

MEXICO

ILLUSTRATION BY
HELENA MORAIS SOARES

"FEET, WHAT DO I NEED
YOU FOR WHEN I HAVE
WINGS TO FLY?"
—FRIDA KAHLO

· GRACE HOPPER ·

COMPUTER SCIENTIST

Once upon a time, there was a little girl called Grace who really wanted to understand how alarm clocks worked. She started taking apart all the clocks she could find. First one, then another, then the third . . . By the time she got to her seventh clock, her mom realized there were no more clocks in the house and told her to stop!

Grace kept tinkering with anything she found interesting. Eventually, she became a professor of math and physics. During the Second World War, she joined the Navy, like her great-grandfather, who had been an admiral.

She was assigned to work on a special project. "Come and meet Mark," they said. She went into a room but instead of a person, she was introduced to the first computer! Called "Mark I," it filled the entire room and—since it was the first—no one knew exactly how to use it. So Grace started studying it. It took a lot of hard work, but thanks to the programs Grace wrote for the Mark I and its successors, U.S. forces were able to decode secret messages sent by their enemies during the war.

When she was old, Grace tried to retire more than once, but she was always called back because of her extraordinary expertise. She eventually became an admiral too, like her great-grandfather.

All her life, Grace went to bed early and woke up at 5:00 a.m. to work on computer coding. She never stopped being curious, and her incredible work showed the world what computers could do.

DECEMBER 9, 1906–JANUARY 1, 1992
UNITED STATES OF AMERICA

ILLUSTRATION BY
KIKI LJUNG

"IF IT'S
A GOOD IDEA,
GO AHEAD
AND DO IT."
—GRACE HOPPER

HOPPE

GRACE O'MALLEY

PIRATE

Once upon a time, on a wild green island, there lived a girl with long ginger hair. Her name was Grace.

When wind howled and waves crashed against the rocks, Grace would stand on the clifftop and dream of sailing out across the stormy seas. "Girls cannot be sailors," her father told her. "And anyway, your long hair would get tangled in the rigging."

Grace didn't like this one bit. She cut her hair short and dressed in boy's clothes to prove to her family that she too could live the life of the sea.

Finally one day, her father agreed to take her sailing, on one condition: "If we meet a pirate ship, hide below deck," he said. But when they were attacked, Grace leaped off the rigging and landed on one of the pirates' backs! Her surprise attack worked—and they beat the pirates off.

Grace was a fine sailor, and she wanted to do something more exciting than catching fish. She became a pirate, and when the English attacked her castle, she fled to the sea rather than submit to English rule. Grace was so successful that soon she had her own fleet of ships, as well as several islands and castles along the west coast of Ireland.

When the English captured her sons, Grace sailed to meet Queen Elizabeth I to try and save them. To everyone's surprise, the queen and Grace became friends. The queen returned her sons and possessions, and Grace helped her fight against England's enemies, the French and Spanish.

CIRCA 1530–1603

IRELAND

HARRIET TUBMAN

FREEDOM FIGHTER

One day, a girl was standing in front of a grocery store in Maryland when a Black man came running past. He was being chased by a white man, who yelled, "Stop that man! He's my slave!"

The girl did nothing. She hoped the man would escape. Her name was Araminta, and she was 12 years old. She was also enslaved.

Just then, the white man hurled a heavy object. He missed the man running away and hit Araminta on the head instead. She was badly injured. But her thick hair cushioned the blow enough to save her life. "My hair had never been combed," she said, "and it stood out like a bushel basket."

A few years later, she married a man named John Tubman. She changed her name to Harriet after her mother. Then the family who kept her enslaved put her up for sale. So Harriet decided to escape.

Harriet hid in the daytime and traveled by night. The shimmering stars served as her guide as she made her way north through the darkness. When she crossed the border into Pennsylvania, she realized for the first time in her life she was free. "I looked at my hands to see if I was the same person now that I was free. There was such a glory over everything . . . I felt like I was in heaven."

She thought about the enslaved man trying to find freedom and her family in Maryland who were still held captive. She knew she had to help them. Over the next 11 years, she went back 19 times and rescued hundreds of enslaved people. She was never captured, and she never lost a single person.

CIRCA 1822–MARCH 10, 1913
UNITED STATES OF AMERICA

"I HAVE HEARD THEIR GROANS AND
SIGHS AND SEEN THEIR TEARS,
AND I WOULD GIVE EVERY DROP OF
BLOOD IN MY VEINS TO FREE THEM."
—HARRIET TUBMAN

SCAN TO
HEAR MORE

HATSHEPSUT

PHARAOH

Long ago, a woman ruled Egypt for more than 20 years. Her name was Hatshepsut, and she was the first woman to ever become pharaoh.

At the time, the idea of a woman being pharaoh was so strange that Hatshepsut had to act as though she was a man in order to convince Egyptians that she was their legitimate leader. She proclaimed herself *king* and not *queen*. She wore men's clothes and sometimes even put on a false beard!

But apparently that wasn't enough. Twenty years after she died, someone tried to erase her from history. Statues of her were smashed, and her name was removed from the records.

Why? Because a female pharaoh freaked people out. What if her success encouraged other women to seek power?

Thankfully, it's not so easy to erase the memory of someone immortalized in stone. Enough traces of her life and work remained for modern archaeologists to piece together her story.

Hatshepsut's mummy, wrapped in linen and perfumed with resins, had been removed from her original grave and hidden, but it was eventually found in the nearby Valley of the Kings. In 2006, an Egyptologist proved her identity by matching a tooth to her mummified jaw.

CIRCA 1508–1458 B.C.

EGYPT

"I HAVE RESTORED THAT WHICH
WAS IN RUINS. I HAVE RAISED UP
THAT WHICH WAS DESTROYED."
—HATSHEPSUT

• HELEN KELLER •

ACTIVIST

Once upon a time, a girl named Helen suffered from a bad fever that left her deaf and blind. Frustrated and angry, she used to lie on the ground, kicking and screaming.

One day, her mom took Helen to a special school for the blind. A talented young teacher named Anne Sullivan met them and decided to try and teach Helen how to speak.

But how can you learn the word *doll* if you cannot see your doll, Anne wondered. How do you say *water* if you've never heard anyone speak?

Anne realized that she had to use Helen's sense of touch. She held Helen's fingers under running water and spelled the word *water* on her hand. Then she spelled the word *doll* while Helen cuddled her favorite doll. Helen suddenly understood that the words stood for the different things!

With her fingers on Anne's lips, Helen felt the vibrations when these words were spoken, and slowly she learned how to make those words herself. Soon, she was speaking out loud for the first time.

She learned how to read Braille by running her fingers over the raised dots. She even learned French, German, Latin, and Greek, too!

Helen gave public speeches and championed the rights of people with disabilities. She traveled the world with her amazing teacher and her beloved dog. She didn't need words to tell them how she felt. She just gave them big, loving hugs.

JUNE 27, 1880–JUNE 1, 1968
UNITED STATES OF AMERICA

ILLUSTRATION BY
MONICA GARWOOD

"THE BEST AND MOST
BEAUTIFUL THINGS IN THE
WORLD CANNOT BE SEEN
OR TOUCHED, BUT THEY
MUST BE FELT WITH THE
HEART."
—HELEN KELLER

HILLARY RODHAM CLINTON

There was a time when only boys could be whatever they wanted: baseball players, doctors, judges, policemen, presidents.

At that time, in Illinois, a girl named Hillary was born.

Hillary was a brave girl with blonde hair and boundless curiosity. She wanted to go out and explore the world, but she was scared of the rough boys in her neighborhood who laughed at her and called her names.

Once, her mother saw her hiding inside. "You have to face things and show them you're not afraid," she told Hillary.

So out she went. She learned how to fight against bullies and soon found others who were fighting too, like people of color fighting against racism and single moms fighting to bring up their kids. Hillary listened to their stories and tried to figure out how she could help.

The best way to fight for justice, she decided, was to go into politics. Because many Americans were not used to seeing a woman politician, they criticized her for silly reasons, like her hairstyle, the sound of her voice, or the clothes she wore. They tried to bully her out of politics. But Hillary had learned how to deal with bullies, and she stood up to them.

Hillary became the first woman nominated by a major party for president of the United States.

There was a time when girls could not be whatever they wanted, but that time is gone.

BORN OCTOBER 26, 1947
UNITED STATES OF AMERICA

"TO EVERY LITTLE GIRL WHO DREAMS BIG:
YES, YOU CAN BE ANYTHING YOU WANT—
EVEN PRESIDENT."
—HILLARY RODHAM CLINTON

· HYPATIA ·

MATHEMATICIAN AND PHILOSOPHER

Once upon a time, in the ancient Egyptian city of Alexandria, there was a huge library. It was the largest library in the world at that point, but it had no books and no paper. People wrote on papyrus (made from a plant), which they rolled into scrolls instead of having flat books like we have today. In this ancient library, there were thousands of scrolls, each handwritten by a scribe and carefully kept on a shelf.

In the library at Alexandria, a father and a daughter sat side by side studying scrolls together. Philosophy, math, and science were their favorite subjects. Their names were Theon and Hypatia.

Hypatia solved equations and put forward new theories about geometry and arithmetic. She liked studying so much that soon she started to write her own books (*oops! scrolls!*). She even built an instrument, called an astrolabe, for calculating the position of the Sun, the Moon, and the stars at any given time.

Hypatia taught astronomy, and her classes were always popular. Students and other scholars crowded in to hear her speak. She refused to wear traditional women's clothes and gave her lectures dressed in scholars' robes like the other teachers. Sadly, all her works were destroyed when the library burned down. But luckily, her students wrote to one another about Hypatia and her brilliant ideas, so people can still learn about this genius of Alexandria.

CIRCA 370–MARCH 415

EGYPT

ILLUSTRATION BY
RIIKKA SORMUNEN

"RESERVE YOUR RIGHT TO
THINK, FOR EVEN TO THINK
WRONGLY IS BETTER THAN NOT
TO THINK AT ALL."
—HYPATIA

IRENA SENDLEROWA

WAR HERO

In Warsaw, Poland, there lived a little girl called Irena who loved her father dearly. One day, a terrible epidemic of typhus broke out in their city. Irena's father was a brave doctor. He could have stayed away from the people who were sick and not put himself at risk. But he chose to be with them and look after them until he, himself, fell ill with the disease.

Before he died, he said to his daughter, "Irena, if you see someone drowning, you must jump in and try to save them."

Irena cherished his words and, when Jews started to be persecuted by the Nazis, she helped Jewish families save their children.

She gave the children Christian names and found Christian families where they could be safe. She wrote their real names and their new names on little slips of paper that she rolled up and hid in marmalade jars. Then she buried all the jars in a friend's garden, under a big tree.

Sometimes, the smaller children would cry when Irena was taking them away. To distract the Nazi guards and cover up the noise, Irena trained a dog to bark when she told it to.

She hid children in sacks, in bags full of clothes, in boxes, even inside coffins!

In three months, she saved 2,500 children.

After the war, she dug up the marmalade jars and reunited many of the children with their families.

FEBRUARY 15, 1910–MAY 12, 2008
POLAND

"I WAS BROUGHT UP TO BELIEVE THAT A PERSON MUST BE RESCUED WHEN DROWNING, REGARDLESS OF RELIGION AND NATIONALITY."
—IRENA SENDLEROWA

ISABEL ALLENDE

WRITER

Not long ago in Chile, there lived a passionate young girl called Isabel. The oldest child of a single mother, Isabel grew up in her grandfather's home. She looked up to him and the way he provided for his family. Isabel wanted to be successful, too.

She loved writing and was fascinated by people and their life stories, so she decided to become a journalist.

One day, she interviewed a famous Chilean poet called Pablo Neruda. "You have such a vivid imagination, you should be writing novels, not articles for a newspaper," he told her.

A few years later, Isabel got some sad news. Her grandfather was dying. She was far from home, in Venezuela, and could not get back to Chile to visit him, so she started writing him a letter.

Once she started writing, she found she couldn't stop. She wrote about her family, about people who were alive, and people who were dead. She wrote about a cruel dictator, about passionate love stories, a terrible earthquake, supernatural powers, and ghosts.

The letter grew so long that it turned into a novel.

The House of the Spirits became wildly successful, making Isabel one of the most famous novelists of our time. She has written more than 20 books and won more than 50 literary awards.

BORN AUGUST 2, 1942

CHILE

ILLUSTRATION BY
PAOLA ROLLO

"WRITE WHAT SHOULD NOT
BE FORGOTTEN."
—ISABEL ALLENDE

JACQUOTTE DELAHAYE

PIRATE

Once upon a time, in Haiti, there was a girl with hair as red as fire. Her name was Jacquotte.

Jacquotte's mother died while giving birth to her little brother. Their father died not long after, and Jacquotte had to find a way to provide for herself and her brother. She decided to become a pirate.

Jacquotte led a gang of hundreds of pirates. Together, while at sea, they ate smoked meat, played games, pressed gunpowder into cannons, and robbed Spanish ships. Jacquotte even had a secret island where she and her pirates lived!

She had many enemies. Both the government and rival buccaneers were after her. In order to escape, she decided to fake her own death and go into hiding. She gave herself a new name and dressed as a man, but her deception didn't last long. No one else had such flaming red hair! She soon returned to piracy and earned the nickname "Back from the Dead Red."

Jacquotte had a girlfriend who was a pirate, too! Her name was Anne Dieu-le-Veut, and she was married with two children. After Anne's husband died, she took command of their ship and joined forces with Jacquotte. They were two of the most feared pirates of the Caribbean. Their stories became legends that pirates told one another, as they lay in their hammocks, beneath the stars, rocked by the waves, dreaming of the adventures that awaited them at dawn.

CIRCA 1630–CIRCA 1663

HAITI

ILLUSTRATION BY
RITA PETRUCCIOLI

"I COULDN'T LOVE A MAN WHO COMMANDS ME, ANY MORE THAN I COULD LOVE ONE WHO LETS HIMSELF BE COMMANDED BY ME."
—JACQUOTTE DELAHAYE

JANE AUSTEN

WRITER

Once upon a time, in the English countryside, there lived a girl who loved books more than anything else. There was nowhere Jane would rather be than curled up on a sofa in her father's library, with her nose in a book. She would get so engrossed in the stories that sometimes she even argued with the characters as though they could talk back.

Jane and her seven siblings put on plays and charades to amuse themselves and their parents. When she was still very young, she started to write her own stories and read them out to her sister Cassandra to make her laugh. Jane's writing was like Jane herself: bright, inventive, witty, and sharp. To her, every detail counted. How a couple squabbled, how a man walked, what maids said to each other—these were all clues revealing people's characters. Jane jotted down everything in her notebooks, ready to use in her novels.

At that time, girls were expected to get married. But Jane didn't want to get married, so she never did.

"Oh, Lizzy! Do anything rather than marry without affection," she wrote in one of her novels.

Jane Austen came to be one of the most famous writers in the history of English literature. You can still visit the beautiful cottage in the little village where she used to sit, writing at a small desk, looking out of the window and into the flower garden.

DECEMBER 16, 1775–JULY 18, 1817

UNITED KINGDOM

ILLUSTRATION BY
SOPHIA MARTINECK

"AH! THERE IS NOTHING
LIKE STAYING AT HOME,
FOR REAL COMFORT."
—JANE AUSTEN

JANE GOODALL

Once, in England, there was a girl called Jane who loved climbing trees and reading books. Her dream was to go to Africa and spend time with the wild animals there.

So, Jane traveled to Tanzania with her notebook and binoculars, determined to study real chimpanzees in their natural environment.

At first, it was hard to get close to them. The chimpanzees would run away the moment she was in sight. But Jane kept visiting the same place every day at the same time. Eventually, the chimps allowed her to get closer. Getting closer was not enough for Jane. She wanted to become friends with them. So she started a "banana club." Whenever she visited the chimpanzees, she would share bananas with them.

At the time, little was known about chimpanzees. Some scientists used to observe them from far away, using binoculars. Others studied chimps in cages. Jane, however, spent hours hanging out with chimpanzees. She tried to speak to them using grunts and cries. She climbed trees and ate the same foods they ate. She discovered that chimpanzees have rituals, that they make and use tools, and that they communicate using at least 120 different sounds. She even discovered that chimpanzees are not vegetarians.

Once, Jane rescued an injured chimpanzee and nursed it back to health. When she released it back into the wild, the chimpanzee turned and gave her a long, loving hug as if to say, "thanks and bye!"

BORN APRIL 3, 1934
UNITED KINGDOM

ILLUSTRATION BY
EMMANUELLE WALKER

"ONLY IF WE UNDERSTAND, WILL
WE CARE. ONLY IF WE CARE,
WILL WE HELP. ONLY IF WE HELP,
SHALL ALL BE SAVED."
—JANE GOODALL

JESSICA WATSON

SAILOR

Once upon a time, there was a girl called Jessica who was afraid of water.

One summer morning, Jessica was playing with her sister and cousins by the pool. At one point, the other children lined up on the side and got ready to jump in together holding hands.

Jessica's mom watched from the window to make sure Jessica was okay. She expected Jessica to step away from the pool, but was amazed to see her daughter step forward with the others. "One . . . two . . . three . . . " *Splash!* The kids landed in the water, shouting and laughing.

From that day on, Jessica started loving the water. She joined a sailing club and decided to sail around the world on her own without stopping. She painted her boat bright pink and christened her *Ella's Pink Lady*.

She packed the boat with steak and kidney pies, potatoes, cans and cans of beans, many bottles of milk, and lots of water, and set sail from Sydney Harbor. She was just 16 years old.

All on her own, Jessica sailed onward. She fought against waves as tall as skyscrapers, she woke up to the most beautiful sunrises, spotted blue whales, and watched shooting stars above her boat.

Seven months later, she arrived back in Sydney. Thousands of people turned out to greet her. They rolled out a special carpet for her. It was bright pink, just like her boat!

BORN MAY 18, 1993
AUSTRALIA

ILLUSTRATION BY
KATHRIN HONESTA

"YOU CAN'T CHANGE
CONDITIONS—JUST THE WAY
YOU DEAL WITH THEM."
—JESSICA WATSON

JILL TARTER

ASTRONOMER

Once there was a girl who wanted to become friends with the stars. Her name was Jill.

"How can we be alone in the universe, when the sky is so big?" she used to wonder.

She couldn't stop thinking about it, so when she grew up, she decided to search the skies for extraterrestrial life. She became an astronomer and director of SETI, the most important center for scientific research into the possibility of life in outer space.

For years, Jill and her team investigated hundreds of star systems, using radio telescopes located around the world. Every night, she looked for signs of civilization on some distant planet.

Nobody knew—and even today nobody knows—what communication systems aliens might be using. But many people believe the universe is too big for us to be its only inhabitants.

Jill especially enjoyed her solitary walks at night under constellations, visible in the starry sky. As she walked to the control room for a midnight shift, she noted, "Orion was right overhead, like an old friend."

None of her research so far has established any scientific proof for extraterrestrial life, but she hasn't lost hope. She likes to remind people that just because one glass of water comes up empty, it doesn't mean there are no fish in the sea.

BORN JANUARY 16, 1944
UNITED STATES OF AMERICA

ILLUSTRATION BY
ZOZIA DZIERŻAWSKA

"THE STORY OF HUMANS IS THE STORY OF IDEAS—SCIENTIFIC IDEAS THAT SHINE LIGHT INTO DARK CORNERS."
—JILL TARTER

• JINGŪ •

EMPRESS

nce upon a time, in Japan, there lived an empress, who was expecting a child.

One day her husband, the emperor, declared war on a group of rebel fighters. Jingū did not think it was a good idea.

Jingū's husband ignored her advice. He lost the battle and died.

While still pregnant, Jingū kept her husband's death secret, put on his clothes, and defeated the rebel fighters herself.

Jingū had a vision that led her to take the Japanese army across the sea to Korea. She believed Korea was "full of marvelous things dazzling to the eye." Some people still admire her fighting spirit, but others will never celebrate the woman who invaded Korea and harmed Korean people.

It is hard to separate the myths from the truths about Jingū. At the time, many people thought she had all kinds of magical powers. Some said she controlled the tides, using two special jewels she had in her jewelry box. Others said that her son, Ōjin, remained in her womb for three whole years, giving his warrior mother time to go on an expedition and return home to give birth.

She was probably just exceptionally talented and tough.

Jingū reigned for more than 70 years.

CIRCA 169–269

JAPAN

ILLUSTRATION BY
ANA GALVAN

"BRANDISHING OUR WEAPONS,
WE SHALL CROSS THE TOWERING
BILLOWS . . . WE SHALL TAKE
POSSESSION OF THE LAND OF
TREASURE."
—JINGŪ

JOAN JETT

ROCK STAR

J oan loved rock 'n' roll. One Christmas, when she was 13 years old, she got her first guitar.

She was ecstatic—but something was missing. Playing on her own was okay, she thought, "But if I really want to be a rock star, I need a band."

Two years later, she had her band together: Sandy on drums, Cherie on vocals, Jackie played bass, and Lita was the band's lead guitarist. With Joan on rhythm guitar and singing, they were . . . The Runaways.

They were 15 years old, loud and proud. Onstage, Joan always wore a red leather jumpsuit, and Cherie often came on in nothing but her underwear.

"You're too young," people said.

"So what?" they shouted back.

"You're too loud," people complained.

They just played louder.

"Girls can't be punk rockers."

"Oh yeah? Just watch us!"

One of their first songs, "Cherry Bomb," was a hit.

Their second album, *Queens of Noise*, became a sensation in Japan.

It wasn't always easy, though. Back home, they toured around in a beat-up old van, traveling from town to town through the night. Sometimes people would shout at them or throw things. But the Runaways didn't care. They lived for the music. They felt raw and alive.

BORN SEPTEMBER 22, 1958
UNITED STATES OF AMERICA

ILLUSTRATION BY
CARI VANDER YACHT

"MY GUITAR IS
NOT A THING. IT
IS AN EXTENSION
OF MYSELF. IT IS
WHO I AM."
—JOAN JETT

JULIA CHILD

CHEF

SCAN TO
HEAR MORE

At six feet two inches, Julia Child was an uncommonly tall girl. When the Second World War broke out, Julia was determined to join the army. She was rejected for being too tall. The navy said she was too tall for them, too. So she became a spy.

One of her first missions was to solve a highly explosive problem. Dotted around the ocean were underwater bombs targeting German submarines. The trouble was that they kept being set off by sharks swimming too close. All the other agents were stumped—but Julia had an idea.

She started cooking.

Mixing together all sorts of disgusting ingredients, she baked cakes that smelled like dead shark when put into the water. Sharks didn't dare get close to them. You know when you spray your arms with insect repellent to keep the bugs away? She did the same, only with sharks and bombs.

After the war ended, Julia and her husband moved to France for his job. Julia's very first mouthful of French food was mind-blowing. She couldn't believe that food tasted so wonderful! No more shark repellent for her. She decided to join Le Cordon Bleu—the finest cooking school in the world—and learn everything the chefs there could teach her.

Julia became an authority on French food and her cookbook, *Mastering the Art of French Cooking*, was a best seller. She even had her own TV shows. *"Bon appétit,"* she said, "except if you're a shark!"

AUGUST 15, 1912–AUGUST 13, 2004
UNITED STATES OF AMERICA

ILLUSTRATION BY
BARBARA DZIADOSZ

"A PARTY
WITHOUT
CAKE IS JUST
A MEETING."
—JULIA CHILD

KATE SHEPPARD

SUFFRAGETTE

There was a time when men believed women were put on Earth only to serve them. They thought women should cook and clean, look after the children, and not worry about anything else. Women, so they thought, should wear "feminine clothes"—which meant long dresses with tightly laced corsets. It didn't matter that when women dressed that way, they could hardly move or even breathe.

Having a job was off limits, playing sports was off limits, and governing the country was definitely off limits. Women were not even allowed to vote!

But Kate thought that women should have the same freedom as men—freedom to say what they thought, to vote for whom they wanted, and to wear comfortable clothes.

One day, she stood up and declared, "Women should be allowed to vote. And they should stop wearing corsets." People were shocked, outraged, and inspired by Kate's radical new ideas.

Kate and her friends gathered so many signatures on their petition that they had to paste sheets of paper together to form a long roll. They carried it into parliament and unrolled it on the floor, like a really long carpet. Imagine 74 ice cream trucks parked in a line—it was even longer than that! It was the longest petition ever presented. The legislators were speechless. Thanks to Kate, New Zealand became the first country in the world where women gained the right to vote.

MARCH 10, 1847–JULY 13, 1934

NEW ZEALAND

ILLUSTRATION BY MALIN ROSENQVIST

"DO NOT THINK YOUR
SINGLE VOTE DOES NOT
MATTER MUCH. THE RAIN
THAT REFRESHES THE
PARCHED GROUND IS MADE
UP OF SINGLE DROPS."
—KATE SHEPPARD

· LAKSHMI BAI ·

QUEEN AND WARRIOR

Once upon a time, in the state of Jhansi, India, there lived a girl who loved fighting.

She studied self-defense, archery, and swordfighting and trained hard at weight lifting and wrestling. She was a brilliant rider, too. She formed her own private army with other girls who were also skilled at fighting.

Lakshmi Bai married Gangadhar Rao, Maharaja of Jhansi, and became queen (*Rani* in Sanskrit). Lakshmi and Gangadhar had a child, but the boy died tragically young. The Maharaja never recovered from the sadness of losing a son and died himself soon after.

At that time, the British ruled India, and they wanted to rule Jhansi, too. They used the death of Lakshmi's son and husband as an excuse and ordered her to leave the palace. First, Rani Lakshmi Bai tried to fight the British in court, but they refused to hear her case. So she assembled an army of 20,000 rebels, which included both women and men.

After a fierce battle, her army was overcome, but even then, Lakshmi Bai, Rani of Jhansi, did not give in. She left the city by jumping her horse down a huge wall and headed east, where she was joined by more rebels—many of whom were girls like her. Rani Lakshmi Bai led her troops back into battle, dressed as a man and on horseback.

One of the British generals remembered her as "the most dangerous of all the rebel leaders."

NOVEMBER 19, 1828–JUNE 18, 1858

INDIA

ILLUSTRATION BY
LIEKE VAN DER VORST

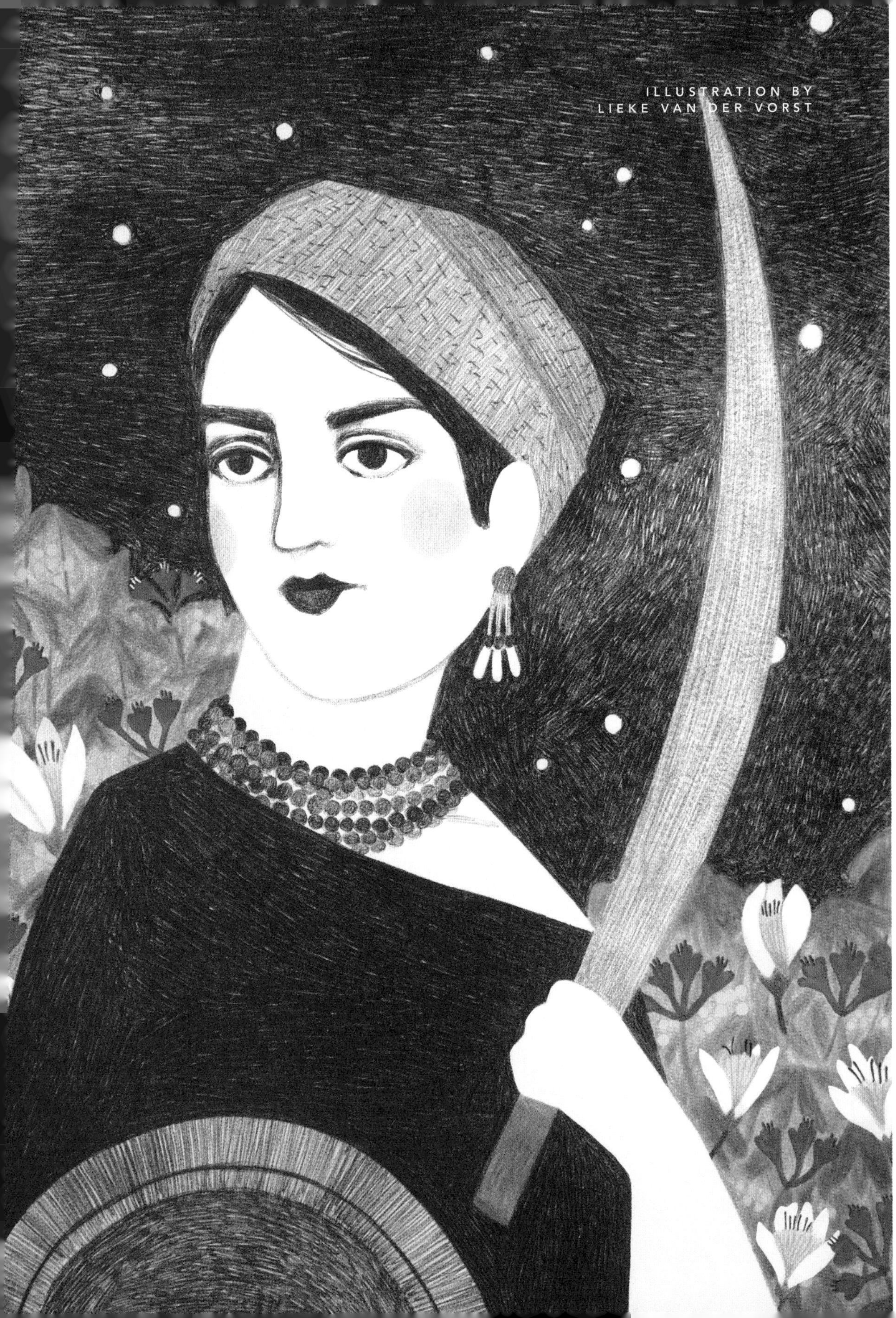

LELLA LOMBARDI

FORMULA ONE RACER

Once there was a girl who liked to help her father deliver meats in their van. Every time they had a delivery, she would jump into the driver's seat, and her father would time her. Her name was Maria Grazia, but everybody called her Lella.

Lella was so good at driving that she set a new record with each delivery. Everyone in town got used to seeing the Lombardis' van driving at full speed down the hills, with salami bouncing around in the back.

When she turned 18, Lella used all her savings to buy a used race car and started racing professionally. When her parents read in the newspaper that she had won the Formula 850 Championship, they weren't really surprised.

Lella didn't care that she was always the only woman in the race. She just drove as fast as she could to become a Formula One race car driver.

Her first attempt was a flop. She didn't even qualify. But the next year, she found a good manager, a sponsor, and a fantastic car: white, with the Italian flag on the nose. During the Spanish Grand Prix, Lella finished sixth, becoming the first-ever female driver to score in a Formula One race.

Despite her success, her team decided to hire another driver—a man— and Lella realized that Formula One still wasn't ready to accept women drivers. She continued to race all her life. No other female driver has yet beaten her Formula One record.

MARCH 26, 1941–MARCH 3, 1992
ITALY

"I'D RATHER HAVE AN
ACCIDENT THAN FALL IN
LOVE—THAT'S HOW MUCH I
LOVE MOTOR RACING."
—LELLA LOMBARDI

· LOZEN ·

WARRIOR

Once upon a time, there was a girl who wanted to be a warrior. Her name was Lozen, and she belonged to one of the Apache tribes, Native American people who originally roamed across what is now Arizona, New Mexico, and Texas.

When Lozen was still a little child, the United States Army attacked the Apache to take control of their land. Lozen saw many of her friends and relatives die in battle and, from that moment on, she vowed that she would dedicate her life to defending her tribe and her people.

"I don't want to learn women's work, and I don't want to get married," she said to her brother Victorio. "I want to become a warrior."

Victorio was the leader of their tribe. He taught Lozen to fight and hunt and always wanted her by his side on the battlefield. "Lozen is my right hand," he used to say. "Strong as a man, braver than most, and cunning in strategy, Lozen is a shield to her people."

Her courage and strength were legendary. People believed she had supernatural powers that allowed her to anticipate the movements of their enemies. She became the spiritual leader of her tribe, as well as a healer. After her brother died, Lozen joined forces with the famous Apache leader Geronimo. She was eventually captured with this last group of free Apache, but her memory is still strong in the heart of all people who fight for freedom.

CIRCA LATE 1840s–1889
UNITED STATES OF AMERICA

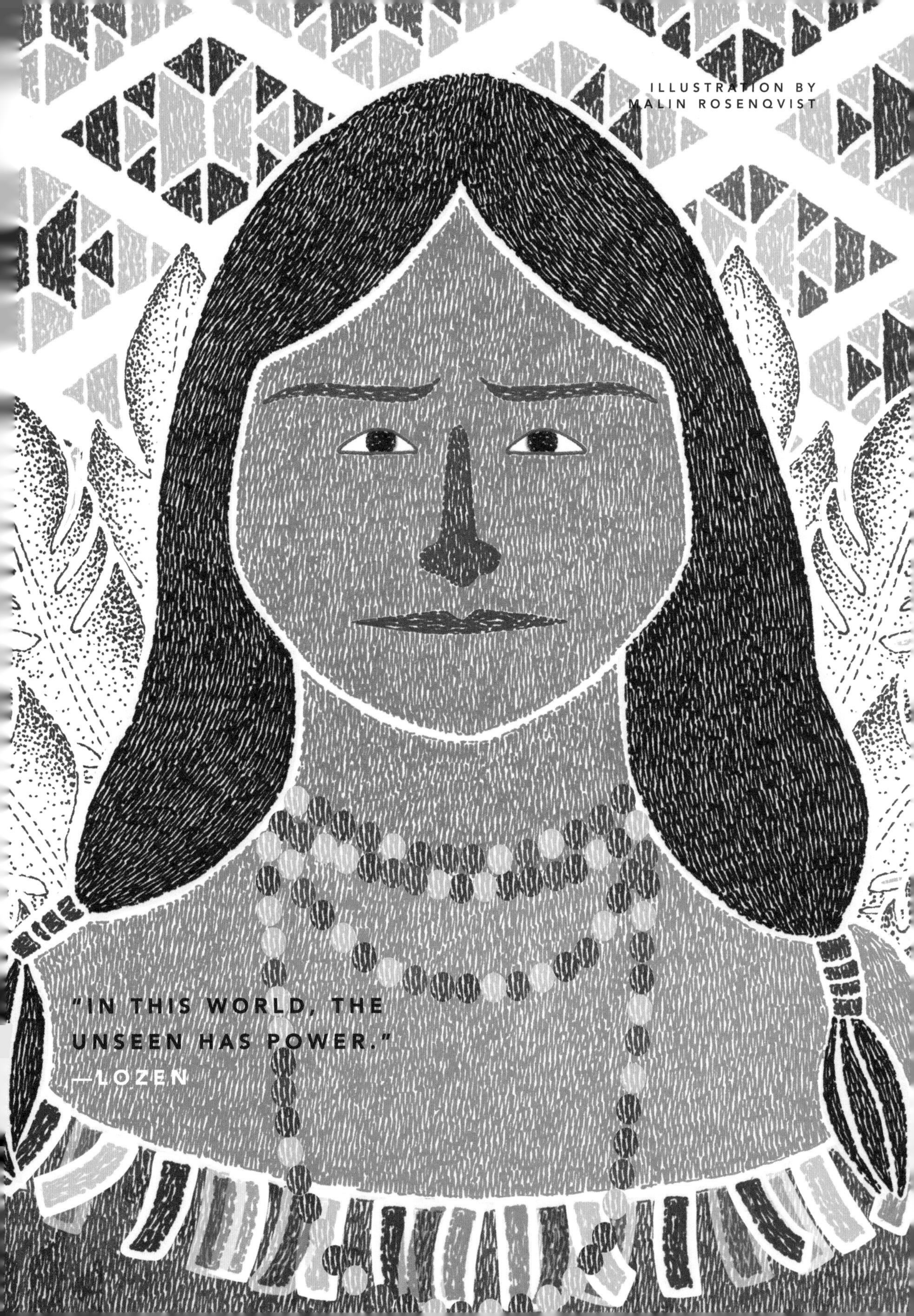

ILLUSTRATION BY MALIN ROSENQVIST

"IN THIS WORLD, THE UNSEEN HAS POWER."
—LOZEN

MAE C. JEMISON

ASTRONAUT AND DOCTOR

Once upon a time, there was a curious girl named Mae who could not make up her mind about what she wanted to be when she grew up.

Sewing dresses for her Barbie dolls, she wanted to be a fashion designer. Reading a book about space travel, she wanted to be an astronaut. Fixing a broken toy, she thought maybe an engineer would be better. And going to the theater, she exclaimed, "Maybe I'll become a dancer."

The world was Mae's laboratory. She studied chemical engineering, African American studies, and medicine. She learned to speak Russian, Swahili, and Japanese. She became a doctor and volunteered in Cambodia and Sierra Leone. Then she applied to NASA to become an astronaut. Mae was selected, and after one year of training, she was sent into space on board the space shuttle *Endeavour*.

She carried out tests on the other members of the crew. Since she was not only an astronaut but also a doctor, her mission was to conduct experiments on things like weightlessness and motion sickness, which can be quite a problem when you're floating upside down in space.

When Mae came back to Earth, she realized that—while she had enjoyed space—her true passion was improving health in Africa. So she quit NASA and founded a company that uses satellites to do just that.

Mae Jemison was the first Black woman in space.

BORN OCTOBER 17, 1956
UNITED STATES OF AMERICA

"ONE THING I WAS
CONSISTENT ABOUT WAS
TESTING LIMITS—MINE
AND OTHER PEOPLE'S—
ESPECIALLY ADULTS.
—MAE C. JEMISON

ILLUSTRATION BY
ALEXANDRA BOWMAN

MALALA YOUSAFZAI

ACTIVIST

Once there was a girl who loved school. Her name was Malala. Malala lived in a peaceful valley in Pakistan. One day, a group of armed men called the Taliban took control of the valley. They frightened people with their guns.

The Taliban forbade girls from going to school. Many people disagreed, but they thought it would be safer to keep their girls at home.

Malala thought this was unfair, and wrote about it online. She loved school very much—so one day, she said on TV, "Education is power for women. The Taliban are closing girls' schools because they don't want women to be powerful."

A short while later, Malala got onto her school bus as usual. Suddenly, two Taliban men stopped the bus and shouted, "Which one of you is Malala?"

When her friends looked at her, the men fired their guns, hitting her in the head and injuring two other girls as well. Malala was rushed to the hospital, but she did not die. Thousands of children sent her get well cards, and she recovered faster than anyone could have imagined.

"They thought bullets would silence us, but they failed," she said. "Let us pick up our books and our pens. They are our most powerful weapons. One child, one teacher, one book, and one pen can change the world."

Malala is the youngest person ever to receive the Nobel Peace Prize.

BORN JULY 12, 1997

PAKISTAN

ILLUSTRATION BY
SARA BONDI

تعليم

"WHEN THE WHOLE WORLD
IS SILENT, EVEN ONE VOICE
BECOMES POWERFUL."
—MALALA YOUSAFZAI

MANAL AL-SHARIF

WOMEN'S RIGHTS ACTIVIST

Once there was a girl who wanted to drive a car. She lived in Saudi Arabia, a country where religious rules forbade women from driving.

One day, she decided to break the rules.

She borrowed her brother's car and drove around the streets of her city.

She posted a video on YouTube showing her at the wheel, so that as many people as possible could see what she was doing and could find the courage to do the same.

"If men can drive, why can't women?" Manal said in the video.

It was a simple question, after all. But the religious authorities didn't like it. "What if other women start to drive? They will get out of control," the authorities shouted.

Manal was arrested the following day and had to promise not to drive again.

Her video, in the meantime, had been watched by thousands of people. A few weeks later, hundreds of brave Saudi women took to the streets with their cars, defying religious authorities.

Manal was put in jail again, but she continued to speak out and encourage women to drive and fight for their rights.

"Don't ask when this ban will be lifted. Just get out and drive," Manal said. Saudi Arabia finally lifted its ban on women drivers in 2018.

BORN APRIL 25, 1979
SAUDI ARABIA

"GO OUT AND DRIVE."
—MANAL AL-SHARIF

MARGARET HAMILTON

COMPUTER SCIENTIST

Once there was a girl who put a man on the Moon. Her name was Margaret, and she was really good with computers.

When she was just 24 years old, she joined MIT, where she learned to write code that would predict the weather. Then Margaret heard that MIT was looking for a programmer for a special joint mission with NASA, the U.S. agency that explores space.

As an engineer, Margaret led the team who programmed the code that allowed the Apollo 11 spacecraft to land safely on the Moon's surface.

Margaret would bring her daughter, Lauren, to work on weekends and evenings. While four-year-old Lauren slept, her mother programmed away, creating sequences of code to be added to the Apollo's command module computer.

On July 20, 1969, just minutes before Apollo 11 touched down on the lunar surface, the computer started spitting out error messages. The entire mission was in danger. Luckily, Margaret had set up the computer to focus on the main task and ignore everything else. So instead of aborting the mission, Apollo 11 landed safely on the Moon.

The Apollo landing was hailed by the world as "one small step for man, one giant leap for mankind." But it wouldn't have happened at all without the brilliant programming skills and cool-headedness of one woman: NASA software engineer Margaret Hamilton.

BORN AUGUST 17, 1936
UNITED STATES OF AMERICA

ILLUSTRATION BY
ÉDITH CARRON

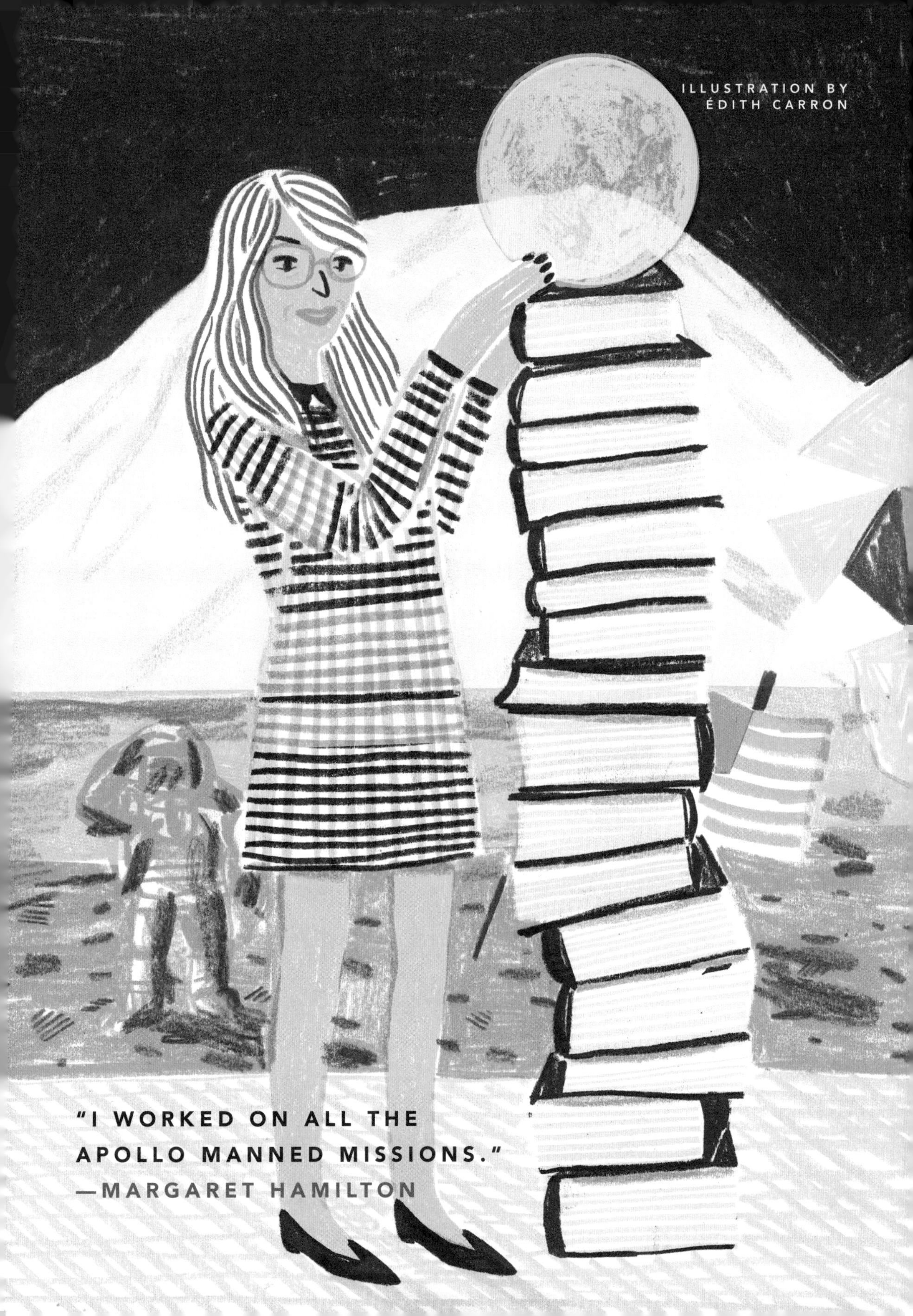

"I WORKED ON ALL THE
APOLLO MANNED MISSIONS."
—MARGARET HAMILTON

MARGARET THATCHER

PRIME MINISTER

Once upon a time, in Great Britain, there was a strong-willed girl named Margaret, who believed in doing what she thought was right. Some people liked her for being honest, but others thought she was rude. Margaret just shrugged and carried on.

She studied chemistry and became a scientist, but her true passion was politics, so she tried to get elected to the British Parliament. The first time she tried, she lost. The second time, too. But Margaret was not one to give up.

She decided to go back to college and study law. She got married and had twins. When the next elections came, she was not even considered, because it was thought that a young mother would be unsuitable for life in Parliament.

Finally, a few years later, her dream came true, and Margaret was elected to Parliament. Once in Parliament, she was so successful she became leader of the Conservative Party and then prime minister—the first female prime minister in British history.

When she took free milk away from primary school children, the public disliked her. But when she won the war against Argentina in the Falkland Islands, people admired her strength and determination.

Margaret was immensely practical. Sometimes she made decisions that people did not agree with, but she stood firmly behind all of her choices. That's why she became known as the "Iron Lady."

OCTOBER 13, 1925–APRIL 8, 2013

UNITED KINGDOM

"IF YOU WANT ANYTHING SAID, ASK A MAN. IF YOU WANT ANYTHING DONE, ASK A WOMAN."
—MARGARET THATCHER

MARGHERITA HACK

ASTROPHYSICIST

Once upon a time, in the *Via delle Cento Stelle* (Street of a Hundred Stars) in Florence, a little girl was born. Her name was Margherita, and she would grow up to become an incredible astrophysicist (a scientist who studies the properties of stars and planets).

While she was studying physics, she became increasingly interested in stars: "We are part of the evolution of the universe," she said. "From the calcium in our bones to the iron in our blood, we're entirely made of elements created in the heart of stars. We really are 'children of the stars'."

Margherita's favorite place was the Arcetri Observatory. High on a hill above Florence, she would scan the skies through a huge telescope, her mind full of questions: How do galaxies evolve? How far are the stars from each other? What can we learn from starlight?

Margherita traveled the world, giving lectures and inspiring others to study the stars. Back in Trieste, she became Italy's first woman director of an astronomical observatory.

Margherita said that some of her best friends were stars. Their names were Eta Boo, Zeta Tauri, Zeta Her, Omega Tau, and 55 Cygni. She even had an asteroid named after her!

For Margherita, being a scientist meant basing your knowledge of the natural world on facts, observations, and experiments, and being passionately curious about the mystery of life.

JUNE 12, 1922–JUNE 29, 2013
ITALY

"THE STARS ARE NOT VERY DIFFERENT FROM US: THEY ARE BORN, THEY GROW OLD, THEY DIE."
—MARGHERITA HACK

ILLUSTRATION BY CRISTINA SPANÒ

MARIA CALLAS

OPERA SINGER

Maria was a clumsy girl. She worried that she was not as pretty or as popular as her sister. But soon she found out that she was very special indeed.

One day, Maria's mother discovered that her little daughter had an amazing voice. She encouraged Maria to sing in order to earn money for their family. Maria's mother tried to enroll her in the Athens Conservatory, but Maria was rejected because she was too young. So her mother found her another teacher.

When the teacher first heard Maria sing, she was speechless. She said it was the most amazing voice she had ever heard. Not only did Maria master all the most difficult arias in a matter of a few months, she sang in a style that went straight to the heart. Maria applied to the Athens Conservatory again, and this time, she was accepted.

One night, she made her debut on the stage of the most prestigious opera house in the world: La Scala in Milan. When she sang, the audience hung on to every note and every word, as her voice carried them away to a place full of passion, rage, joy, and love. At the end of Maria's performance, they jumped to their feet, clapping and shouting, and showered the stage with roses.

Maria came to be known simply as "La Divina," the divine one—the most famous soprano ever.

DECEMBER 2, 1923–SEPTEMBER 16, 1977

GREECE

"I WILL ALWAYS
BE AS DIFFICULT
AS NECESSARY TO
ACHIEVE THE BEST."
—MARIA CALLAS

MARIA MONTESSORI

PHYSICIAN AND EDUCATOR

Once upon a time, there was a teacher who worked with children with disabilities. Her name was Maria, and she was also a doctor.

Instead of applying old teaching methods, Maria watched children to see how they learned. In her school, children were not forced to do what the teacher told them to do. They could move about freely and choose whatever activity they loved the most.

Maria's innovative techniques proved to be very effective for children with disabilities, so she decided to open a school and apply the same teaching methods. She called her school the Children's House.

For the Children's House, Maria invented child-sized furniture: small, light chairs that children could move easily and low shelves, so they could reach things without needing a grown-up.

Maria also invented toys that encouraged children to discover the world in practical and independent ways. In her classes, children discovered how to button and unbutton their shirts, how to carry a glass of water without spilling it, how to set the table by themselves.

"Children who are self-sufficient," she said, "who can tie their shoes, dress or undress themselves, [will feel] joy and sense of achievement."

Maria Montessori's method is applied in thousands of schools, and it helps children all over the world grow up strong and free.

AUGUST 31, 1870–MAY 6, 1952

ITALY

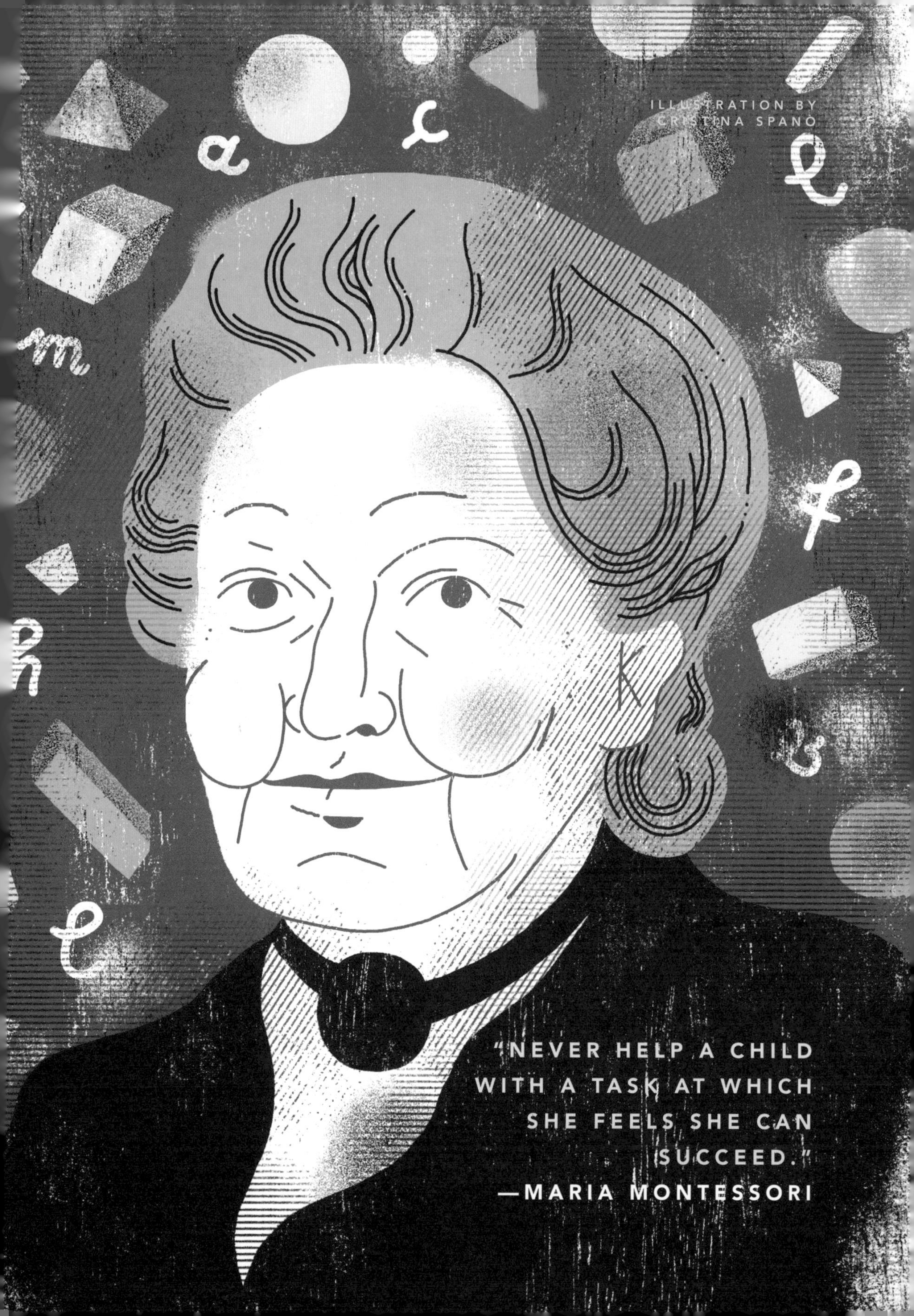

ILLUSTRATION BY
CRISTINA SPANO
"NEVER HELP A CHILD
WITH A TASK AT WHICH
SHE FEELS SHE CAN
SUCCEED."
—MARIA MONTESSORI

MARIA REICHE

MATHEMATICIAN AND ARCHAEOLOGIST

In a small house in a Peruvian desert, there lived an adventurous German mathematician called Maria Reiche.

Etched into the dry desert rocks were hundreds of lines. No one knew what they were for, or why they were there, or even how old they were.

These mysterious lines, called Nazca lines, became Maria's passion. She flew with the Peruvian Air Force to map the lines and, when there were no planes to fly, she just climbed the tallest ladder she could find to observe the lines from above. Some lines had been covered by dust so she used brooms to clean them.

As she studied the lines, she discovered something incredible. They were not just random scratches. They were enormous drawings made by the people who lived there thousands of years ago. There was a hummingbird! Intertwined hands! Flowers! A spider! All sorts of geometrical shapes!

Why would these ancient people create drawings that could be seen only from the sky? What were they? Maria was determined to solve the mystery.

She found that the lines corresponded to the constellations in the night sky. "It's like a giant map of the heavens," she said.

When Maria moved from Germany to Peru, she wasn't looking for giant mysterious drawings. But when she found them, she knew she would spend the rest of her life trying to figure them out. She became known as "The Lady of the Lines."

MAY 15, 1903–JUNE 8, 1998
GERMANY

"WHEN I FIRST CAME TO PERU
BY SEA, THE SHIP WENT PASSING
THROUGH THE CENTER OF FOUR
CONSECUTIVE RAINBOWS: FOUR
ARCS, ONE INSIDE THE OTHER!"
—MARIA REICHE

· MARIA SIBYLLA MERIAN ·

NATURALIST

Maria was a little girl who loved art. Every day, she would gather flowers to paint. Sometimes, she found caterpillars on the flowers and made paintings of how they changed, day by day, into beautiful butterflies.

At that time, people believed that butterflies magically sprouted out of mud. Maria knew better, but no one believed her.

Years passed and Maria became a great watercolor artist. She wrote about her discoveries, but at the time, scientists only took books in Latin seriously, and Maria's was in German.

One day, Maria and her daughter decided to move to a new city: Amsterdam. There, Maria found display cases filled with exotic insects collected from South America. Maria thought, "If I could study these insects in their natural habitat, I could write a book that people would notice."

She sold her paintings and set sail to South America. In the rainforests of Suriname, Maria and her daughter climbed tall jungle trees to study the insects high up. Maria wrote her new book in Latin, and this time, it was a huge success. Everybody learned that butterflies and moths come from caterpillars, not mud! The process is called *metamorphosis* (from the Greek word meaning *to change shape*). Today, we know that many animals metamorphosize: frogs, moths, beetles, crabs . . . and all thanks to the work of Maria Sibylla Merian!

APRIL 2, 1647–JANUARY 13, 1717
GERMANY

ILLUSTRATION BY
AMANDA HALL

"IN MY YOUTH, I SPENT MY
TIME INVESTIGATING INSECTS."
—MARIA SIBYLLA MERIAN

MARIE CURIE

SCIENTIST

Once, in Poland, there was a secret school. People called it the Floating University.

The foreign government at that time was very strict about what people could and couldn't study. Girls were not allowed to go to college at all.

Marie and her sister went to the secret school, but they were tired of hiding. One day, they heard that in Paris there was a university called the Sorbonne, which accepted girls, so they decided to move to France.

Marie was fascinated by metals and magnets. She found out that some minerals were radioactive. They gave off powerful rays and glowed in the dark. To analyze these minerals' properties, Marie would set them on fire, melt them, filter them, and stay up all night to watch them glow. Radiation is used to treat many diseases, but it is also very dangerous. Just imagine that, after all these years, Marie's notebooks and instruments are still radioactive! If you want to look at them, you have to wear protective clothing and gloves.

Marie's husband, Pierre, was so intrigued by her research that he decided to drop his work on crystals to join her. Together, they discovered two new radioactive elements: polonium and radium.

Marie Curie won two Nobel Prizes for her work, and she could have made a lot of money from her discoveries. She chose, instead, to make her research available to anyone for free.

NOVEMBER 7, 1867–JULY 4, 1934

POLAND

"NOTHING IN LIFE
IS TO BE FEARED.
IT IS ONLY TO BE
UNDERSTOOD."
—MARIE CURIE

• MARY ANNING •

PALEONTOLOGIST

In a tiny, cramped house on the southern coast of England, there lived a girl called Mary. Her house was so close to the sea that sometimes the storms would flood it.

The winds and storms that swept along the coast often revealed fossils in the cliffs along the shoreline. Fossils are the remains of prehistoric plants or animals that died a long time ago.

Mary could not go to regular school because her family was too poor, but she still learned to read and write. She studied geology to learn more about rocks and anatomy to learn more about the skeletons of the prehistoric animals she found.

One day, she saw a strange shape jutting out of a rock. Mary took out her special little hammer and carefully chipped away at the rock. Bit by bit, she uncovered a 30-foot-long skeleton. It had a long beak, but it wasn't a bird. Rows of sharp teeth, but it wasn't a shark. Flippers, but it wasn't a fish. And a long thin tail! It was the first-ever discovery of that kind of fossil, and she named it *ichthyosaur*, meaning *fish-lizard*.

At the time, people believed that the Earth was only a few thousand years old. Mary's fossils helped prove that there had been life on our planet for hundreds of millions of years.

Scientists from all over the world came to see Mary, the self-taught scientist who loved walking by the sea.

MAY 21, 1799–MARCH 9, 1847
UNITED KINGDOM

ILLUSTRATION BY MARTINA PAUKOVA

"MY NAME IS WELL KNOWN THROUGHOUT EUROPE."
—MARY ANNING

MARY EDWARDS WALKER

SURGEON

Once upon a time, there was a girl called Mary who wore whatever clothes she wanted: boots, pants, ties, shirts.

At that time, girls were expected to wear tightly laced corsets and layers of petticoats under their skirts. It was hard to move or even breathe in clothes like that. But unlike all her friends' parents, Mary's mom and dad thought that everyone, including girls, should wear whatever they liked. Her father, a carpenter, thought that all of his children would be happier and healthier in comfortable trousers and shirts, especially in the hot, humid summers.

Mary was happy about that—she much preferred boys' clothes anyway.

Mary, her sisters, and her brother were encouraged by their father to study. Mary wanted to be a doctor, so she attended medical school and graduated as one of the first female doctors in the United States.

At her wedding to a fellow doctor, she wore trousers and a coat, because she liked that outfit more than a traditional wedding dress.

When the Civil War broke out, she stepped forward to serve in the Union Army.

A few times, Mary was arrested for dressing in men's clothes. But to Mary, those were just clothes—she just wore what she wanted.

She saved many lives during the Civil War and was awarded a Congressional Medal of Honor once it had ended. She wore the medal her whole life, on the collar of her coat, next to her tie.

NOVEMBER 26, 1832–FEBRUARY 21, 1919
UNITED STATES OF AMERICA

ILLUSTRATION BY
ELIZABETH BADDELEY

"LET THE GENERATIONS KNOW
THAT WOMEN IN UNIFORM ALSO
GUARANTEED THEIR FREEDOM."
MARY EDWARDS WALKER

MARY KOM

BOXER

Once upon a time, in India, there was a little girl called Mary. Mary's family was very poor and struggled to put food on the table. Mary wanted to help her family live a better life, so she decided to become a boxer.

One day, she boldly walked up to the coach in a boxing gym. "Will you train me?" she asked. "You're too tiny," he said. "Go away."

But when the coach finished for the day, he found her still waiting for him by the gate. "I want to do this. Put me in the ring," she said to him.

Reluctantly, he took her on, and she started training hard. She began competing and won many fights. But she hadn't told her parents—she didn't want to worry them.

One day, her dad read about her in a newspaper. "Is this you?" he asked, worried. "Yes," said Mary, proudly. "What if you get hurt?" her mother asked. "We don't have the money for doctors!"

"I will work hard and save as much as I can. Don't worry," Mary replied.

She slept in hostels, ate vegetables and rice because she could not afford meat, skipped breakfast because she only had money for lunch and dinner, and she became a champion.

Her parents watched her fights on TV. Mary won medal after medal. She even won a medal at the Olympics! She provided for her family and made her village proud.

BORN MARCH 1, 1983

INDIA

"WITHOUT BOXING, I CAN'T
LIVE. I LOVE BOXING."
—MARY KOM

MATILDE MONTOYA

DOCTOR

Once upon a time, in Mexico, there lived a woman called Soledad, who had a little girl whose name was Matilde. Soledad soon realized that her daughter was exceptionally bright. She could read and write by the time she was four and was ready for high school by the time she was 12.

When she turned 16, Matilde started training as a midwife. But she had bigger dreams. She wanted to be a doctor.

When she joined the National School of Medicine, she was the only female student. Lots of people told her that a woman could never be a doctor, but she had her mom and many friends on her side.

At the end of her first year, the university tried to expel Matilde.

Matilde wrote a letter to the president of Mexico asking for his help. He wrote to the university telling them to stop being so unfair to her. She finished her course, but then the university stopped her from going in for her final exam.

Again, she wrote to the president, and again he stepped in. This time, he passed a law that allowed all women to study medicine and become doctors.

The president himself traveled all the way to the university to see her take her final exam. It was a historic moment.

The next day, newspapers across the country celebrated the story of "La Señorita Matilde Montoya," Mexico's first-ever female doctor.

MARCH 14, 1859–JANUARY 26, 1939

MEXICO

ILLUSTRATION BY
CRISTINA PORTOLANO

MAUD STEVENS WAGNER

TATTOO ARTIST

Once there was a girl who liked tattoos. Her name was Maud, and she was a circus performer.

Maud was a great aerialist and contortionist. People would come to see her fly through the air every night.

One day, she met a man called Gus Wagner who had his body completely covered with tattoos: monkeys, butterflies, lions, horses, snakes, trees, women—anything you can think of!

"I am a walking, talking work of art!" he used to say.

Maud liked his tattoos so much that she agreed to go out with him, if he gave her a tattoo.

Gus first made one tattoo on her body, then another, and another . . . until Maud's body was also completely covered with tattoos.

Maud was a quick learner and soon began working as a tattooist for other circus performers and for the public, all while she continued to perform as an acrobat on the circus and carnival circuit.

At the time, tattoos were unusual, and people would flock to the circus to gawk at the scantily clad women, their bare skin covered with ink.

Maud and Gus worked so well together that they became inseparable. They eventually got married and spread the art of tattooing beyond circus sideshows and across the country.

Maud is the first known female tattoo artist in the United States.

FEBRUARY, 1877–JANUARY 30, 1961

UNITED STATES OF AMERICA

MAYA ANGELOU

WRITER

Once there was a little girl who didn't speak for five years. She thought her words could hurt people and promised to never make a peep again. Her name was Maya.

People thought Maya was crazy, but she was simply scared. "I know you will speak again one day," her grandmother kept telling her. "You will find your voice," her beloved brother said.

Maya listened to them and began to memorize everything she heard or read: poems, songs, short tales, random conversations. "It was like putting a CD on. If I wanted to, I'd run through my memory and think, that's the one I want to hear," she later recalled.

She became so good at memorizing words that when she started to write, it was like music was flowing from her pen. She wrote about her childhood, growing up in a town where Black people were treated badly for the color of their skin.

Her writing became the voice of the civil rights movement and all the people fighting for the rights of African Americans. She constantly reminded us that everyone, Black or white, male or female, has equal rights.

In addition to writing many books, Maya was so talented that she wrote songs, plays, and movies, and acted onstage and onscreen. "See me now, Black, female, American, and Southern," she once said to a group of Black students. "See me and see yourselves. What can't you do?"

APRIL 4, 1928–MAY 28, 2014

UNITED STATES OF AMERICA

• 134 •

"MY MISSION IN LIFE IS NOT MERELY TO
SURVIVE, BUT TO THRIVE; AND TO DO SO
WITH SOME PASSION, SOME COMPASSION,
SOME HUMOR, AND SOME STYLE."
—MAYA ANGELOU

MAYA GABEIRA

SURFER

Once upon a time, there was a girl who liked big waves. Not the ones that you splash around in at the seaside. Not even the ones that you see from the pier. She liked super-mega-gigantic monster waves and wanted to become the Superwoman of Surfing.

"Not again, Maya," her mom would wail, as her daughter headed off to the beach. "You're always wet and cold, and everyone else surfing is a guy!" But Maya didn't care. Surfing was her passion. "And as for the guys, well, they'd better get used to me!" she said.

She started traveling the world in search of the biggest waves possible: Australia, Hawaii, Portugal, and beyond. Maya would jump on a plane and go anywhere to catch the next big one. Once, in South Africa, she rode a wave 14 meters high—the highest ever for a female surfer. She won every major competition and became the highest-paid big wave surfer in the world. But one day, while she was surfing in Portugal, a wave caught her by surprise. The wall of water crashed over her, dragging her underwater. She broke bones and almost drowned before her partner rescued her and gave her CPR. After such a scary incident, most people would have been afraid to go back in the water and maybe thought about a career change.

Not Maya.

As soon as she healed, Maya went right back to the same beach in Portugal. "I love it," she says. "The surf around here is epic."

BORN APRIL 10, 1987

BRAZIL

"I RAN A LOT, SURFED A LOT, AND WORKED A LOT"
—MAYA GABEIRA

MELBA LISTON

COMPOSER AND TROMBONIST

Once there was a small girl named Melba who wanted to play the trombone. When she was seven, a traveling music store came to town. She saw a bright, shiny brass instrument, and Melba just knew she had to have one. "That?" exclaimed her mother. "For a little bitty girl? Why, it's almost as tall as you are!" But Melba insisted. "It's the most beautiful thing I've ever seen."

Melba started to play her trombone every day. She studied music with her grandfather but was mostly self-taught. "I'll learn on my own. I'll just play it by ear," she said. It was hard, but she loved the bold, brassy sound the instrument made. Within a year, she was good enough to play solo trombone on the local radio station.

When she was still a teenager, Melba toured the United States with a band led by trumpet player Gerald Wilson. A few years later, she was hired to accompany Billie Holiday—one of the greatest jazz singers of all time—on a tour in the South.

The tour wasn't as successful as they'd hoped. When Melba returned home, she decided to stop playing for a while. But her passion was too strong and she returned to writing and playing music. She even came out with a solo album, *Melba Liston and her 'Bones* (short for *trombones*). She also arranged music for other musicians, weaving rhythms, harmonies, and melodies into gorgeous songs for all the jazz greats of the twentieth century.

JANUARY 13, 1926–APRIL 23, 1999
UNITED STATES OF AMERICA

"I HAD TO PROVE MYSELF."
—MELBA LISTON

MICHAELA DEPRINCE

BALLERINA

Once, a girl named Michaela lost her parents during a terrible war.

Michaela had *vitiligo*, a skin condition that caused white spots on her neck and chest. Because of how she looked, the people at the orphanage called her "the devil's daughter." Little Michaela was lonely and scared—but so was a girl called Mia. When Michaela was afraid, Mia would sing her songs. When Mia could not sleep, Michaela would tell her a bedtime story. They became best friends.

One day, the wind blew a magazine to the gates of the orphanage. On the cover was a picture of a beautiful lady in a sparkly dress, her toes pointed. "She's a ballerina," Michaela's teacher told her.

"She looks so happy," four-year-old Michaela thought. "I want to be like her." Soon afterward, she was taken on a long journey. She and Mia got separated. To stop herself from being scared, Michaela started to dream.

She dreamed that she and Mia had a mom and that she was a ballerina.

At the end of the journey, a lady came up to her saying that she wanted to adopt not only Michaela but Mia, too! Michaela's dreams were coming true. So where was her tutu? She started searching around. "What are you looking for?" asked her new mom. Michaela showed her the magazine.

"You can be a ballerina, too," her mom said, smiling.

Michaela now dances with the Dutch National Ballet.

BORN JANUARY 6, 1995
SIERRA LEONE

ILLUSTRATION BY
DEBORA GUIDI

"NEVER BE AFRAID TO BE A POPPY
IN A FIELD OF DAFFODILS."
—MICHAELA DEPRINCE

MICHELLE OBAMA

LAWYER AND FIRST LADY

Once upon a time, there was a girl who was always afraid.

Her name was Michelle Robinson, and she lived in a tiny apartment in Chicago with her family.

"Maybe I'm not smart enough," she worried. "Maybe I'm not good enough." And her mother would say, "If it can be done, you can do it."

"Anything is possible," said her dad.

Michelle worked hard. But still, sometimes people told her not to aim too high. They said she would never achieve something big because "she was just a Black girl from the South Side of Chicago."

But Michelle chose to listen to her parents. "Anything is possible," she thought. So she graduated from Harvard and became a lawyer at a big firm. One day, her boss asked her to mentor a young lawyer. His name was Barack Hussein Obama.

They fell in love and got married a few years later.

Eventually, Barack told her he wanted to become President of the United States. At first, she thought he was crazy, but then she remembered: "If it can be done, you can do it." So she quit her job and helped him on his campaign.

Barack won the election, and Michelle became the first Black First Lady of the United States. "No one is born smart," she likes to point out. "All of that comes with a lot of hard work."

BORN JANUARY 17, 1964

UNITED STATES OF AMERICA

"ALWAYS STAY TRUE TO YOURSELF AND
NEVER LET WHAT SOMEBODY ELSE SAYS
DISTRACT YOU FROM YOUR GOALS."
—MICHELLE OBAMA

MILLO CASTRO ZALDARRIAGA

DRUMMER

Once there was a small girl of Cuban, Chinese, and African heritage who dreamed of playing the drums. She lived on an island full of music, colors, and delicious papayas. Her name was Millo.

Everyone on the island knew that only boys were allowed to play drums. "Go home," they would shout at Millo. "This is not for girls."

They didn't know that Millo's passion for drums was stronger than a coconut crab. During the day, she would listen to all the sounds around her. The sound of palm trees dancing in the wind, the sound of hummingbirds flapping their wings, the sound of jumping into a puddle with both feet—SPLASH!

At night, she would sit on the beach and listen to the sound of the sea. "Why can't I also be a drummer?" she would ask to the breaking waves.

One day, Millo convinced her father to take her to a music lesson. Timbales, conga, bongos . . . she could play anything! The teacher was so impressed that she started to give Millo lessons every day. "I will play in a real band," Millo kept saying. When her sister Cuchito put together Anacaona, Cuba's first ever all-girl dance band, 10-year-old Millo joined as drummer. They soon had everyone dancing.

Millo became a world-famous musician. She even played at an American president's birthday party when she was just 15.

BORN CIRCA 1922

CUBA

THE MIRABAL SISTERS

ACTIVISTS

When a cruel dictator named Rafael Trujillo took power in the Dominican Republic, four sisters started to fight for freedom. They were the Mirabal sisters: Minerva, Patria, Maria Teresa, and Dedé.

People called them *Las Mariposas*, the butterflies.

They distributed pamphlets and organized a movement to protest Trujillo and restore democracy in their country. Trujillo didn't like it.

To him, girls like the Mirabal sisters were good company for parties. They were supposed to compliment him, receive flowers and gifts, smile, and say "thank you." They were not supposed to raise their voices, disagree, and try to overturn his regime! The Butterflies' fierce independence scared him, so he tried several different strategies to silence them.

He put them in jail and barred Minerva from practicing law. He imprisoned Minerva and her mother in a hotel room. He even tried to seduce Minerva! But Minerva said no. She didn't care about becoming the girlfriend of a powerful tyrant. She only cared about freedom for her country.

The sisters' courage inspired Dominicans and gave them the strength to oppose Trujillo's regime. Eventually, he was taken down.

On the tall obelisk that Trujillo put up to celebrate his power, there's now a mural honoring the Mirabal sisters, four butterflies who defied a tyrant.

PATRIA, FEBRUARY 27, 1924–NOVEMBER 25, 1960
MINERVA, MARCH 12, 1926–NOVEMBER 25, 1960
MARIA TERESA, OCTOBER 15, 1935–NOVEMBER 25, 1960
DEDÉ, MARCH 1, 1925–FEBRUARY 1, 2014
DOMINICAN REPUBLIC

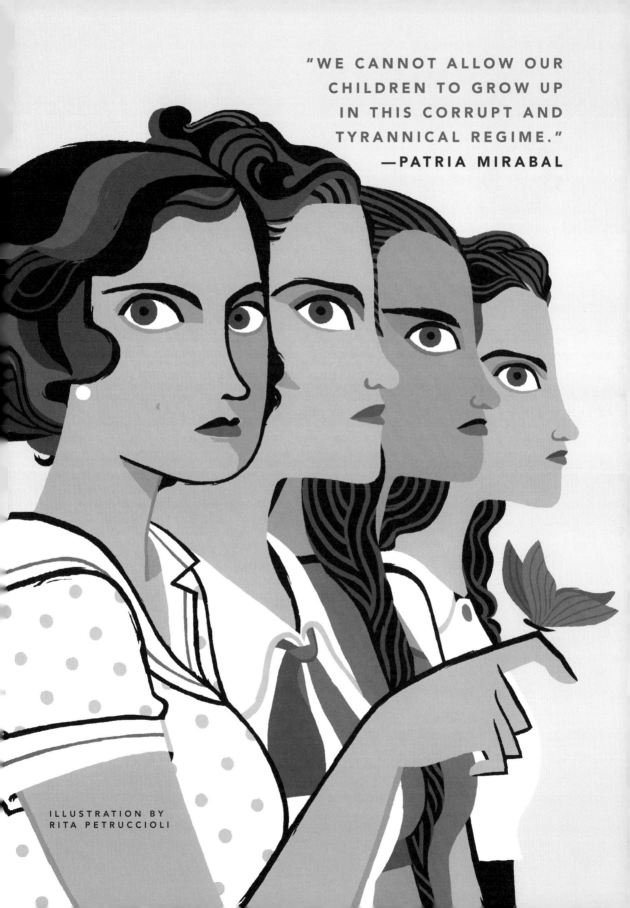

"WE CANNOT ALLOW OUR CHILDREN TO GROW UP IN THIS CORRUPT AND TYRANNICAL REGIME."
—PATRIA MIRABAL

ILLUSTRATION BY RITA PETRUCCIOLI

MIRIAM MAKEBA

ACTIVIST AND SINGER

Once upon a time, the people of South Africa were treated very differently according to the color of their skin. It was illegal for Black and white people to spend time with each other or to fall in love and have children. This cruel system was called *apartheid*.

Into this world came a little girl who loved to sing. Every Sunday, Miriam went to church with her mother. She was so desperate to sing in the choir that she used to sneak into the room whenever they were rehearsing.

Miriam grew up and recorded more than 100 songs with her all-girl band, the Skylarks.

She sang about life in South Africa—what brought her joy, what made her sad, what got her angry. She sang about dancing and about apartheid.

The people loved her songs, especially one called "Pata Pata," which was her biggest hit. But the government did not like the anti-apartheid message of Miriam's music. They wanted to silence her voice of protest. When Miriam left the country on tour, they took away her passport and wouldn't let her back into the country.

Miriam toured the world and became a symbol of the proud African fight for freedom and justice. People started calling her "Mama Africa."

After 31 years, she was allowed back home. Shortly afterward, apartheid was finally crushed.

MARCH 4, 1932–NOVEMBER 9, 2008
SOUTH AFRICA

"EVERYBODY STARTS TO
MOVE AS SOON AS 'PATA
PATA' STARTS TO PLAY."
—MIRIAM MAKEBA

MISTY COPELAND

BALLERINA

It was a beautiful night when Misty stepped onstage before a hushed audience to dance the leading role in a ballet called *Firebird*. Misty was the only Black woman in one of the world's most famous dance companies, and it was the first time she had danced as a prima ballerina.

As the curtain rose, her arms moved gracefully like the wings of a bird, she turned pirouettes and soared across the stage in long, beautiful jumps. The audience was transfixed.

When the final curtain fell, she revealed something no one could have imagined. She had hurt her leg and been in great pain throughout the whole performance. She had six fractures in her left shin and needed surgery. It seemed impossibly cruel that the very night she had achieved her dream, she was told she might never dance again.

For Misty, that was unacceptable. She loved ballet too much. Dance had found Misty when she was 13 years old, living in a motel with her mom and her five siblings. Dance had found her when she never thought she could earn a living by doing something she was passionate about.

So she went through the surgery, through therapy, and worked harder than ever to be fit enough to dance again with the American Ballet Theatre. Later, she danced in *Swan Lake*, a true black swan, stronger and more elegant than ever.

BORN SEPTEMBER 10, 1982
UNITED STATES OF AMERICA

"DANCE FOUND ME."
—MISTY COPELAND

ILLUSTRATION BY
PING ZHU

NANCY WAKE

SPY

Once there was a girl who became a secret agent. When she was just 16 years old, she traveled by herself from Australia to France and convinced a newspaper to hire her. When the Second World War broke out, she joined the French Resistance (the *Maquis*) in their fight against the Nazis.

Later, after escaping to England, Nancy parachuted back into France to help train and organize resistance fighters and rescue British pilots who had been shot down. She got them fake identity papers and then ferried them across the mountains to Spain so they could get back to Britain safely.

She outwitted the German secret police (the *Gestapo*) at every turn and was soon at the top of their Most Wanted list. They nicknamed her "The White Mouse," because she seemed impossible to catch!

Nancy was also a great soldier. She was an excellent shot and never lost her nerve. When her unit suffered a surprise attack by the Germans, she took command of a section whose leader had been killed and, with exceptional coolness, organized a retreat with no further losses.

When the war ended and France was finally liberated, Nancy was awarded the George Medal by the British. The French gave her three Croix de Guerre medals and the Médaille de la Résistance. They later made her a Knight of the Legion of Honor—their highest award. The Americans awarded her the Medal of Freedom.

AUGUST 30, 1912–AUGUST 7, 2011
NEW ZEALAND

ILLUSTRATION BY
MONICA GARWOOD

"FOR GOODNESS SAKE, DID
THE ALLIES PARACHUTE ME
INTO FRANCE TO FRY EGGS
AND BACON FOR THE MEN?"
—NANCY WAKE

NANNY OF THE MAROONS

QUEEN

O nce upon a time, in Jamaica, there lived an escaped slave with royal African ancestors. She was the leader of a group of escaped slaves called the Maroons and became known as Queen Nanny.

At the time, Jamaica was occupied by the British. They enslaved Africans and sent them to Jamaica to work on sugarcane plantations. But Queen Nanny wanted freedom for herself and for her people, so she escaped, freed many other slaves, and led them into the mountains where they built a village called Nanny Town.

The only way to Nanny Town was along a narrow path through the jungle. Queen Nanny taught the Maroons to cover themselves with leaves and branches to blend in with the jungle. As British soldiers walked through the forest in single file, they had no idea they were surrounded. But at the sound of a signal, the "trees" around them suddenly leaped to life and attacked.

Nanny Town had one problem, though. Its inhabitants were hungry.

One night, weak with hunger and worried for her people, Queen Nanny fell asleep. She dreamed of one of her ancestors who told her: "Don't give up. Food is at hand."

When she woke up, she found pumpkin seeds in her pockets. She planted them on the hillside, and soon her tribe had plenty of food.

From then on, the hill near Nanny Town was called Pumpkin Hill.

CIRCA 1686–1733

JAMAICA

NELLIE BLY

REPORTER

In a village in Pennsylvania, there was a girl who always dressed in pink. Her name was Nellie.

When her father died, the family fell on hard times. She went out looking for a job to help her mom make ends meet.

One day, Nellie read an article in a local newspaper. It was called "What Girls Are Good For." In the article, girls who worked were described as a "monstrosity" because the author believed that a woman's place was in the home. Furious, Nellie wrote a passionate letter to the editor.

Impressed by her writing style, the editor offered her a job as a reporter. Nellie soon proved to be a brave investigative journalist. She moved to New York and joined the *New York World*, a newspaper run by a famous man called Joseph Pulitzer. Once, she pretended to be mentally ill and got herself checked into a mental institution to expose how badly the patients were treated. She was fearless, clever, and compassionate.

The newspaper set her a challenge. Author Jules Verne had written a popular novel called *Around the World in Eighty Days*. Could she do it in less time? It took Nellie just a few hours to pack a small bag and set sail from New York in a steamer. Traveling by ship, rail, and even donkey, she kept up a grueling pace. People placed bets on whether she would succeed or fail. Finally, 72 days, 6 hours, 11 minutes, and 14 seconds later, she arrived back in New York. She made it!

MAY 5, 1864–JANUARY 27, 1922

UNITED STATES OF AMERICA

"I HAVE NEVER WRITTEN A WORD THAT DID NOT COME FROM MY HEART. I NEVER SHALL."
—NELLIE BLY

THE NEW.

NELLIE BLY

BEST REPORTER IN THE U.S.

ILLUSTRATION BY ZARA PICKEN

NETTIE STEVENS

GENETICIST

O nce upon a time, there was a teacher called Nettie Stevens who decided she wanted to become a scientist. She saved as much money as she could and—when she was 35—she moved to California to attend Stanford University.

While she was at the university, she became obsessed with finding out why it was that boys become boys and girls become girls. The answer, she was sure, lay in studying cells.

Humanity had been concerned with this question for almost 2,000 years. Scientists and philosophers had invented all sorts of theories to explain it. Some said it depended on the body temperature of the dad. Others said it was about nutrition . . . basically, no one had a clue.

In order to crack this mystery once and for all, Nettie started studying mealworms.

After studying their cells for hours under a microscope, she made an important discovery: female larvae had 20 large chromosomes, while male larvae had only 19 large chromosomes plus one smaller one.

"Bingo!" shouted Nettie, eyes still glued to the microscope.

A scientist called Edmund Wilson made a similar discovery at about the same time, but he failed to realize quite how important it was. Wilson thought that sex was also affected by the environment, but Nettie said, "Nope. It's all down to the chromosomes." And she was right.

JULY 7, 1861–MAY 4, 1912
UNITED STATES OF AMERICA

"HOW COULD YOU THINK YOUR QUESTIONS WOULD BOTHER ME? THEY NEVER WILL, SO LONG AS I KEEP MY ENTHUSIASM FOR BIOLOGY."
—NETTIE STEVENS

NINA SIMONE

SINGER

Nina was a gifted, proud girl. When her mom was at church, Nina, unnoticed, climbed up the organ bench and learned to play "God Be with You Till We Meet Again." She was three years old.

When she was five years old, her mother's employer offered to pay for piano lessons, and Nina started training to become a classical pianist.

She was committed, hardworking, and hugely talented.

At 12, she gave her first concert. Her parents were sitting in the front row, but they were forced to move to the back of the hall to make room for some white people who'd come in. Nina refused to start playing until her parents were returned to seats in the front.

Nina poured her passion and pride into her music, and she could not stand racism. She wanted Black people to be proud, to be free, and to embrace their talents and their passions, free of judgement.

That's why she wrote songs like "Brown Baby" and "To Be Young, Gifted, and Black." Nina Simone knew how racism hurt Black people, and she wanted them to find strength in her songs. "The worst thing about that kind of prejudice . . . " she said, "is that while you feel hurt and angry and all the rest of it, it feeds your self-doubt. You start thinking, perhaps I am not good enough."

Nina decided to cultivate her talent, rather than her fear, and eventually, she became one of the most famous jazz singers in the world.

FEBRUARY 21, 1933–APRIL 21, 2003
UNITED STATES OF AMERICA

ILLUSTRATION
BY PALESA
MONARENG

"I'LL TELL YOU
WHAT FREEDOM IS
TO ME: NO FEAR."
—NINA SIMONE

POLICARPA SALAVARRIETA

SPY

Once upon a time, in Bogotá, Colombia, there was a seamstress who was also a spy. Her real name was secret, but most people knew her as Policarpa Salavarrieta, or "La Pola."

When she was a child, Policarpa's godmother taught her how to sew. Little did she know that one day, her sewing skills would help bring about a revolution.

At the time, Colombia was ruled by faraway Spain. Many people, called *royalists*, were proud that they had a Spanish king. Others were revolutionaries like Policarpa. They wanted Colombia to be free.

The royalists were always on the lookout for revolutionaries. Policarpa had to keep changing her name to avoid being captured.

She worked as a seamstress in the houses of royalists. While she was altering clothes for the ladies, she gathered information about royalist plans, which she passed on to her revolutionary friends.

One day, a messenger carrying information provided by Policarpa was caught, and her secret identity was uncovered. She was arrested and told that her life would be spared only if she gave them the names of her friends. She looked them straight in the eye and refused. She was a fierce young woman who would not be scared.

Policarpa still inspires women and men from Colombia and all over the world to fight for freedom and justice without fear.

CIRCA 1795–NOVEMBER 14, 1817
COLOMBIA

"I HAVE MORE
THAN ENOUGH
COURAGE."
—POLICARPA
SALAVARRIETA

RITA LEVI-MONTALCINI

SCIENTIST

When Rita's nanny died of cancer, she decided to become a doctor. She was particularly fascinated by neurons (the stuff our brain is made of). So after graduation, Rita worked with an extraordinary professor named Giuseppe Levi and a group of outstanding fellow scientists from her class.

They were in the middle of some very important research when a cruel dictator passed a law saying that Jewish people were not allowed to work at the university. She escaped to Belgium with her professor, who was also Jewish. But when the Nazis invaded Belgium, she had to escape again. Rita returned to Italy.

It is hard to work as a scientist when you have to hide all the time and have no access to a lab, but Rita did not give up.

She turned her bedroom into a small research station. She sharpened sewing needles to create surgical instruments. She placed a small operating table in front of her bed, where she dissected chickens and studied cells under a microscope.

When her city was bombed, Rita escaped again, then again. From hideout to hideout, no matter how difficult, wherever she went, she kept on working. For her work in the area of neurobiology, she was awarded the Nobel Prize for Physiology or Medicine—which made her the third person from her medical school class to win a Nobel Prize!

APRIL 22, 1909–DECEMBER 30, 2012
ITALY

"ABOVE ALL, DON'T FEAR
DIFFICULT MOMENTS. THE
BEST COMES FROM THEM."
—RITA LEVI-MONTALCINI

ROSA PARKS

ACTIVIST

Once upon a time, Montgomery, Alabama, was a segregated city. Black people and white people went to different schools, prayed in different churches, shopped in different stores, rode different elevators, and drank from different water fountains. Everyone rode the same buses, but they had to sit in different areas: white people up front, Black people at the back. Rosa Parks grew up in this black-and-white world.

It was hard for Black people, and many were angry and sad because of segregation. But if they protested, they were thrown in jail.

One day, 42-year-old Rosa was sitting in the back of a bus on her way home from work. It was crowded, and there were not enough seats in the front section (the one reserved for whites), so the driver told Rosa to give up her seat so a white person could sit down.

Rosa said no.

She spent the night in jail, but this one brave act showed people that it was possible to say no to injustice.

Rosa's friends declared a boycott. They asked every single Black person not to use any of the buses in the city until the law was changed. Word spread fast and wide. The boycott lasted for 381 days. It ended when bus segregation was declared unconstitutional by the U.S. Supreme Court.

It took 10 years for segregation to be banned in any other state, but it happened, finally, thanks to Rosa's first brave "No."

FEBRUARY 4, 1913–OCTOBER 24, 2005

UNITED STATES OF AMERICA

"I WOULD LIKE TO BE REMEMBERED
AS A PERSON WHO WANTED TO
BE FREE . . . SO OTHER PEOPLE
WOULD BE ALSO FREE."
—ROSA PARKS

SCAN TO
HEAR MORE

RUTH BADER GINSBURG

SUPREME COURT JUSTICE

Once upon a time, there was a girl who dreamed of becoming a great lawyer. "A lady lawyer?" people would mock her. "Don't be ridiculous! Lawyers and judges are always men."

Ruth looked around her and saw that they were right. "But there's no reason why that shouldn't change," she thought. She attended Harvard Law School and Columbia Law School as one of their brightest students.

Her husband, Marty, was also a student at Harvard. "Your wife should be home baking cookies and looking after the baby," people used to say. But Marty didn't listen. Ruth was a terrible cook! And besides, he loved taking care of their daughter and was proud of his brilliant wife.

Ruth was passionate about women's rights. She argued six landmark cases on gender equality before the U.S. Supreme Court. Then she became the second female Supreme Court Justice in the country's history.

There are nine justices on the Supreme Court. "If I'm asked when will there be enough women on the Supreme Court, I say, 'When there are nine,'" explained Ruth. "People are shocked—but there've been nine men, like forever, and nobody's ever raised their eyebrows at that."

Even in her eighties, Ruth did 20 push-ups every day and became a style icon, thanks to the extravagant collars she wore in court with her judge's robes.

MARCH 15, 1933–SEPTEMBER 18, 2020
UNITED STATES OF AMERICA

ILLUSTRATION BY
ELEANOR DAVIS

"I DISSENT."
—RUTH BADER GINSBURG

RUTH HARKNESS

EXPLORER

Along time ago, zoos didn't know much about how to care for the animals they acquired. It was rare for an exotic animal to survive the trip to the United States. Visitors were used to seeing dead, stuffed animals. So when Ruth's husband decided to bring back a live panda from China, it was a big deal. But things didn't go according to his plan. Just a few months after arriving in China, he died.

Ruth was a fashion designer in New York City and knew little about China. But she missed her husband and loved adventures. So she thought, "I'll finish what Bill started. I'll go to China and bring back a live panda."

In China, Ruth hiked through the thickest forests, climbed up to ancient monasteries, followed rivers by day, and made fires by night. One night, she heard a sound. Ruth followed the noise into the forest and found a baby panda in a tree hollow. She took it in her arms and didn't know what to do. She gave the panda milk. When she was back in the city, she bought a fur coat so the baby panda would feel better when she held it.

She called the panda Su Lin and brought it to a zoo in Chicago. Although no one should steal a baby panda from its natural habitat, at the time, this was the only way people knew how to share their discoveries and educate others about foreign wildlife. As a result of Ruth's actions, tens of thousands of people learned that all wild animals deserve respect and love.

SEPTEMBER 21, 1900–JULY 20, 1947
UNITED STATES OF AMERICA

ILLUSTRATION BY
CLAUDIA CARIERI

"I DON'T KNOW WHETHER IT WILL
BE HUMANLY POSSIBLE TO GET A
PANDA OR NOT, BUT I FEEL THAT
IF IT IS, I WILL."
—RUTH HARKNESS

SEONDEOK OF SILLA

QUEEN

Once upon a time, in Silla, one of the three kingdoms of Korea, there was a very clever young woman who became queen. Her name was Seondeok. A nobleman called Lord Bidam didn't like this at all and led an uprising against Seondeok with the slogan "Girls can't be kings!" He saw a falling star and said it was a sign that her reign would end.

But Seondeok flew a burning kite and told the people that her star was back in the sky.

That was not the first time that Seondeok amazed everyone with a clever stunt. When she was a child, her father (the king) was given a packet of peony seeds and a painting of peonies by the Emperor of China. "These will be beautiful flowers," she said, looking at the illustration on the packet, "it's just a shame they won't have a sweet scent."

"How do you know that?" her father asked.

"If they did, there would have been bees or butterflies in the picture."

When the flowers bloomed, it turned out she was right: they were indeed odorless.

The young queen sent scholars and students to China to learn Chinese languages and customs, forging strong ties of friendship between their countries.

Seondeok was the first queen of Silla, after 26 kings.

CIRCA 610–FEBRUARY 17, 647

KOREA

ILLUSTRATION BY
KIKI LJUNG

"WHAT IS HARDER THAN
GAINING PEOPLE'S
TRUST IS HAVING TO
ABANDON THEM."
—SEONDEOK
OF SILLA

SERENA AND VENUS WILLIAMS

TENNIS PLAYERS

Once upon a time, there was a pair of sisters in the city of Compton who spent their afternoons at the tennis court with their father. Their names were Serena and Venus.

Every day, their father brought a basket of tennis balls to the court and showed the girls how to play. Serena was just four years old at the time. She was so small that when she sat on the bench, her feet didn't touch the ground.

Growing up, she was often the youngest player in the tournaments her father entered her in—but that didn't stop her from winning.

In Compton, there were gangs who would sometimes cause trouble, but when they saw Serena and Venus playing tennis, they stood by the court in awe and made sure no one disturbed them. They were inspired by the sisters' passion and determination.

Serena and Venus trained hard, giving their all to tennis. By the time they were teenagers, they were so strong that their father declared they were on their way to becoming the best tennis players in the world.

And that's exactly what happened! Both sisters have been ranked number 1 in the world. They continue to wow tennis fans and make the whole city of Compton very proud.

SERENA, BORN SEPTEMBER 26, 1981
VENUS, BORN JUNE 17, 1980
UNITED STATES OF AMERICA

"IF YOU WANT TO
BE THE BEST, YOU'VE
GOT TO EMULATE
THE BEST."
—SERENA WILLIAMS

SIMONE BILES

GYMNAST

Once there was a girl who could fly. Her name was Simone Biles. She was a gymnast, the greatest in American history. When Simone took to the mat, people couldn't take their eyes off her. She was so fast, so strong, so flexible, so agile! She flew through the air with grace and speed, twisting and turning, and landing perfectly each time.

Simone started gymnastics when she was just six years old. By the time she was 18, she had already won so many medals that when she traveled to Rio de Janeiro, Brazil, for the Olympics, everyone expected her to win not one but five medals.

One day, a journalist asked her, "How do you deal with that kind of pressure?"

"I try not to think about it. Right now, my goal is to be more consistent on the uneven bars."

"What about the goal of winning a gold medal?"

"A medal can't be a goal," Simone replied, smiling. "It's like my mom always says: 'If doing your best means you come out on top, that's awesome. If it means that you finish fourth, that's awesome, too.'"

Simone's mom adopted her when Simone was three. She taught Simone that staying humble and doing your best is the only way to live a meaningful life and inspire everyone around you.

At the Olympics in Rio, Simone won five medals—four of them gold!

BORN MARCH 14, 1997
UNITED STATES OF AMERICA

ILLUSTRATION BY
ELINE VAN DAM

"I WAS BUILT THIS WAY
FOR A REASON, SO I'M
GOING TO USE IT."
—SIMONE BILES

SONITA ALIZADEH

RAPPER

When Sonita was 10 years old, her parents told her, "We have to sell you into marriage." They started buying her nice clothes and taking more care of her than they had done before.

Sonita did not know exactly what all this meant, but she knew she did not want to get married. She wanted to study, to write, and to sing songs. She told her mother so. Her mother said to her, "We need the money to buy a bride for your older brother. There is no choice. We must sell you."

At the last moment, the marriage arrangements fell through. War broke out in Afghanistan, where the family lived, and Sonita and her brother were sent away to live in a refugee camp in Iran. Sonita went to a school nearby, and she started writing down her songs.

When Sonita was 16 years old, her mom came to visit her. She told Sonita that she had to go back to Afghanistan because they had found another husband who wanted to buy her. Again, Sonita said no. Sonita loved her mom, but she did not want to get married. She wanted to be a rapper.

She wrote a hard-hitting song called "Brides for Sale" and uploaded it on YouTube. The video went viral, and Sonita became famous. She won a scholarship to study music in the United States. "In my country, a good girl should be silent," says Sonita, "but I want to share the words that are in my heart."

BORN 1996

AFGHANISTAN

"I AM TIRED OF THE SILENCE."
—SONITA ALIZADEH

ILLUSTRATION BY
SAMIDHA GUNJAL

SYLVIA EARLE

MARINE BIOLOGIST

Once upon a time, there was a young scientist who loved to dive at night, when the ocean was dark and it was impossible to tell if the fish are asleep or awake.

"At night," she said, "you see lots of fish you don't see in the daytime."

Her name was Sylvia, and she led a team of aquanauts. She and her team lived underwater for weeks, diving out of all kinds of underwater vehicles and studying life in the ocean like no one before.

One night, Sylvia wore a special suit. White and gray and as big as a space suit, it had a huge, domed helmet with four round windows to see out of. Six miles offshore, she dived deeper than anyone had ever been without a rescue tether. Down where the dark is blacker than a starless night, with only the feeble light of an underwater lamp, she put her foot on the ocean floor, just as the first man, in a similar costume but miles above her head, had put his footprint on the surface of the Moon.

"Without the ocean," she explained, "there would be no life on Earth. No humans, no animals, no oxygen, no plants. If we don't know the ocean, we can't love it."

Sylvia studied hidden currents, discovered underwater plants, and waved to deep-sea fish. "We must take care of the oceans," she says. "Will you join me in a mission to protect the Earth's blue heart?"

BORN AUGUST 30, 1935
UNITED STATES OF AMERICA

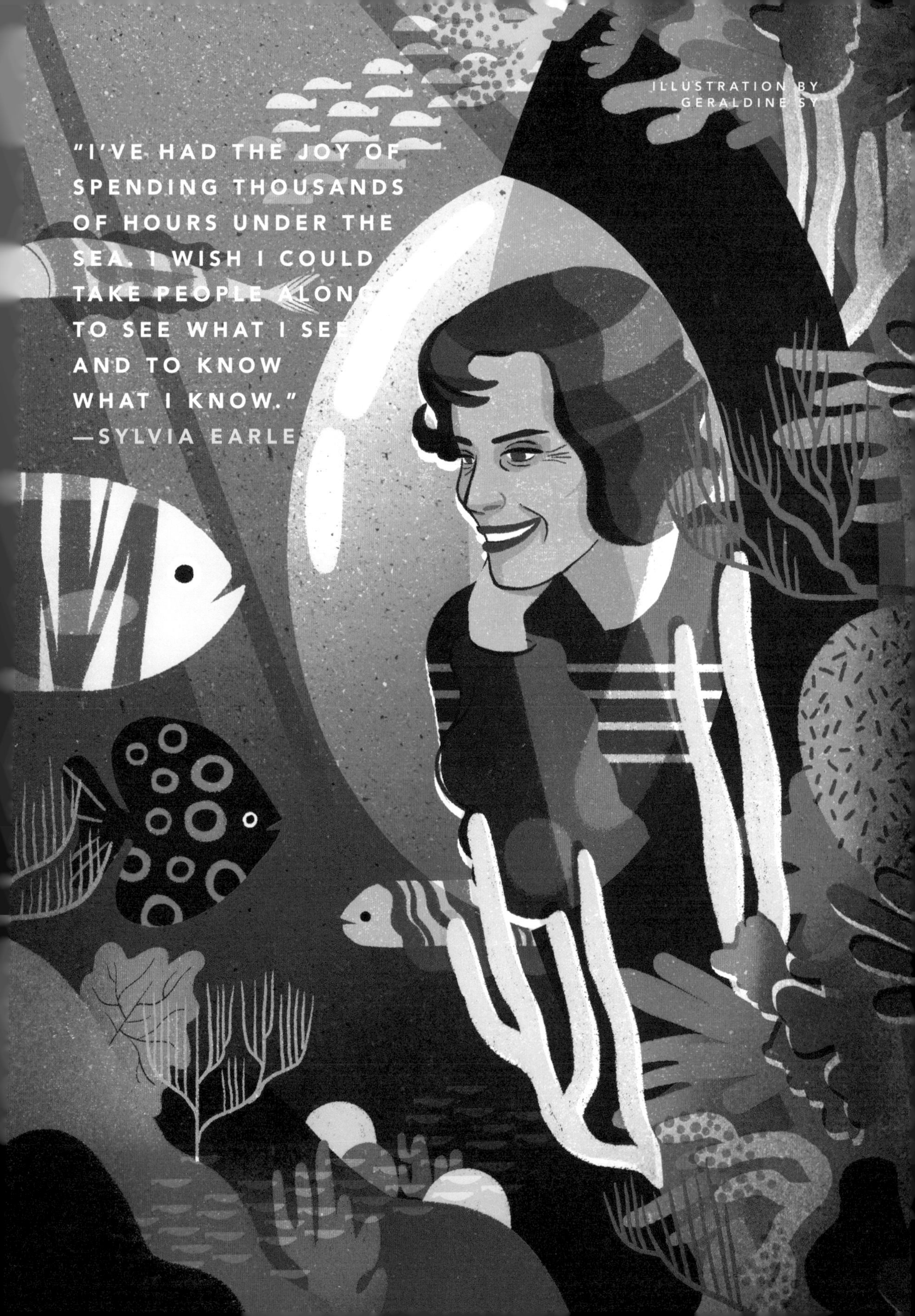

ILLUSTRATION BY
GERALDINE SY
"I'VE HAD THE JOY OF SPENDING THOUSANDS OF HOURS UNDER THE SEA. I WISH I COULD TAKE PEOPLE ALONG TO SEE WHAT I SEE AND TO KNOW WHAT I KNOW."
—SYLVIA EARLE

TAMARA DE LEMPICKA

PAINTER

In an elegant house in Saint Petersburg, Russia, a painter came to paint a portrait of a 12-year-old girl named Tamara.

Tamara did not like his work and thought she could do much better.

A few years later, at the opera with her aunt, Tamara spotted a man in the crowd. She knew instantly that this was the man she would marry—and so she did. His name was Tadeusz.

There was a revolution in Russia, and Tadeusz was thrown in jail. Tamara managed to get him released and organized their escape to Paris.

Paris was the center of the art world at that time, and it was here that Tamara realized her childhood dream of becoming an artist. She became famous. Celebrities lined up to be painted by Tamara.

When World War II broke out, Tamara moved to the United States. Slowly, her bold and striking style fell out of fashion. When a show of hers got bad reviews, she lost her temper and swore never to exhibit again.

Tamara moved to Mexico, where she lived in a beautiful house until her death at the age of 82, with her daughter Kizette by her side.

She asked that her ashes be scattered over the volcano of Popocatépetl, a fitting end for an artistic genius with an explosive personality.

Today, her paintings are worth millions of dollars. Tamara would be proud to know that the singer Madonna is one of her biggest fans.

MAY 16, 1898–MARCH 18, 1980
POLAND

"I LIVE LIFE IN THE
MARGINS OF SOCIETY,
AND THE RULES OF
NORMAL SOCIETY DON'T
APPLY TO THOSE WHO
LIVE ON THE FRINGE."
—TAMARA DE LEMPICKA

VIRGINIA WOOLF

WRITER

Once upon a time, a little girl living in London created a newspaper about her family. Her name was Virginia.

Virginia was witty, cultured, and very sensitive. Whenever something bad happened, she would feel incredibly sad for weeks. When she was happy, she was the happiest kid on Earth.

"I live in intensity," Virginia wrote in her diary.

Virginia suffered from an illness known as depression. These mood swings affected her throughout her life. But whatever her mood, Virginia was always writing. She kept a diary, she wrote poems, she wrote novels, she wrote reviews. Writing was a way for her to see her own feelings more clearly, and by doing so, shed light on everyone's feelings.

There was a person Virginia loved as much as writing: her husband, Leonard.

Virginia and Leonard were incredibly happy together and loved each other dearly, but sometimes Virginia's depression made it hard for her to feel joy. At that time, there was no effective treatment for depression, and many people did not believe it was real.

Today, depression can be treated. But whether you are happy or sad or somewhere in between, it is always a great idea to record your moods in a diary. You may become a writing genius like Virginia and help other people understand their feelings and live lives full of dreams.

JANUARY 25, 1882–MARCH 28, 1941
UNITED KINGDOM

ILLUSTRATION BY
ANA JUAN

"I AM ROOTED, BUT I FLOW."
—VIRGINIA WOOLF

WANG ZHENYI

ASTRONOMER

Once upon a time, in China, there was a young girl who liked to study all sorts of things. She loved math, science, geography, medicine, and writing poetry. She was also great at horse riding, archery, and martial arts. Her name was Wang Zhenyi.

Wang Zhenyi traveled widely and was curious about everything, but above all, she loved astronomy. She spent hours studying the planets, the Sun, the stars, and the Moon.

At that time, people thought that a lunar eclipse was a sign that the gods were angry. Wang Zhenyi knew this couldn't be true and decided to prove it with an experiment. She put a round table—the Earth—in a garden pavilion, and from the ceiling she hung a lamp—the Sun. Off to one side, she placed a big round mirror—the Moon.

Then she started to move these objects exactly as they move in the sky—until the Sun, Earth, and Moon stood in a line, with the Earth in the middle. "There you go! A lunar eclipse happens every time the Moon passes directly through the Earth's shadow."

Wang Zhenyi also understood the importance of making math and science accessible for common people, so she got rid of all the aristocratic language and wrote a paper explaining the force of gravity.

Her reputation spread far and wide. In her poems, she often wrote about the importance of equality between men and women.

1768–1797

CHINA

"ARE YOU NOT CONVINCED,
DAUGHTERS CAN ALSO BE HEROIC?"
—WANG ZHENYI

ILLUSTRATION BY
ANA GALVAÑ

WANGARI MAATHAI

ACTIVIST

Once upon a time, in Kenya, there was a woman called Wangari. When lakes started to dry up and streams started to disappear near her village, Wangari knew she had to do something. She called a meeting with some of the other women.

"The government cut down trees to make room for farms, but now we need to walk for miles to collect firewood," one said.

"Let's bring the trees back," exclaimed Wangari.

"How many?" they asked.

"A few million should do it," she replied.

"A few million? Are you crazy? No nursery is big enough to grow that many!"

"We're not buying them from a nursery. We'll grow them ourselves at home."

So Wangari and her friends gathered seeds from the forest and planted them in cans. They watered and looked after them until the plants were about a foot tall. Then they planted the saplings in their backyards.

It started with a few women. But, just like a tree sprouting from a tiny seed, the idea spread and grew into a widespread movement.

The Green Belt Movement expanded beyond Kenyan borders. More than 51 million trees were planted, and Wangari Maathai was awarded the Nobel Peace Prize for her work. She celebrated by planting a tree.

APRIL 1, 1940–SEPTEMBER 25, 2011

KENYA

"THE TIME IS NOW."
—WANGARI MAATHAI

WILMA RUDOLPH

ATHLETE

Long ago, before the vaccine for polio was discovered, children were not protected against this terrible disease. Wilma was a little child when she contracted polio and was left with a paralyzed leg.

"I'm not sure she's ever going to walk again," the doctor said.

"You will walk again, honey. I promise," whispered Wilma's mom.

For two years, her mom took Wilma to the city for treatment. Every day, her 21 brothers and sisters took turns massaging her weak leg. Wilma had to use a brace to walk, and the mean kids in her neighborhood made fun of her. Sometimes, when her parents were not home, she tried to walk without it. It was hard, but Wilma slowly got stronger.

By the time she was 12, her mom's promise came true. Wilma could walk by herself! She even started playing basketball. She loved jumping and running, so she did not think twice when her coach asked if she wanted to join the track team.

Wilma competed in 20 races and won every one of them.

"I don't know why I run so fast," she said. "I just run."

Wilma became the fastest woman in the world. She broke three world records at the 1960 Olympics.

Wilma always said that the key to winning was knowing how to lose. "Nobody wins all the time," she said. "If you can pick up after a crushing defeat and go on to win again, you are going to be a champion someday."

JUNE 23, 1940–NOVEMBER 12, 1994
UNITED STATES OF AMERICA

"MY DOCTORS TOLD ME
I WOULD NEVER WALK
AGAIN. MY MOTHER TOLD
ME I WOULD. I BELIEVED
MY MOTHER."
—WILMA RUDOLPH

XIAN ZHANG

ORCHESTRA CONDUCTOR

Once upon a time, there was a country where pianos were hard to find. Pianos were not sold in stores, and they were not played in concerts. They simply were nowhere to be found.

One day, a man had a smart idea. He bought all the required pieces and built a piano himself. He did not build it to play it, though. He built it for his three-year-old daughter, Xian Zhang.

Xian Zhang loved playing and wanted to become a concert pianist, but her teacher told her that her hands were too small. He encouraged her to learn composition, to conduct an orchestra instead.

One night, before the final rehearsal of *The Marriage of Figaro* (a beautiful opera), the orchestra conductor called Xian Zhang and told her, without further explanation, "Tomorrow, you are going to conduct."

"Thank you," she squeaked. She was terrified!

She was tiny, only 20 years old. When she stepped onto the podium, some of the musicians laughed at her.

She did not blink. She did not smile. She just raised her baton and waited.

After 10 minutes, the whole orchestra was following her with respect.

"My life changed overnight," she said. Today, Xian Zhang is one of the most important orchestra conductors in the world.

BORN 1973

CHINA

"WHEN GIRLS SEE OTHER
WOMEN DOING THIS JOB,
THEY WILL FEEL THAT THEY
CAN DO IT, TOO."
—XIAN ZHANG

· YAA ASANTEWAA ·

WARRIOR QUEEN

Once upon a time, in a land rich with gold, there lived a strong queen who ruled over the Asante kingdom. Her name was Yaa. Her people believed in the magical powers of a golden stool which was so sacred that even the king and queen were not allowed to touch it. It was said that the heart and soul of the Asante people—past, present, and future—was contained in this golden throne.

One day, a governor-general appointed by the British announced that the British Empire would be taking over the Asante lands. "We also demand your Golden Stool to sit upon. Bring it here immediately."

The Asante leaders were shocked and insulted—but their enemy was powerful. One by one, they urged surrender.

Not Yaa Asantewaa. She stood up.

"If you, the men of Asante, will not go forward, then we will. We the women will," she said. "We will fight the white men."

Yaa led an army of 5,000 into battle against the well-equipped British soldiers. After a fierce fight, Yaa's army was defeated. She was captured and deported to the Seychelles Islands.

She never saw her beloved land again, but her country continued to be inspired by her bravery. A few years after her death, the Asante Empire regained its independence. To this day, Yaa Asantewaa's people sing songs about their beloved queen and her proud, fighting spirit.

CIRCA 1840–OCTOBER 17, 1921

GHANA

ILLUSTRATION BY
NOA SNIR

"IF YOU, THE MEN OF
ASANTE, WILL NOT GO
FORWARD, THEN WE WILL.
WE, THE WOMEN WILL."
—YAA ASANTEWAA

YOKO ONO

ARTIST

Once upon a time, a little girl called Yoko lived in a beautiful house in Tokyo. When war broke out, her house was bombed. Yoko and her family fled for their lives. Suddenly, she and her brother had no toys, no beds, no snacks, no clothes. They had to beg for food. Other children taunted them because they had once been rich, and now they were the poorest of the poor.

When she grew up, Yoko became a performance artist. You didn't just look at Yoko's art, you were part of it. For example, she asked people to cut up her clothes while she was still wearing them.

One day, a musician called John Lennon went to visit one of Yoko's exhibitions. He found her art beautiful and became a fan.

John and Yoko started writing letters to each other, and they eventually fell madly in love. They recorded songs together and created photography projects and even movies.

At the time, the United States was at war with Vietnam. Yoko knew how bad war could be. She wanted to help the peace movement. Many protesters held "sit-ins" but, being Yoko, she wanted to do something different. Instead of a sit-in, John and Yoko had a "bed-in," where they stayed in bed for a week surrounded by television cameras and journalists.

They even recorded a song to sum up their simple, strong message: "Give peace a chance."

BORN FEBRUARY 18, 1933

JAPAN

ILLUSTRATION BY
MICHELLE CHRISTENSEN

"JUST START THINKING
PEACE, AND THE MESSAGE
WILL SPREAD QUICKER
THAN YOU THINK."
—YOKO ONO

YUSRA MARDINI

SWIMMER

SCAN TO HEAR MORE

Once, in Damascus, Syria, there was a swimmer called Yusra. Every day, she and her sister trained with their dad at the local swimming pool. Syria was at war, and one day a bomb was dropped on the swimming pool. Luckily, Yusra was not there at the time.

Shortly afterward, her house was destroyed by another bomb. It was another narrow escape. All of a sudden, Yusra and her family had nothing left and nowhere to live, so they decided to flee the country.

Yusra had heard that Germany was a good place for swimmers. The journey was long and getting there would be hard, but that did not put Yusra off. She and her sister joined a group of other refugees for a month-long journey across several countries and then aboard a rubber dinghy to the island of Lesbos. The boat was only meant for six or seven people. There were 20 crammed aboard. Suddenly, the motor broke down. "We can't die at sea," Yusra thought. "We are swimmers!" And so she jumped into the water with her sister and another boy.

They kicked and swam and dragged and pushed the boat for more than three hours, until they finally reached the shore.

When they reached Germany, the first question Yusra asked was, "Where can I find a swimming club?"

Not only did she find one, but in 2016 she was also part of the first refugee team ever to compete in the Olympics.

BORN MARCH 5, 1998
SYRIA

ILLUSTRATION BY
JESSICA COOPER

"I WANT ALL REFUGEES
TO BE PROUD OF ME."
—YUSRA MARDINI

· ZAHA HADID ·

ARCHITECT

When Zaha turned 10, she decided that she wanted to be an architect. Zaha was a very determined girl, and she grew up to be one of the greatest architects of our time. She became known as the "Queen of the Curve" because the buildings she designed had so many bold, sweeping lines.

One day, she boarded a plane at the airport. The pilot explained that there would be a short delay before they could take off. Zaha was outraged and insisted that they put her on a different flight immediately. It was impossible, the crew said: the baggage was already on board. But Zaha insisted—and she got her way. She usually did.

That was just who she was.

Zaha liked to cross boundaries, to do things everyone else thought were impossible. That is how she created the kind of buildings no one else could even imagine. She designed fire stations, museums, villas, cultural centers, an aquatic center, and much more.

Zaha forged her own path. She was never afraid of being different. One of her mentors said she was like "a planet in her own inimitable orbit."

She always knew what she wanted and did not rest until she got it. Some say that is the key to achieving anything big in life. Zaha was the first woman to receive the Royal Gold Medal from the Royal Institute of British Architects.

OCTOBER 31, 1950–MARCH 31, 2016
IRAQ

ILLUSTRATION BY
NOA SNIR

"I ALWAYS THOUGHT I WAS
POWERFUL, SINCE I WAS A KID."
—ZAHA HADID

• WRITE YOUR STORY •

Once upon a time, _____

_____

_____

_____

_____

_____

_____

_____

_____

_____

_____

_____

_____

_____

_____

_____

_____

_____

DRAW YOUR PORTRAIT

· REBELS' HALL OF FAME ·

Here's to the rebel girls and boys who were early believers in *Good Night Stories for Rebel Girls* on Kickstarter. They come from all over the world, and they're going to change the world.

NIGISTE ABEBE

PIPER ABRAMS

HAIFA AND LEEN AL SAUD

SHAHA F. AND WADHA N. AL-THANI

NEDA ALA'I-CHANGUIT

RAFFAELLA AND MADDALENA ALBERTI

MADELEINE ALEXIS

WILLOW ALLISON

LEIA ALMEIDA

VIOLET AMACK

BROOKLYN ANDERSON

SOFIA ANDREWS

ANDHIRA JS ANGGARA

GRACE ANKROM

OLIVIA ANN

SYLVIE APPLE

ALEJANDRA PIEDRA ARCOS

CAMILA ARNOLD

CAROLINA ARRIGONI

EVANGELINE ASIMAKOPOULOS

PHOEBE ATKINS

AUDREY B. AVERA

AZRAEL

MISCHA BAHAT

KIERA BAIRD

EMERY AND NYLAH BAKER

MOLLY AND SCARLET BARFIELD

EVA BARKER

ISABELLA BARRY

PIPPA BARTON

CRISTINA BATTAGLIO

SOFIA BATTEGODA

JENNIFER BEEDON

EMMA BEKIER

TAYLOR BEKIER

VIVIENNE BELA

MADELINE BENKO

EMMA BIGKNIFE

PIA BIRDIE

HANNAH BIRKETT

ALEXIS BLACK

KATIE BLICKENSTAFF

ADA MARYJO AND ROSE MARIE BODNAR

GABRIELLA MARIE BONNECARRERE WHITE

RIPLEY TATE BORROMEO

MEGAN BOWEN

LILA BOYCE

MARLEY BOYCE

MOLLY MARIE AND MAKENNA DIANE BOYCE

JOY AND GRACE BRADBURY

MAGNOLIA BRADY

EVA AND AUGUST BRANCATO

CORA AND IVY BRAND

TALA K AND KAIA J BROADWELL

AUDREY AND ALEXANDRA BROWN

SCARLETT BRUNER

MARLOWE MARGUERITE BÜCKER

KATIE BUMBLEBEE

VIVIAN AND STACY BURCH

CLARA BURNETTE

MIA A. BURYKINA

ZOE BUTTERWORTH

CASSIA GLADYS CADAN-PEMAN

GIGI GARITA AND LUNA BEECHER CALDERÓN

FINLEY AND MANDIE CAMPBELL

SCARLETT AND CHARLI CARR

KAITLYN CARR

EMILIE CASEY

LUCIENNE CASTILLO

KYLEE CAUSER

OLIVIA ANNA CAVALLO STEELE

NEVEYA CERNA-LOMBERA ESTRADA

ELLE CHANDLER

JOSIE CHARCON

LYN CHEAH

ANNA MARY CHENG

ELINOR CHIAM

LEELA CHOUDHURI

MILA CHOW

BEATRICE CICCHELLI

COCO COHEN

ABIGAIL COLE

EMILY ROBBINS COLEY

SOPHIA CONDON

EMILY COOLEY

ALLISON COOPER

STELLA AND MATILDE CORRAINI

GIORGIA CORSINI

LOGAN COSTELLO

EMILY CLARE AND CHARLOTTE GIULIA COSTELLO

CAMILLE AND ARIANE COUTURE

ISABEL CRACKNELL

ROSE CREED

SOPHIA AND MAYA CRISTOFORETTI

NATALIE SOPHIA AND CHLOE SABRINA CRUZ

GABRIELA CUNHA

EVIE CUNNINGHAM

ADA CUNNINGHAM

EVENING CZEGLEDY

ANTONIA AND INDIANA D'EGIDIO

KYLIE DAVIS

ELLA-ROSE DAVIS

BRENNA DAVISON

ELIZABETH DEEDS

ILARIA AND ARIANNA DESANDRÉ

ROSALIE DEVIDO

ALISSA DEVIR

PAOLA AND ANTONIO DI CUIA

EMILIA DIAZ

NEVAEH DONAZIA

HADLEY DRAPER LEVENDUSKY

HATTIE AND MINA DUDEN

SELMA JOY EAST

ALDEN ECKMAN

EUGENIO AND GREGORIO

SOPHIA EFSTATHIADIS

JULIA EGBERT

AILLEA ROSE ELKINS

ANNA ERAZO

RAMONA ERICKSON

MADELINE "MADDIE" ESSNER

ELENA ESTRADA-LOMBERA

SCOUT FAULL

LILLIAN FERGUSON

AURELIA FERGUSON

HEIDI AND ANOUSHKA FIELD

PAIGE AND MADELYN FINGERHUT

MARILENA AND TERESA FIORE

MARGARET AND KATHERINE FLEMING

VIDA FLORES SMOCK

LILY AND CIARA (KIKI) FLYNN

SABINE FOKKEMA

MIA AND KARSON FORCHELLI

HANNAH FOSS

SARA BON AND HANNAH LEE FOWLER

SYLVIE FRY

MOLLY CHARLOTTE FUCHS

KATARINA GAJGER

OLIVIA GALLAGHER

TAYLOR GALLIMORE

ANN GANNETT BETHELL

MADELINE AND LUCY GERRAND

MAREN AND EDEN GILBERT TYMKOW

FABULOUS GIRL

CAMILLA GOULD

SYAH GOUTHRO

EMMA GRANT

ISLA GREEN

CARA AND ROWAN GREEN

VICTORIA GREENDYK

MARIAH GRIBBLE

SAGE GRIDER

SUSIE GROOMES

EMMA, LUCY, AND FINLEY GROSS

CLAUDIA GRUNER

PAZ GUELFI-SALAZAR

VIOLA GUERRINI

IRIS GUZMAN

ABIGAIL HANNAH

ANNA-CÉLINE PAOLA HAPPSA

ALANNA HARBOUR

EVELYN AND LYDIA HARE

GWYNETH AND PIPER HARTLEY

ABIGAIL AND CHRISTA HAYBURN

SOFIA HAYNES

EVIE AND DANYA HERMAN

MACY HEWS

CLARE HILDICK KLEIN

AUREA BONITA HILGENBERG

RUBY GRACE HIME

AVA HOEGH-GULDBERG

JANE HOLLEY-MIERS

FARAH HOUSE

ARYANNA HOYEM

SASKIA AND PALOMA HULT

JORJA HUNG

HAYLIE AND HARPER HUNPHREYS

NORA IGLESIAS POZA

DEEN M. INGLEY

AZALAYAH IRIGOYEN

MIRIAM ISACKOV

JADI AND ALEXANDRA

MAYA JAFFE

FILIPPA JAKOBSSON

HADDIE JANE

ELEANOR HILARY AND CAROLINE KARRIE

JANULEWICZ LLOYD

JEMMA JOYCE TOBER

MARLEE AND BECCA K. ICKOWICZ

SLOANE AND MILLIE KAULENTIS

JESSICA AND SAMANTHA KELLOGG

MALENA KLEFFMAN

BRONWYN KMIECIK

CHARLOTTE KNICKERBOCKER

VIOLET KNOBLOCK

RACHEL BELLA KOLB

GABBY AND COCO KOLSKY

MILA KONAR

DARWYN AND LEVVEN KOVNER

OLIVIA KRAFT

SHAYNA AND LAYLA KRAFT

ZORA KRAFT

LUCY AND LOLA KRAMER

MORGAN AND CLAIRE KREMER

CLARA LUISE KUHLMANN

VIVIENNE LAURIE-DICKSON

JULIA LEGENDRE

BOWIE LEGGIERE-SMITH

ARIANNA LEONZIO

DARCY LESTER

ARABELLA AND KRISTEN LEVINE

EMILIA LEVINSEN

SOFIA LEVITAN

GWYNETH LEYS

ERICA A. AND SHELBY N. LIED

IRENE LINDBERG

AUDREY LIU-SHEIRBON

SYDNEY LOERKE

ROXANNE LONDON

SIENA AND EMERY LONG

GIULIA LORENZONI

BRIE LOVE

LILY KATHRYN LOWE

ELLAMARIE MACARI-MITCHELL

NATALIA MACIAS

ALISON AND CAROLINE MACINNES

MACKENZIE AND MACKAYLA

IESHA LUCILE MAE

AISLINN MANUS

LUCIA MARGHERITA

MOXIE MARQUIS

LEONOR AND LAURA MARUJO TRINDADE

CARYS MATHEWS

EVELYN AND TEAGAN MCCORMICK

VIOLET MCDONALD

JOSEPHINE, AYLIN AND SYLVIA MCILVAINE

ALIZE AND VIANNE MCILWRAITH

ANNABELLE MCLAUGHLIN

MAGGIE MCLOMAN

FIONA MCMILLEN

SOPHIA MECHAM

RYLIE MECHAM

MAILI MEEHAN

AVA MILLER

MORGAN MILLER

NOA MILLER

KATHERINE MILLER

PHOEBE MOELLENBERG

ALEXANDRA LV MOGER

LUBA AND SABRINA MIRZA MORIKI

FRIDA MORTENSEN

SARAH MOSCOWITZ

VIOLET J. MOURAS

MABEL MUDD

GEORGIANA MURRAY

NOOR NASHASHIBI

BEATRICE NECCHI

SYDNEY NICHOLS

ELLEN NIELSEN

DYLAN AND MARGAUX NOISETTE

VALENTINA NUILA

SUMMER O'DONOVAN

KSENIA O'NEIL

RIN O'ROURKE

ZELDA OAKS

OLIVIA SKYE OCAMPO

EMMA OLBERDING

CLAIRE ORRIS

ELEANORA OSSMAN

CHAEYOUNG AND CHAEWON OUM

KHAAI OWENS

MAJA AND MILA OZUT

POPPY OLIVIA PACE

OLIVIA PANTLE

SIMRIN MILA AND SIANA JAYLA PATEL

ANNAMARIA AND ELIO PAVONE

TINLEY PEHRSON

OAKLEY PEHRSON

SIENA PERRY

SCARLETT PETERS

ALEXANDRA AND GABRIELLE PETTIT

FEI PHOON

SUNNY AND HARA PICKETT

MACYN ROSE PINARD

BRESLYN, ARROT, AND BRAXON PLESH

STOCK-BRATINA

MADISYN, MALLORY, AND RAPHAEL PLUN-
KETT

FRANCES SOPHIA POE

ELSA PORRATA

ALEXANDRA FRANCES RENNIE

ANNA AND FILIPPO RENZI

AVA RIBEIRO

MIKAYLA RICE

ZOE RIVERA

ARIA AND ALANA ROBINSON

CLEO ROBINSON

SOFIA, BEATRICE, AND EDOARDO ROCHIRA

SOPHIE ROMEO

ELLA ROMO

LUCY ROTE

SOFÍA RUÍZ-MURPHY

SILVIA SABINI

ELIZABETH SAFFER

VIOLA SALA

MANUELA SALES STEELE

ESMIE SALINAS

KAYLA SAMPLE

KYRA SAMPLE

MIA AND IMANI SANDHU

SOFIA SANNA

KENDRA SAWYER

LUCY SCHAPIRO

NORAH ELOISE SCHMIT

BELLA SCHONFELD

ELISENDA SCHULTZ

MOLLY SCOTT

KYLIE AND KAITLYN SCOTT

NATALIE SER TYNG WANG

AMAYA AND KAVYA SETH

CRISTINA AND EVELYN SILVA

SHAI SIMPSON

ELLA AUSTEN AND KAILANI MEI SKOREPA

PHOEBE SMITH

ARLENE SMITH

OLIVIA-LOUISE SMITH

SARA SNOOK

EVERLY SNOW

GENEVIEVE AND EMERY SNYDER

SELIA SOLORZANO

AURORA SOOSAAR

AVA STANIEWICZ

RHYAN STANTON

BROOKE STARCHER

ANNABEL WINTER STETZ

SHELVIA STEWART

MAIA STRUBLE

EMMA STUBBS

GJ STUCKEY

NAVAH AND MOLLY STUHR

MYA SUMMERFELDT

SYDNEY SUTHERLAND

SIMONE SWINGLE

VICTORIA SZRAMKA

LOLA-IRIS AND LINLEY TA

OLIVIA TAPLEY

HAILEY ADAMS THALMAN

SOPHIE AND VIOLET THI BRANT

LUANA THIBAULT CARRERAS

REBECCA THROPE

PENELOPE TRAYNOR

JULIA TRGOVCEVIC

CAROLINE TUCKER

CORA ELIZABETH TURNER

SONIA TWEITO

ZOOEY TYLER WALKER

AGNES VÅHLUND

FINLEY VARGO

SARAH VASILIDES

SOPHIE VASSER

NOEMI VEIT

RIDHI VEKARIA

GABRIELLA VERBEELEN

NAYARA VIEIRA

FABLE VITALE

GRACE MARIA WAITE

RAEGAN AND DARBY WALSH

TOVA ROSE WASSON

JOSEPHINE WEBSTER-FOX

ELIZABETH WEBSTER-MCFADDEN

ZOE AND TESSA WEINSTEIN

HARPER WEST

LAUREN WEST

STELLA WEST-HUGHES

ANNA WESTENDORF

ELLIA AND VICTORIA WHITACRE

ELEANOR MARIE WHITAKER

MADELYN WHITE

KAYLA WIESEL

GRACE WILLIAMS

TESSANEE AND KIRANNA WILLIAMS

SAM WILSON

VICTORIA PAYTON WOLF

GEMMA WOMACK

TEDDY ROSE WYLDER HEADEY

CHLOE YOUSEFI

HANNAH YUN FEI PHUA

AZUL ZAPATA-TORRENEGRA

SLOANE ZELLER

WILLA AND WINNIE ZIELKE

· ILLUSTRATORS ·

Sixty extraordinary female artists from all over the world created the portraits of the trailblazing Rebels in this book.

ALEXANDRA BOWMAN, USA, 103
ALICE BARBERINI, ITALY, 139, 191
AMANDA HALL, USA, 121
ANA GALVAÑ, SPAIN, 49, 89, 187
ANA JUAN, SPAIN, 9, 185
BARBARA DZIADOSZ, GERMANY, 93, 159
BIJOU KARMAN, USA, 5
CARI VANDER YACHT, USA, 91
CLAUDIA CARIERI, ITALY, 17, 123, 171
CRISTINA AMODEO, ITALY, 53, 165
CRISTINA PORTOLANO, ITALY, 7, 39, 131
CRISTINA SPANÒ, ITALY, 113, 117
DALILA ROVAZZANI, ITALY, 57
DEBORA GUIDI, ITALY, 111, 141, 175
ÉDITH CARRON, FRANCE, 109
ELEANOR DAVIS, USA, 169
ELENI KALORKOTI, SCOTLAND, 67
ELENIA BERETTA, ITALY, 45
ELINE VAN DAM, NETHERLANDS, 15, 177
ELISABETTA STOINICH, ITALY, 3, 33
ELIZABETH BADDELEY, USA, 127
EMMANUELLE WALKER, CANADA, 83
GAIA STELLA, ITALY, 119
GERALDINE SY, PHILIPPINES, 11, 181
GIULIA FLAMINI, ITALY, 13, 133
HELENA MORAIS SOARES, PORTUGAL, 59, 149
JEANETTA GONZALES, USA, 155
JESSICA M. COOPER, USA, 199
JUSTINE LECOUFFE, USA, 25, 71
KAROLIN SCHNOOR, GERMANY, 43
KATE PRIOR, USA, 23, 107

KATHRIN HONESTA, INDONESIA, 63, 85
KIKI LJUNG, BELGIUM, 41, 61, 173
LEA HEINRICH, GERMANY, 19, 55
LIEKE VAN DER VORST, NETHERLANDS, 97
LIZZY STEWART, UK, 27
MALIN ROSENQVIST, SWEDEN, 95, 101
MARIJKE BUURLAGE, NETHERLANDS, 35
MARTA LORENZON, ITALY, 47
MARTA SIGNORI, ITALY, 115, 143, 183
MARTINA PAUKOVA, SLOVAKIA, 125, 137
MICHELLE CHRISTENSEN, USA, 197
MONICA GARWOOD, USA, 21, 69, 153
NOA SNIR, ISRAEL, 195, 201
PALESA MONARENG, UK, 31, 161
PAOLA ESCOBAR, COLOMBIA, 163
PAOLA ROLLO, ITALY, 51, 77
PING ZHU, USA, 151, 193
PRIYA KURIYAN, INDIA, 29, 129
RIIKKA SORMUNEN, FINLAND, 73
RITA PETRUCCIOLI, ITALY, 79, 147
SALLY NIXON, USA, 65, 167
SAMIDHA GUNJAL, INDIA, 179
SARA BONDI, ITALY, 105
SARAH MAZZETTI, ITALY, 99
SARAH WILKINS, NEW ZEALAND, 37, 145
SOPHIA MARTINECK, GERMANY, 81
THANDIWE TSHABALALA, SOUTH AFRICA, 135, 189
ZARA PICKEN, USA, 157
ZOZIA DZIERŻAWSKA, POLAND, 75, 87

· ACKNOWLEDGMENTS ·

Gratitude is one of our favorite feelings. It has accompanied the creation of this book from its inception through the moment you hold it in your hands. Now, as you are about to finish it, we have a few women who are special to us and who we want to thank:

Our mothers, *Lucia* and *Rosa*, who always believed in us and showed us the phenomenal power of a rebel heart, day after day; our newborn niece, *Olivia*, for giving us one more reason to fight the tough fights; *Antonella*, for always being a big sister, despite being the youngest; *Annalisa*, *Brenda*, and *Elettra* who are the most precious friends anyone could ever hope for; *Christine*, who—after a 20-minute meeting—decided that 500 Startups would become the first investor in Timbuktu Labs; *Arianna*, for her unshaken enthusiasm in all things *Timbuktu* and for her precious collaboration on the research for this book; *Vilma*, for the rock she is; *nonna Marisa*, for her trusting heart and luminous eyes; *nonna Giovanna*, for always keeping it real with the sassiest productivity quotes on earth; *zie Lelle*, for all the laughs.

A heartfelt "thank you" to the (as we're writing) 20,025 backers whose support helped us bring *Good Night Stories for Rebel Girls* to life.

We couldn't have done this without you.

ABOUT THE AUTHORS

ELENA FAVILLI is a *New York Times* best-selling author, journalist, and breaker of glass ceilings. She is the cofounder of Rebel Girls and serves on the board, leading all impact initiatives. Elena has written for the *Guardian, Vogue, ELLE, COLORS* magazine, *McSweeney's, RAI, Il Post,* and *La Repubblica,* in addition to authoring four books within the Rebel Girls series.

FRANCESCA CAVALLO is a *New York Times* best-selling author, activist, and entrepreneur. Recipient of the 2018 *Publishers Weekly* Star Watch Award for her work at Rebel Girls, Francesca launched some of the most successful crowdfunding campaigns in the history of publishing. In 2019, she founded Undercats, a company with the mission of radically increasing diversity in children's media.

REBEL GIRLS is a global, multi-platform empowerment brand dedicated to helping raise the most inspired and confident global generation of girls through content, experiences, products, and community. Originating from an international best-selling children's book, Rebel Girls amplifies stories of real-life women throughout history, geography, and field of excellence. With a growing community of nearly 20 million self-identified Rebel Girls spanning more than 100 countries, the brand engages with Generation Alpha through its book series, award-winning podcast, events, and merchandise. With the 2021 launch of the Rebel Girls app, the company has created a flagship destination for girls to explore a wondrous world filled with inspiring true stories of extraordinary women.

LISTEN TO MORE EMPOWERING STORIES ON THE REBEL GIRLS APP!

Download the app to listen to beloved Rebel Girls stories, as well as brand-new tales of extraordinary women. Filled with the adventures and accomplishments of women from around the world and throughout history, the Rebel Girls app is designed to entertain, inspire, and build confidence in listeners everywhere.

JOIN THE REBEL GIRLS COMMUNITY

Rebel Girls' books and podcast have won awards, including:

- 2020 Discover Pods Award, Best Kids & Family Podcast
- 2020 Webby Award, Best Kids & Family Podcast
- 2020 New York Festivals Radio Award, Gold in Education Podcasts
- 2020 Corporate Content Award, Best Use of Content in a Social Context
- 2019 People's Choice Podcast Award, #1 in Education
- 2018 Australian Book Industry Award, International Book
- 2018 Publishers Weekly Star Watch Superstar
- 2017 Blackwell's, Book of the Year
- 2017 Foyles, Book of the Year

Connect with Rebel Girls!

    Facebook: facebook.com/rebelgirls

    Instagram: @rebelgirls

    Twitter: @rebelgirlsbook

    Web: rebelgirls.com

    App: rebelgirls.com/app

If you liked this book, please take a moment to review it wherever you prefer!

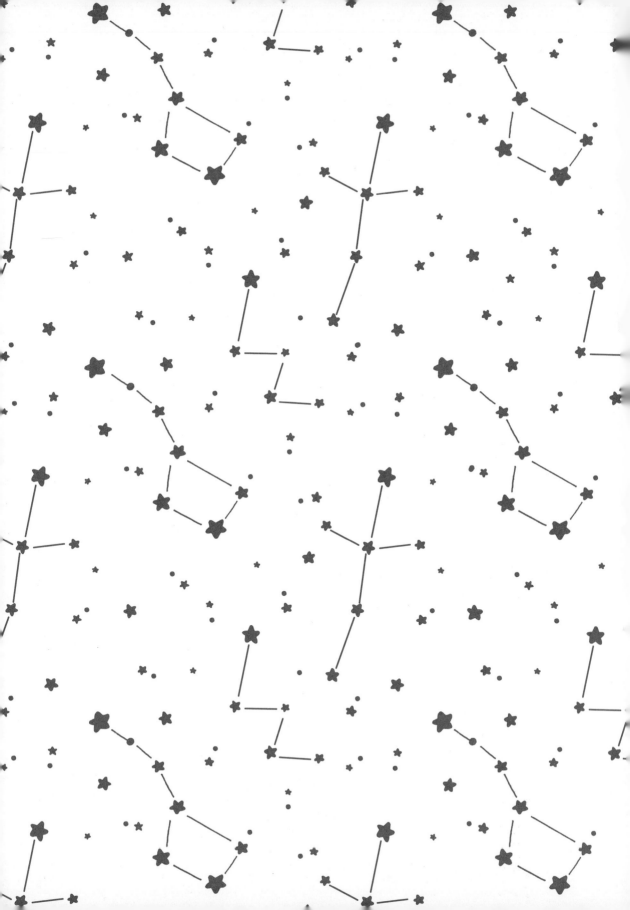